College in Black and White

SUNY Series

FRONTIERS IN EDUCATION
Philip G. Altbach, Editor

The Frontiers in Education Series draws upon a range of disciplines and approaches in the analysis of contemporary educational issues and concerns. Books in the series help to reinterpret established fields of scholarship in education by encouraging the the latest synthesis and research. A special focus highlights educational policy issues from a multidisciplinary perspective. The series is published in cooperation with the Graduate School of Education, State University of New York at Buffalo.

Class, Race, and Gender In American Education
—Lois Weis (ed.)

*Excellence and Equality: A Qualitatively Different
Perspective on Gifted and Talented Education*
—David M. Fetterman

Change and Effectiveness in Schools: A Cultural Perspective
—Gretchen B. Rossman, H. Dickson Corbett,
and William A. Firestone

The Curriculum: Problems, Politics, and Possibilities
—Landon E. Beyer and Michael W. Apple (eds.)

*The Character of American Higher Education and
Intercollegiate Sport*
—Donald Chu

Crisis in Teaching: Perspectives on Current Reforms
—Lois Weis, Philip G. Altbach, Gail P. Kelly,
Hugh G. Petrie, and Sheila Slaughter (eds.)

*The High Status Track: Studies of Elite Schools and
Stratification*
—Paul William Kingston and Lionel S. Lewis (eds.)

College in Black and White

African American Students in
Predominantly White and in Historically
Black Public Universities

Walter R. Allen
Edgar G. Epps
Nesha Z. Haniff
Editors

State University of New York Press

Published by
State University of New York Press, Albany

© 1991 State University of New York

For information, address State University of New York
Press, State University Plaza, Albany, N.Y., 12246

Production by E. Moore
Marketing by Fran Keneston

Library of Congress Cataloging-in-Publication Data

College in black and white : African American students in
    predominantly white and in historically Black public universities /
    Walter R. Allen, Edgar G. Epps, and Nesha Z. Haniff, editors.
        p.   cm. — (SUNY series, frontiers in education)
    Includes bibliographical references.
    ISBN 0-7914-0485-4 (alk. paper). — ISBN 0-7914-0486-2 (pbk.:
alk. paper)
        1. Afro-American college students.   2. Motivation in education.
    3. Vocational interests—United States.   I. Allen, Walter Recharde.
    II. Epps, Edgar G., 1929– .   III. Haniff, Nesha Z., 1948–   . IV. Series.
    LC2781.C58 1991
    378.1'982—dc20   90-32306
                                                        CIP

10 9 8 7 6 5 4 3 2

Dedication

Resistance and striving have been hallmarks in the history of Africans in America. Education is now, and always has been, a vital weapon in the Black arsenal for freedom struggle. As our students continue the quest for higher education and the power that knowledge represents, may they draw inspiration from the past, a sense of purpose from the present and hope from the future. Today's African American college students are part of a proud tradition, walking in the footsteps of those who passed before and blazing a path for those yet to follow. In this sense the rocky road toward Black liberation reaches backward as it strains forward.

Education can be a powerful force for individual and societal transformation. For this reason the African American community has long stressed educational achievement and through perseverance, sacrifice, faith and struggle we have managed to tear down school door barriers.

We dedicate this book to our students, hoping that they will strive in all aspects to develop themselves to the fullest capacity. May our students recognize the privilege, seize the opportunity and fulfill the obligation of learning. May they also become willing workers in the daunting task of making a new world, contributing to the advancement of their people, their community, this nation and the world.

Contents

ix

PART II
THE UNDERGRADUATE YEARS:
EMPIRICAL RESEARCH FINDINGS

PART III
THE GRADUATE AND PROFESSIONAL YEARS:
EMPIRICAL RESEARCH FINDINGS

PART IV
PRACTICAL ISSUES IN THE HIGHER EDUCATION
OF BLACK AMERICANS

Foreword

Access to higher education is an integral part of African Americans' long struggle for equality. Before the Civil War, the first private historically Black colleges were established in Ohio (at Wilberforce in 1856) and Pennsylvania (at Cheney State in 1837 and Lincoln in 1854). After emancipation, and with the assistance of northern philanthropy, private schools and colleges were established for the education and religious "salvation" of the former slaves. The latter half of the nineteenth century and the first decades of the twentieth century witnessed the expansion of church-related institutions, the development of public schools and colleges for African Americans, and the entrenchment of the "separate-but-equal" concept of segregated education.

While the separate educational system was growing in the South, a few African Americans braved racism and discrimination to earn baccalaureate and graduate degrees from white institutions in the North. Denied academic appointments in northern white colleges, many of these scholars moved south to become the teachers of the next generations of African American teachers and professionals.

A recent book by James D. Anderson (1988) provides a striking description of African Americans' commitment to education as a means of improving their chances of achieving equal opportunity. In addition, Anderson clearly demonstrates that African Americans were not passive recipients of the largesse of white beneficence. They were aggressive actors in the process of developing institutions that they thought would provide them with the keys to occupational and economic achievement.

Throughout the history of the African American experience in America, white Americans have expressed doubts about the intellectual capabilities of people of African descent. Whites have also expressed concerns about the proper role of African Americans in the social and economic

xiii

structure of American society. These doubts were expressed first as beliefs that African Americans did not have the mental capacity to cope with the cognitive demands of higher education; and second as a belief that there was no place in the American social and economic system for well-educated African Americans. There was a fear that highly educated African Americans might demand "social equality" with a people who considered them to be morally and intellectually inferior.

In spite of strong opposition from southern whites (and many northerners), public education in the South—including a system of segregated colleges and universities—slowly developed during the years from 1870 to 1940. These institutions, along with private historically Black colleges, graduated almost all of the Black teachers, preachers, doctors, lawyers, and social service workers prior to World War II. As recently as 1964, historically Black institutions graduated more than half of all African Americans earning degrees in the United States.

This record of achievement took place during a period when state legislatures provided meager resources for Black education, and when public institutions were required to focus on "agricultural and mechanical" rather than liberal arts education. With the crumbling of official segregation barriers in the South and the relaxing of nonlegal barriers in the North by the middle of the 1960s Blacks began to enroll in historically white institutions in unprecedented numbers. Thus, the successes of the Civil Rights Movement both broadened opportunities for African Americans, and, at the same time, exposed them to new arenas within which they encountered, once again, racism and discrimination.

Opening the doors of historically white institutions to African Americans caused some educators and policy makers to raise questions about the continued existence of historically Black institutions. Why, it was asked, are these colleges necessary now that admission to predominantly white institutions is possible? It was assumed by many white scholars that the historically Black institutions were academically inferior (Jencks and Riesman 1968); therefore, now that they had a choice, African American students would choose the "superior" white institutions. However, proponents of historically Black institutions argued that Black colleges and universities served a population that would be ignored by white institutions, Black institutions had a long history of success in educating poorly prepared students, and that Black colleges were important social, cultural, and economic resources within their communities.

The research reported in this volume addresses a number of important issues that must be faced by Americans concerned with equal opportunity in higher education. How are African American students faring on predominantly white campuses? What are the relative advantages or disadvantages for an African American student of attending a historically Black institution or a traditionally white institution? On each type of campus, what factors affect student retention or attrition? Are males and females encountering different types of obstacles or support systems on Black and white campuses? These are a few of the many questions that can be asked about the experiences of African American students in higher education during the decades since predominantly white institutions became desegregated.

Answers to such questions are complex, and, while many issues are addressed in this volume, there is still much that needs to be done. For example, earlier work (Gurin and Epps 1975) described the diversity that exists among historically Black colleges and universities. They differ in size, geographic location (for example, rural-urban; or North-South), quality of faculty, quality of laboratories and libraries, types of students they attract (some institutions attract students nationwide, while others are almost exclusively from within the state), range of major fields of study offered, and the availability of graduate programs.

Of course, there is great diversity among traditionally white institutions as well. The point to be emphasized is that categories such as Historically Black Colleges and Universities (HBCU) or Historically White Colleges and Universities (HWCU) mask this diversity. We must be concerned with the qualities and characteristics of institutions that support and encourage student success, and those aspects that alienate students and detract from their ability to matriculate successfully at a particular institution.

In his work on student attrition, Tinto (1975) discussed academic and social integration of students as factors that influence students' decisions to remain in school or to drop out. We should expect greater social integration of African American students at HBCUs than at HWCUs. This expectation is supported by some of the chapters in this volume. However, as the research of Phillip Hart (1984) has shown, some traditionally white institutions are remarkably successful in retaining and graduating African American students, while some historically Black institutions are much less successful. Comparisons of this kind are always problematic because they fail to take into account the availability of resources at various institutions. Institutions with generous resources are able to provide a broad range of social, academic and financial support for students when they choose to allocate resources for such purposes.

Some researchers (Shade 1982) contend that African Americans stress social rather than instrumental cognition. If Shade's observations are correct, we would expect African American students to fare better in settings that provide opportunities for self-expression, creativity, and innovation rather than in settings that stress traditional forms of teaching and learning. There are some suggestions in the research reported in this volume that institutions in which nontraditional teaching is experienced by African American students are more successful in retaining and graduating African Americans than are institutions where traditional instruction is emphasized.

It has been noted recently that there is a trend for African American students to transfer out of white institutions and into HBCUs (Patel 1988). How widespread this trend is has yet to be determined. Also, we do not know the extent of transfers from HBCUs to HWCUs. Knowledge of the reasons why students move from one type of institution to another and the magnitude of such transfers would add to our knowledge of how students experience higher education in different settings.

It is reported in several studies in this volume that African American students are economically and academically disadvantaged relative to white students and that students at historically Black institutions are more disadvantaged than those at traditionally white institutions. These disadvantages are, to be sure, experienced by only a portion of African American students, but at some institutions, the disadvantaged constitute a majority. This reflects the impoverished circumstances in which many African Americans continue to find themselves as well as the impoverished elementary and secondary schools which many African Americans attend. Thus, the ills of the society are reflected in the schools and are further reflected in the colleges and universities attended by these young people. The vicious cycle of racism, poverty, and underachievement continues to haunt many African American students even though they have graduated from high school and have entered postsecondary education.

While we can ask colleges and universities to do much more than they are now doing to make higher education more accessible and achievable for African Americans, it is clear that other efforts are needed as well. For example, much more attention must be paid to the relationship between poverty and school quality at the elementary and secondary levels. In addition, there is a need for incentives to motivate students to aspire to high standards of academic achievement and high levels of attainment. Finally, there is great need for more humane financial assistance programs, better recruitment and retention programs, and a commitment on the part of all institutions of higher education toward the elimination of racism and sexism on campus. I hope the research reported in this book will provide a stimulus for policy makers to take a more aggressive stance in support of an equal educational opportunity for all Americans.

EDGAR G. EPPS

Acknowledgments

At the end of a long journey one feels keenly the sense of obligation to those who assisted along the way. This is particularly true when the journey has been difficult. The task of bringing this book to fruition has been fraught with challenge and struggle. For this reason I owe a tremendous debt of gratitude to many people. My co-editors, Edgar G. Epps and Nesha Z. Haniff each made invaluable contributions to this project and to my scholarly development. Edgar Epps influenced my thinking from graduate school until the present, nearly twenty years. From him I gained an understanding of the important place of education in the lives of African Americans and of the myriad individual, institutional, community factors that shape Black educational outcomes. He also impressed upon me the need to join scholarly excellence with social responsibility in the pursuit of career. His is the model I seek to emulate in my teaching, graduate student training, research, writing and community service.

Nesha Haniff was a supportive presence, an essential collaborator and willing worker throughout the life of this project at Michigan. Without her assistance this book most certainly would have stagnated at some earlier stage. At critical points in the process her words of encouragement, her sage advice, her brilliant insights and her most able editorial skills saved the day.

I also owe special votes of thanks to several colleagues on whom I have leaned heavily for intellectual support and guidance since graduate school and the early years of my career. Margaret Spencer, Bruce Hare and Aldon Morris have each been profoundly important influences, helping to shape my thinking and to encourage my work. I am extremely grateful for all their help.

The research collaborators who assisted this project were an able, industrious and distinguished group. They accepted the difficult task of representing the project "on the ground," serving as liaisons between the study and their respective universities. Only with their help was the successful implementation of the study insured. To a greater or lesser extent, research collaborators served as co-directors for this project. The research collaborators and their universities follow: A. Wade Smith, Arizona State University; Roselle Davenport Wilson and Ronald Woods, Eastern Michigan University; Tom Shick, Westina Matthews and Clovis White, University of Wisconsin—Madison; Oscar Love and Russell Thomas, Memphis State University; Melvin Oliver, University of California—Los Angeles; Bruce Hare, State University of New York—Stony Brook; Henry Frierson, University of North Carolina—Chapel Hill; Robert Davis, North Carolina A & T University; Stella Hargett, Morgan State University; Geraldine Brookins, Jackson State University; Alex Swan, Texas Southern University; Jeffrey Smith, North Carolina Central University; Barbara Barrett, Florida A & M University; Lawrence Delzine, Central State University; and Clarence Thornton, Southern University.

Important assistance to the project was also provided by an Advisory Board consisting of the following members: Peter Dual, Richard English, Edgar Epps, James McPartland and Gail Thomas. This board provided invaluable oversight and advice, helping the Director make key project decisions along the way.

At the center of the project has been the finest administrative, secretarial and clerical group that one could wish for. Garry Fleming was Assistant Project Director during the study's early years. He was simply excellent and indispensable in this role. In subsequent years Blondell Strong, Marcia Hall, Anne-Marie Debritto, Rosario Montoya and Diana Tumminia worked effectively as administrative assistants to the Project Director. I have also benefitted from the services of an extraordinary secretarial corps: Marina Shoemaker, Rose Chinnock, Efuru Perkins, Adrienne DeJesus, Stan Barrett, Michele White, Mary Breijak and Deborah Jones. Together they managed the day-to-day business of the project and typed countless drafts of the manuscript.

Perhaps the most important contributors to this project, and certainly the most delightful, were the undergraduate and graduate student employees at the University of Michigan and the University of California—Los Angeles. These students brought an enthusiam, vision and meaning to the study without which it would have been greatly impoverished. It is additionally gratifying that most went on to achieve distinction in their chosen fields, earning doctorates or professional degrees in Social Work, Engineering, Planning, Law, Business or Medicine. Of particular note in the Michigan group were: Marcia Hall, Anne Marie Debritto, Blondell Strong, Angelle

Cooper, Arlene Mays, Jonathan Stern, Jo Anne Hall, Cheryl Presley and Rosario Montoya. Most notable among the U.C.L.A. group were Diana Tumminia and Heidi Kim. Other students also made important contributions to the work of this study: Jon Van Camp, Angelia Wimberly, Winifred Nweke, John Wallace, Mary Kirkland, Robin Spencer, Michelle Hurst, Angela Haddad, Paul Fleuranges, Evelyn Bogen, Deborah Daughtry, Richard Tabler, Karen Wilson, Jacqueline Smith, Michele Jones, Aubrey Scott, Matthew Lynes, Ahn Bui, Lawrence Bobo, Carolyn Drummond, Michael Sudarkasa, Mary Kirkland, Godfrey Cadogan and Lisa Gibson.

In addition, we thank the participating universities, their Presidents/ Chancellors, Registrars and students for their willingness to assist with this study. In each instance, the university community was open to this inquiry and committed to better understanding the circumstances of Black college students. Greatest gratitude here is owed to the participating students who spent countless uncompensated hours of their valuable time completing our questionaires, and in some instances sharing their ideas in person, by phone or through the mail. These students were clearly motivated by altruistic goals and the desire to contribute to positive change in U.S. higher education; hoping by their efforts to assist with elimination of the remaining vestiges of racial, ethnic and gender discrimination.

A study of this magnitude is simply not possible without adequate financial support. This project has been fortunate to gain the necessary resources to complete the task, thanks to many sponsors. Foremost among our sponsors has been Marion Faldet and the Spencer Foundation. The foundation's initial funding gave impetus to the project while its subsequent funding helped to maintain our momentum. Marion Faldet was the first foundation representative to discern the importance of this project and to offer substantial backing. However, Velma Burtley of the C.S. Mott Foundation and Gladys Chang Hardy of the Ford Foundation also believed. Under their supervision, the Ford and Mott Foundations funded the data collection phases of the research. Benjamin Payton, Alison Bernstein and Linn Cary at Ford Foundation were also very important to the success of this project. At Mott Foundation, Suzanne Feurt provided similar help. Funding from Marta White and the Joyce Foundation supported the coding, keypunching and analysis of our data. Supplemental assistance for analysis and write-up was provided by Charles Moody, Office of Minority Affairs and the following University of Michigan offices: Vice President for Research, Dean of Literature, Science and the Arts and the President. The Center for Afroamerican and African Studies, under directors Ali Mazrui, Niara Sudarkasa, Thomas Holt and Lemuel Johnson contributed office space and support services for the life of the project. At the University of

California—Los Angeles supplemental assistance for completing this book was provided by the Provost, College of Letters and Science and the Dean of Social Sciences.

A very special debt of gratitude is owed to my wife Wilma. She has loved me and supported my work for over twenty years. When my need was greatest she was able to help with an idea, to offer encouragement and to lend a hand. Without her my life and work would have lacked zest. I also wish to acknowledge my children, Bryan, Binti and Rena, each of whom in his or her own way contributed to this project. I thank my wife and children for their many sacrifices, for encouraging me to continue the quest.

Since so many have given so much to this project, it is inevitable that I will overlook someone. I apologize profusely, in advance, for such oversights. Those who were essential to the work of this study know who you are, you should also know the depth and breadth of my gratitude.

It can also be expected with a project of this size that many errors will inevitably escape detection, some will be quite glaring others minor. While responsibility for the conduct and completion of this study is willingly shared, I am reluctant to accept any blame for its shortcomings. If I must then I am willing to share responsibility with the many contributors, insisting that my share of accolades be greater than is deserved and my share of criticism considerably less than is warranted.

WALTER R. ALLEN

WALTER R. ALLEN

Introduction

The decade of the 1960's marked a watershed in American history, when, in response to the Civil Rights Movement, our society made major efforts to address some of the wrongs imposed on its Black citizens for centuries. Increasing Black access to higher education was seen as a major solution to the problem of racial inequality, and the decade witnessed the beginning of a dramatic increase in the enrollment of Black students in predominantly white colleges and universities. This response by institutions of higher learning to the Civil Rights Movement was abetted by unusually favorable conditions within higher education; public support for higher education was high, and colleges and universities were experiencing a period of continual expansion.

Today, thirty years later, both the mood of the country on racial issues and the state of higher education have changed. The national moral response to Black demands for equality has been tempered by ambivalence and the persistent problems associated with downturns in the nation's economy. Higher education generally has moved from a period of boundless expansion and optimism to one of retrenchment and financial constraint. This has been reflected in a dilution in higher education's commitments to Blacks and other minorities. The enrollment of Black students in four-year, predominantly white institutions, has fallen short of anticipated goals and has, in fact, declined from 1975 to 1985. Black faculty and administrators have remained a minute proportion of the tenured and senior staff in white colleges and universities. In addition, studies of Black students suggest that many have negative experiences in white institutions, suffering lower achievement and higher attrition.

1

Higher education's complacency on this issue has been shaken recently by the outbreak of ugly racial incidents on a number of college campuses across the United States. This has led to considerable self-examination at many colleges and universities, and, in some cases, a revitalization of the commitment to Black and minority students. But how to implement this commitment is by no means clear.

Despite a generation of experience with a significant presence of Black students in white institutions of higher education, we have only a limited and imprecise understanding of the factors that affect the increases and decreases in an institution's enrollment of minority students, and, once enrolled, of the factors that provide these students with an institutional and educational experience that is personally gratifying and academically successful. Thus, even when an institution is ready to commit more resources to the minority endeavor, the institution's leadership lacks clear directions on how best to expend these resources.

To a considerable extent, our lack of hard knowledge in this arena is due to the fact that the historic change in higher education's opening to Black and minority students has been the subject of very little systematic, quantitative, and analytic research. This volume uses data from the National Study of Black College Students and other sources to address this problem by contributing to the growing body of knowledge about Black student experiences and outcomes in U.S. higher education.

BACKGROUND TO STUDY

The study which forms the basis for this volume has been nearly fifteen years in the making. The germ of the idea for this study was planted in 1975. At the time, I was a new Assistant Professor in sociology at the University of North Carolina-Chapel Hill. In this capacity and as one of the few African American faculty at the institution, I was often called upon to serve on committees concerned with the status of "minorities and the disadvantaged" in the University.

Successive committees examined the situations of the African American faculty, students and staff and determined them to be severely disadvantaged relative to their white peers. In this respect, the situation for African Americans at the University of North Carolina was very much the same as on most other predominantly white campuses across the nation.

As each committee sought to fulfill its charge to report on the status of "minorities" and to formulate solutions, certain realities emerged with startling consistency. Chief among these was the recognition of a tremendous void in the empirical information which was actually available. Time and time again, genuine efforts to address the problems were stymied by an absence of reliable systematic data. In numerous other instances, individuals and offices not genuinely committed to correcting the readily apparent problems resorted to the convenient excuse of inconclusive or nonexistent empirical evidence as justification for inaction, thus thwarting pressures for change. It was quite clear that little progress would result without the generation of reliable, comprehensive data.

Into this void came the National Study of Black College Students. The project was intended first and foremost to produce desperately needed data on the characteristics, experiences, and achievements of Black students at the University of North Carolina. Second, the project sought to generate data which captured the specific reality of Black students, therefore conscious decisions were made to restrict the sample to Black students and to incorporate measures that tapped the reality of Black students. The data resulting from this study were to be systematically analyzed with the empirical findings to provide the basis for recommended changes in University policies and practices.

From 1976 through 1979 several waves of data were collected on African American students who attended the University of North Carolina-Chapel Hill. In 1980 the first comparative data were collected, comparing Black students who attended North Carolina to those who attended the University of Michigan-Ann Arbor. Subsequently the study was expanded to incorporate a national sample of Black undergraduate, graduate and professional students on eight historically Black and eight predominantly white campuses.

During these early years the research project was funded by seed grants from the Spencer Foundation and with faculty research grant funds being provided by the Universities of Michigan and North Carolina. Study instruments and procedures underwent successive revision through 1981 when funding from the Spencer Foundation supported the establishment of the current collaborative multicampus design. Over the ensuing years, the project was generously funded by grants from the Ford Foundation, the Charles Stewart Mott Foundation, the Rockefeller Foundation and the Joyce Foundation.

The research design for the National Study of Black College Students has been distinguished by the involvement of research collaborators from each participating campus. Collaborators were involved in questionnaire construction, sample selection, and campus liaison. As compensation, research collaborators received consultant payments and copies of the data sets for their respective campuses. Since the creation of a collaborative network of Black scholars doing research on Black students in higher education was another conscious goal of the study, various opportunities were created for study collaborators to meet regularly, to participate jointly in national conferences, and to publish joint research papers from the data.

The involvement of African American and other graduate students with related interests as research assistants was another important offshoot of the study. Our intention was to provide Black students specifically—and other students more generally—with professional training and experience in all phases of social-science research. Several dissertations, graduate student presentations during national meetings, and publications including graduate students as coauthors resulted from this research.

BLACK STUDENTS IN HIGHER EDUCATION: THE RESEARCH RECORD

Over the past thirty years, profound changes have occurred in Black student patterns of college attendance in the United States. Whereas previously, the overwhelming majority of Black college students were enrolled in historically Black institutions, by 1973 that percentage had dropped significantly to roughly one-fourth of Black enrollment (Anderson 1984). Three-fourths of all Black students in college currently attend predominantly white institutions of higher learning (National Center for Education Statistics 1982). An estimated fifty-seven percent of all baccalaureate degrees awarded to Black students during 1978–1979 were granted by predominantly white colleges and universities (Deskins 1983).

However, Black students on predominantly white campuses continue to be severely disadvantaged relative to white students in terms of persistence rates (Astin 1982; and Thomas 1981), academic achievement levels (Nettles et al. 1985; and Smith and Allen 1984); enrollment in advanced degree programs (Hall, Mays, and Allen 1984); and overall psychosocial adjustments (Allen 1982, 1985, and 1986; and Fleming 1984). Black students on historically Black campuses are disadvantaged relative to students (both Black and white) on white campuses in terms of family socioeconomic status (Thomas 1984; and Morris 1979), and high-school academic records (Astin and Cross 1981). Caliber of university instructional faculty and facilities (Fleming 1984), academic specializations selected (Thomas 1984), and enrollment in advanced study (Pearson and Pearson 1985; and Blackwell 1982) are also lower for Black students on Black campuses.

Past research suggests that the fit between Black students and white colleges is, indeed, not a very good one. Black students differ in fundamental ways from the white students who are commonly served by these schools. They, therefore, experience more adjustment difficulties, more limited academic success, and higher attrition rates with definite consequences for their aspirations.

Studies of Black students attending predominantly white postsecondary institutions commonly incorporate the following concerns regarding Black students:

1. Their social and economic characteristics (Allen 1982; and Blackwell 1982);
2. Their levels of adjustment in predominantly white institutions (Fleming 1984); and
3. Their academic success (attrition rate) in these institutions (Braddock and Dawkins 1981; and Nettles et al., 1985)

Black students in college are different from their white peers in several respects. For example, the parents of Black students are typically urban, have fewer years of education, earn less, and work at lower status jobs than is true for the parents of white students (Blackwell 1982).

Yet, despite social, and economic disadvantages, Black college students have equal, or higher, aspirations compared to their white counterparts (Allen 1986, and 1985). However, Black students are less likely to attain their aspirations than white students. Lower educational attainment is pronounced for Black students in general, and for Black females in particular (Hall, Mays, and Allen 1984; Smith and Allen 1984; and Gurin and Epps 1975). Black students attending predominantly white colleges apparently experience considerable adjustment difficulty. Many of the adjustment problems are common to all college students but African American students also experience additional problems. For instance, many of these students often find it necessary to create their own social and cultural networks given their exclusion (self-and/or otherwise imposed) from the wider university community. Of all problems faced by Black students on white campuses, those arising from isolation, alienation, and lack of support seem to be most serious (Allen 1986, and 1985).

Whether it is because of adjustment or other difficulties, Black students on the average have weaker academic records than their white peers. These academic difficulties for Black students on white campuses are often compounded by the absence of remedial/tutorial programs and information-sharing with whites, whether faculty and/or students (Hall, Mays, and Allen 1984). Despite the initial difficulties most Black students experience, many make the required adjustments and are academically successful in predominantly white institutions (Allen 1986; and Peterson et al. 1978).

Unlike studies of Black students on white campuses, studies of these students on Black campuses assume a proper fit between students and institution. Comparisons of Black students on Black campuses with those on white campuses are more often based on conjecture than fact. The presumption is that predominantly white campuses provide superior environments for Black student education. Much is made of differences between student populations at historically Black and predominantly white colleges. The typical parents of Black students on Black campuses earn less money, have lower educational achievement, hold lower status jobs, and are more often separated or divorced (Thomas 1984). Consistent with observed economic discrepancies, typical Black students on Black campuses have lower standardized test scores and weaker high-school backgrounds than do typical Black students on white campuses (Astin and Cross 1981).

A natural outgrowth of the research has been the recognition of the "special mission" of Black colleges. To a large extent, Black colleges enroll students who might not otherwise be able to attend college because of financial or academic barriers (Thomas, McPartland, and Gottfredson 1980). These institutions pride themselves on their ability to take poor and less-prepared Black students where they are, correct their academic deficiencies, and graduate them equipped to compete successfully for jobs or graduate/professional school placements in the wider society (National Advisory Committee on Black Higher Education and Black Colleges and Universities 1980).

When Black student campuses are compared on the dimension of psychosocial development, those on Black campuses fare much better. In an early study, Gurin and Epps (1975) found that Black students who attend Black colleges possessed positive self-images, strong racial pride, and high aspirations. More recently, Fleming (1984) demonstrated psychosocial adjustment to be more positive for Black students on Black campuses when compared with those on white campuses.

In sum, the evidence suggests that Black students on Black campuses are more disadvantaged in socioeconomic *and* academic terms than are Black (or white) students on white campuses. However, Black students on Black campuses display more positive psychosocial adjustments, significant academic gains, and greater cultural awareness/commitment than is true for their peers on white campuses.

Researchers have identified persistent differences by gender in college experiences and outcomes. As might be expected, these differences cross the color line. In one of the earlier, more comprehensive comparisons of Black men and women attending Black colleges, Gurin and Epps (1975) found that women's goals were lower on all measures of educational and occupational aspirations; males were three times more likely to plan on pursuing the Ph.D.; women were more likely to aspire to jobs in the "female sector'' of the economy, jobs that required less ability and effort while providing lower prestige; and males were more likely to be influenced in their goals and aspirations by the college attended.

In general, Black females were found to experience clear disadvantages when compared to Black men on the Black campuses studied. Gurin and Epps (1975) studied Black students enrolled in ten traditionally Black institutions from 1964–1970. Roughly ten years later, Fleming (1984) studied a comparable sample of three thousand black college students which was expanded to incorporate students attending predominantly white colleges. Fleming found that white males on white campuses, and Black males on Black campuses, derived far more benefits from college than was true for Black women. Patterns were reversed for the Black males studied by Fleming; they suffered most on white campuses and were most satisfied on Black campuses. On white campuses, Black males were withdrawn and unhappy, feeling themselves to have been treated unfairly. In addition, they experienced considerable academic demotivation. At the other extreme were Black males on Black campuses who, like white males on white campuses, felt potent and ''in charge.''

Findings from a study of Black students on white campuses further elaborate gender differences in educational experiences and outcomes (Smith and Allen 1984; Allen 1986). Analysis of a national sample of over seven hundred undergraduate students revealed that Black males were more likely than Black females to have both high aspirations and good grades. This was a surprising finding given the fact that, on average, Black females in this sample out-performed Black males in the classroom as measured by grades. When Black males and Black females with comparable achievement levels were compared, the males consistently reported higher postgraduate aspirations. Thomas (1984) found that their occupational aspirations were highest and least traditional when Black females attended private colleges.

A critical reading of the research literature on Black students in U.S. higher education reveals fundamental gaps in our knowledge. To be sure, the evidence attesting to severe problems with Black student access to U.S. higher education is overwhelming and incontestable. Black students who comprise 13 to 15 percent of all college-aged youth, are only 10.7 percent of the nation's high-school graduates and a mere 8.8 percent of college undergraduates (American Council on Education 1988). Beyond the concern with Black rates of access to higher education is the concern with success rates. Again, the literature provides conclusive evidence. Black students have lower academic achievement levels in college and higher attrition or dropout rates than do white students. Black students also express greater dissatisfaction with the college experience and are less likely to pursue advanced study.

The literature is decisive in documenting the twin problems of limited access and success for Black students in higher education. Where previous research fails is in the examination of complex relationships underlying the creation and persistence of Black student disadvantages in higher education. Prior studies have not provided a systematic, comprehensive perspective on the complex societal, institutional, interpersonal, and individual factors implicated in the creation and persistence of Black disadvantage in higher education. In short, the area is underdeveloped both theoretically and methodologically. Studies that provide comprehensive explanation of student outcomes are nonexistent.

From a critical view, the literature on Black students in higher education has been underdeveloped theoretically. Few if any studies provide an overarching theory or emphasize a theoretical approach to the problem. Instead, researchers have tended to approach the question narrowly, ignoring the relationship of Black student status in college to the status of Blacks in the larger society. For the most part, researchers have used an applied perspective, seeking easy solutions to the problem of Black access to and success in higher education. Inevitably, the narrowness of the perspective has limited the possibilities of achieving lasting, effective solutions.

Associated with the theoretical underdevelopment of research in this area is a noticeable lack of sophisticated methodological and statistical approaches. Thus, one finds the field to be characterized more so by analytic approaches which are descriptive and simplistic. In those rare instances where advanced, sophisticated statistical analyses were employed, findings were often compromised because the samples that are used tend to be geographically restricted and nonrandom. Perhaps the most serious and recurrent methodological flaw in studies of Black college students, however, has been the failure to explicitly match the methodology of a study to its theoretical and practical aims. Researchers have relied heavily on data which were not specific to the experience of Black college students, were superficial or insufficiently detailed, and were cross-sectional rather than longitudinal.

THE NATIONAL STUDY OF BLACK COLLEGE STUDENTS: METHODS AND DATA

The National Study of Black College Students (NSBCS) seeks to empirically examine the educational experiences of Black students in U.S. higher education and ultimately to provide solutions to the myriad problems which these students face. Since 1981, the study has collected mail survey data from over four thousand undergraduate, graduate, and professional

Black students on sixteen public university campuses across the country. Participating students completed questionnaires which provided information about their family backgrounds, high-school and college academic experiences, interpersonal relationships on the campus, problems with racism and discrimination, adjustment to college, and academic progress/performance in college.

The study was based at the University of Michigan in Ann Arbor where all operations of mailing, receiving, processing, coding, punching, and computer tabulation of questionnaires were conducted. All of the schools participating in this study were public, four-year universities since these are the type of institutions which currently account for the majority of Black student enrollment and degree completion. The participating institutions were selected on the basis of regional diversity and accessibility.

The selection of students for participation in the study was random, based on lists of currently enrolled Black students supplied by the various university Registrar offices. In each case, a probability sample in the form of a systematic random sample was drawn. Prior to selection, students were stratified by year of enrollment (in the case of years where data collected were cross-sectional) and by program (in the case of graduate and professional students). Four waves of data were collected by the National Study of Black College Students:

1. *1981 Cross-Sectional Study* of 1,050 Black undergraduate, graduate, and professional students across the different levels and years of enrollment. The participating universities were: Arizona State University at Tempe, Memphis State University in Tennessee, State University of New York at Stony Brook, University of California at Los Angeles, University of Michigan at Ann Arbor, and University of North Carolina in Chapel Hill. The 1981 adjusted response rates were: undergraduate, 27 percent (695); and graduate professional, 37 percent (353).

2. *1982 Base-Year Longitudinal, White Schools Study* of 1,300 Black first-year undergraduate, graduate, and professional students. The participating universities were eight predominantly white institutions: Arizona State University, Eastern Michigan University in Ypsilanti, Memphis State University, State University of New York at Stony Brook, University of California at Los Angeles, University of Michigan at Ann Arbor, University of North Carolina at Chapel Hill, and the University of Wisconsin at Madison. The adjusted response rates for 1982 were: undergraduates 39 percent (902); and graduate professionals, 47 percent (407).

3. *1983 Base-Year Longitudinal Study, Black Schools Study* of 1,134 Black undergraduate, graduate, and professional students. The participating schools were eight traditionally Black institutions: Central State Univer-

sity in Wilberforce, Ohio; Florida A & M University at Tallahassee; Jackson State University in Jackson, MS; Morgan State University, Baltimore, Md.; North Carolina Central University in Durham; North Carolina A & T University in Greensboro; Southern University in Baton Rouge, La.; and Texas Southern University in Houston. The 1983 adjusted response rates were: undergraduates, 25 percent (833); and graduate professional, 28 percent (247).

4. *Spring 1985 First Longitudinal Follow-Up, White Schools Study* of 456 Black undergraduate, graduate, and professional students responding from the 1982 predominantly white state universities base-year group. The Spring 1985 adjusted response rates were: undergraduate, 35 percent (283); and graduate professional, 46 percent (173).

5. *Fall 1985 First Longitudinal Follow-Up, Black Schools Study* of 471 Black undergraduate, graduate, and professional students from the 1983 historically Black universities base-year group. The Fall 1985 adjusted response rates were: undergraduates, 48 percent (384); and graduate professional, 57 percent (87).

The studies reported in this volume use only data from the 1981, 1982, and 1983 waves of the National Study of Black College Students.

The National Study of Black College Students data files are among the most extensive and comprehensive currently available. To our knowledge, no other studies provide data of comparable breadth, depth and relevance on the experiences of Black Americans in U.S. higher education. However, this study, like all studies, suffers from some limitations relative to the quality of data obtained.

To begin, we focus on a group that is notoriously difficult to study; studies of African Americans, young people, or college students are routinely plagued by low response rates. This research looks at young, Black college students; thus, response problems are confounded. In addition, finite resources, timing of the study and other issues require that researchers make difficult choices. Who will be in the sample? How detailed should questions be? How long will the field study last? These are the difficult questions to be addressed as one plans and executes a research project. As the researcher chooses, certain consequences or trade offs result for the quality of data obtained.

Since its inception, this project has sought to achieve the optimal balance between often competing concerns, such as representativeness of the sample, validity and reliability, questionnaire length, study response rates, relevance to Black students' lives, and costs of research. From the necessary trade offs have come unique, rich, and powerfully revealing datasets.

THE ROLE OF IDEOLOGY IN THE STUDY
OF BLACK COLLEGE STUDENTS

Ideology represents the silent partner in research. It is the hidden agenda operating alongside theory and method to shape the outcome of a particular study. Rarely is the contribution of ideology acknowledged, for to do so is to fly in the face of cherished traditions. Convention would have us adopt a view of research as strictly objective and empirical, free from the soiling influence of personal values, preferences, or assumptions about what is normal. In fact, ideology or the value-stance of the researcher plays an important role in all research.

Contrary to popular opinion, the data do not "speak" for themselves. Instead, the message of the data is channeled through researchers who function as translators or mediums. Inevitably, these researchers hear—or better still, see—the data differently. They are influenced in this respect by their personal characteristics *and* their values. Thus it is that researchers using the same theory, methodological approach, and data will often reach diametrically opposed conclusions.

Generally speaking, ideology has received insufficient attention as a variable in the research process. Even less attention has been given to the role of ideology in research on the status of African Americans in U.S. higher education. Researchers have tended to assume or apply paradigms that are not necessarily cognizant of nor sensitive to the circumstances of Black people in this country. Many choose to study Black college students exactly as white college students are studied. Such approaches fail to make allowances in conceptualization, theory, method, or interpretations for the different histories of these two groups or, for that matter, their very different present and future.

Traditional paradigms for the study of higher education also tend to view the educational process in consensus terms. Educational institutions, the educational process, and the place of education in society are represented in the literature, as encompassing society's basic values. In this sense, educational systems are believed to echo the "common voice" of a culture.

In ways both explicit and implicit, classical theorists such as Rousseau, Durkheim, Dewey, and others portray educational systems as cultural signatures. To understand a culture's schools is to understand that culture. Societies are seen as rationally organizing their educational systems to achieve the goal of creating good citizens—citizens who are versed in the requisite skills and values of the society and who are prepared to participate fully in the life of that society.

It is only from a consensus framework that the following quote could emerge—a quote which presumes a consensus between schools, community, family, and individual which is not necessarily reflective of the experiences of Blacks in America:

> It is in our public schools that the majority of our children are being formed. These schools must be guardians par excellence of our national character. (Durkheim 1925/1961:3–4)

In light of our history, first as an enslaved population, then as rural peasants and later as an urban proletariat—and throughout a discriminated caste group—African Americans have maintained ambivalent ties to this country's educational system.

More often than not, schools in this country have been the setting for Black contest and struggle, as African Americans fought for full citizenship and participation in the society. Historically, educational institutions and educators have been among the most active and effective instruments for the oppression of black people. Schools systematically denied Blacks equal access while helping to establish the "pseudoscience" literature which proclaimed African Americans' deficit and provided rationales for their continued subjugation.

For reasons of self-protection and survival, therefore, African Americans have found it necessary to adopt an adversarial stance vis-a-vis the U.S. educational system. In response to a system which, at best, ignored them but, more often, persecuted them, Blacks have been required to adopt a self-consciously conflictual stance. Thus, Dewey's, Durkheim's, and Rousseau's espoused ideals about education simply do not fit the reality of African Americans in a country founded on the principle of Black subordination.

Instead of being at one with the educational system, Blacks have found themselves at odds with that system. In this respect, acts of defiance and challenge become acts of self-affirmation. Carter G. Woodson reminds us that:

> The same educational process which inspires and stimulates the oppressor with the thought that he is everything and has accomplished everything worthwhile, depresses and crushes at the same time the spark of genius in the Negro by making him feel that his race does not amount to much and never will measure up to the standards of other people. The Negro thus educated is a hopeless liability to the race. (Woodson 1933/1969:xxxiii)

An essential tension exists between African Americans and American society. This tension is played out in the educational arena as in other spheres of life. Blacks look upon schools as potential routes to upward mobility and thus seek to take from them that which is positive and uplifting. Blacks also know the schools as tools of oppression. Thus, they strive to reject aspects which would crush their self-image, aspirations and striving.

This drama of stress and strain, of uneasy peace between student and teacher and between community and school, borne of conflicts over racial/cultural content and goals must find fuller expression in the literature if that literature is to be taken seriously. Thus it is that this book—(and the study on which it is based)—consciously addresses the politics of the Black-white cultural and ideological struggle in higher education. We embrace Richard Shaull's premise offered in his introduction of Paulo Freire's seminal text, *Pedagogy of the Oppressed.*

> There is no such thing as a *neutral* educational process. Education either functions as an instrument which is used to facilitate the integration of the younger generation into the logic of the present system and bring about conformity to it, *or* it becomes "the practice of freedom," the means by which men and women deal critically and creatively with reality and discover how to participate in the transformation of their world. (Freire 1982:15)

To the extent that the serious theoretical, methodological, and ideological issues referenced in this introduction are recurrent, our knowledge about Black student access to and success in college suffers. The observation that these issues are indicative of shortcomings shared more broadly in the field is axiomatic. Thus, if one looks critically at the literature and reviews the work of regular contributors (such as Allen, Astin, Braddock, Blackwell, Fleming, Nettles, Peterson, and Thomas) it is clear that all can be criticized—more or less vigorously—for failings on the noted issues of theory, method, and ideology. The studies reported here sought to overcome shortcomings previously associated with this area. Needless to say, many of these problems remain, for these are not perfect studies. However, these studies do represent substantial improvement over prior research in several key aspects.

BOOK OUTLINE

This book reports findings from the National Study of Black College Students, a study of Black college students' characteristics, experiences, and achievements in U.S. higher education. The study's chief purpose is to examine connections between Black student adjustment, achievement, and career aspirations as related to student background, institutional context, and interpersonal relationships. Over four thousand undergraduate, graduate, and professional students on sixteen campuses across the nation (eight historically Black and eight predominantly white) participated in this study. This book approaches the study of Blacks in college from an interdisciplinary perspective, reporting the findings of history, psychology, geography, sociology, and education as they relate to and clarify the circumstances of Black students in U.S. higher education. This book begins with papers that survey the broader issues and data pertinent to assessments of African American experiences in colleges and universities. The papers in section one derive from other data sources and are intended to frame the historical, geographic, and empirical context for the interpretation of findings from the National Study of Black College Students.

The second and third sections of this book are concerned with the specific consideration of empirical results from the National Study. Section two presents findings from the analysis of undergraduate student data, while section three presents results from the graduate and professional student data.

The final section of the volume summarizes key findings from this research, offers an assessment of broader political and theoretical issues in the study of Black college students. This section also presents examples of successful interventions. Appendix materials offer detailed discussion of technical issues of the study.

Part One

Orienting Perspectives to the Study of Black Students in U.S. Higher Education

Each paper in this section provides an orientation and context for looking at the experiences, status, and outcomes for Black students in U.S. higher education. The results from nationally focused studies that used data from sources other than the National Study of Black College Students are examined.

The studies look at time trends in Black student enrollment and degree attainment. They also model the process whereby Black students elect major fields of study and they compare academic achievement patterns between Black and white students on selected college campuses.

These papers provide a useful overview of salient issues, key variables, and significant research findings important in the study of Black student experiences and outcomes in college. The papers by Donald R. Deskins, Jr., Gail E. Thomas, and Michael T. Nettles were presented during a preliminary meeting of contributors to this book. Contributors were expected to benefit from the delineation of a common context for consideration of their specific research topics from the National Study of Black College Students data.

Deskins' paper, "Winners and Losers: A Regional Assessment of Minority Enrollment and Earned Degrees in U.S. Colleges and Universities, 1974-84", provides an in depth look at the performance of Black students not only in relation to white students, but in relation to other minority groups as well. This is a good starting point for this book since this information provides an important reference point in examining with discernment, universities' reports on minority enrollment and graduation.

Trent's paper is one of the few in this book which addresses gender as well as race. The National Study of Black College Students examined gender only peripherally. This is a serious limitation of the study. Whatever has been done has been put to good use as papers in the following sections will show. However, what Trent presents is a critical handle on the issue of gender and race. Higher education's response to the matriculation of minority women is not as rosy as one would think. Again this is precisely the orientation with which to begin the collection of readings in this book.

Finally Thomas' paper examines the college selection process for Black students. What is it that most Black students study in college, in what fields do they graduate? This paper again touches on the issue of gender noting not only the choice of fields for Black men but also for Black women. The context for understanding the Black student's—both male and female—choice of field, is set here in a manner which provides insight.

Together these papers are valuable as points of reference and comparison to the empirical findings from the National Study of Black College Students reported in section II and III of this book. The nuances of minority enrollment and successes in Deskins' paper, the fate of minority women in higher education and the content of the education that Black students receive in institutions of higher learning provide us with significant research findings in the study of Black students experiences and outcomes in college.

DONALD R. DESKINS, JR.

Chapter One

Winners and Losers: A Regional Assessment of Minority Enrollment and Earned Degrees in U.S. Colleges and Universities, 1974–1984*

INTRODUCTION

Enrolling in college and subsequently earning a degree is clearly an indicator of status attainment in American society. Degree recipients are not only the beneficiaries of newly acquired status, but also possess a valued education that greatly enhances the chance of assuming important leadership positions and obtaining a larger share of the economic pie. Collectively, an earned college degree is enormously important to minority groups if they are to become major players in mainstream, political, social, and economic activities. Degree attainment is particularly important to those minority groups who have long been underrepresented on the nation's campuses and who strive to achieve equity. The extent to which these groups are participating in institutions of higher learning in this country, if measured over time, provides an excellent means to determine group progress, the basis upon which to speculate on what impact minorities are to have on America's future.

In spite of some progress made in minority enrollment during the later half of the 1970s, the gap is widening for African Americans who, since then, are now noticeably becoming absent from the nation's campuses. In contrast, Asian presence has been steadily increasing for at least a decade, and there are presently no signs of a trend change in the near future. It is the purpose of this paper to determine who are the winners and losers in this race for educational attainment. To do so requires a comprehensive examination of national and regional patterns of enrollment and degrees earned in the United States by minorities and for those nonminority populations who are also major players. Included among the minority groups considered in this assessment are Black (B), Hispanic (H), Asian (A), and Native American (NA). White (W), nonresident alien (NRA), total minority (TM) and total-all (T) will also be used as a basis for comparison.

Sufficient data is available for this undertaking: namely, the comprehensive data on enrollment and degrees conferred generated by the Higher Education General Information Survey (National Center for Educational Statistics 1976, 1978, 1980, 1982, and 1984). These data have been available annually since 1972 and are particularly useful to this task.

In order to determine if there is internal variance in enrollment and earned-degree data for the groups considered, four regions are used: Northeast (NE), Midwest (MW), South (S), and West (W). These regions have been used by the U.S. Bureau of the Census and are comprised of groupings of states according to economic and social conditions (U.S. Bureau of the Census 1980). The regions resulting from this state clustering are assumed to be homogeneous. It is upon this basis that they will be utilized in this study. States by region are as follows: *West*—Alaska, Arizona, California, Colorado, Hawaii, Idaho, Montana, New Mexico, Nevada, Oregon, Utah, Washington, Wyoming; *Midwest*—Illinois, Indiana, Iowa, Kansas, Michigan, Minnesota, Missouri, Nebraska, North Dakota, Ohio, South Dakota, Wisconsin; *South*—Alabama, Arkansas, Florida, Georgia, Kentucky, Louisiana, Mississippi, North Carolina, Oklahoma, South Carolina, Tennessee, Texas, Virginia, West Virginia; *Northeast*—Connecticut, Delaware, District of Columbia, Maine, Maryland, New Hampshire, New Jersey, New York, Pennsylvania, Rhode Island, Vermont.

Since the data base for this analysis is enormous, only summary tables—usually at the national level—will be integrated in the text. Detailed data on the regional level is found in the text which serves as a foundation for this examination and as reference materials for the reader.

ENROLLMENT

An idea of who the winners and losers are in aggregate enrollment becomes apparent when total enrollment from 1974 to 1984 are examined (Table 1.1). In 1980, enrollment for all groups (total) peaked at 10,586,465 (peak values are underlined) with enrollment for white, Black, Native American, and total minority also peaking in the same year (1980), indicating that the level of participation in higher education was also diminishing for these groups. Two years later, Hispanic enrollment also peaked and subsequently subsided. During the ten years between 1974 and 1984, only two groups—Asians and nonresident aliens—have yet to show signs of decline. Acknowledging that group degree-attainment is dependent on admissions and enrollment, aggregate data on enrollment at the national level shows that Asians and nonresident aliens are ahead in this race of relative gains, and all other groups to varying degrees are losing ground.

On the undergraduate level, Blacks, Native Americans, whites, nonresident aliens, and total have declined since 1980 (Table 1.1). Declines are observed for total minority, and Hispanics in 1982, with Asian undergraduate enrollment showing no signs of decline over the ten-year span examined.

For graduate enrollment, on the other hand, the peaked period enrollment for groups show much more variance (Table 1.1). Since 1976, the level of Black enrollment in graduate programs has been declining, along with that for Native American and white enrollees. Signs of decline for Hispanic, total minority, and total at this level, did not appear until 1980. Again, Asian and nonresident alien enrollment continues to increase for the period, giving them a decided edge over all other groups in eventually earning graduate degrees.

Aggregate enrollment in professional programs (Table 1.1) which includes those enrolled in medical, law, and dental programs, and a wide variety of other areas show that Native American enrollment peaked in 1976 and the categories of whites and total both peaked in 1980. By comparison, Black, Hispanic, Asian, total minority, and nonresident alien enrollment peaked in 1984.

Clearly, at the national level, aggregate Black enrollment in higher education has been in sharp decline for the longest time, closely followed by Native Americans. Enrollment declines for the white and total categories are next, followed by Hispanics. Asian and nonresident aliens show continued growth, therefore placing them as the clear winners in this quest for educational attainment while Blacks are the clear losers.

Rates of Change

Between 1976–1984, total enrollment in institutions of higher learning at the national level increased by 6.5 percent (Table 1.2). During this time span, total minority enrollment increased at a much higher rate (11.8 percent) reaching 1,713,776 in 1984—the highest number of minorities enrolled in institutions of higher education in the nation's history.

TABLE 1.1
Enrollment in Higher Education in the United States, 1974–1984 By Race/Ethnicity

Year	Black	Hispanic	Asian	Native American	Total Minority	Nonresident Alien	White	Total
Total Enrollment								
1974	821,930	287,431	114,266	52,876	1,276,503	189,768	7,965,963	9,416,868
1976	942,962	348,236	174,797	66,433	1,532,828	197,997	8,025,833	9,753,178
1978	960,804	370,366	203,250	66,264	1,601,680	231,281	8,059,106	9,892,067
1980	999,691*	413,549	244,112	72,535	1,737,012	279,068	8,570,621	10,586,465
1982	946,558	434,427	282,465	71,312	1,734,562	291,265	8,418,022	10,440,049
1984	894,179	429,755	321,371	68,471	1,713,716	348,260	8,328,692	10,390,668
Undergraduate Enrollment								
1974	745,414	267,975	97,057	48,700	1,159,146	121,928	6,847,447	8,129,521
1976	866,455	323,445	152,237	61,293	1,403,830	128,949	6,899,156	9,431,535
1978	887,505	344,958	177,838	61,407	1,471,708	154,869	6,938,999	8,565,576
1980	926,909	389,303	214,519	67,855	1,599,186	199,250	7,426,149	9,215,349
1982	833,043	406,272	251,466	67,036	1,607,617	193,250	7,360,247	9,161,314
1984	839,071	398,716	284,409	63,988	1,577,184	190,088	7,280,449	9,047,721
Graduate Enrollment								
1974	64,827	15,561	14,382	3,458	98,228	64,937	901,347	1,064,539
1976	65,326	20,244	18,485	3,887	107,942	66,087	906,626	1,080,655
1978	61,871	21,055	20,612	3,785	107,323	73,368	890,801	1,071,492
1980	59,978	24,246	23,487	3,878	111,589	85,916	897,198	1,094,703
1982	50,801	20,997	23,479	3,365	98,642	94,969	822,821	1,016,432
1984	51,064	23,256	27,893	3,514	105,727	154,830	816,560	1,077,117
Professional Enrollment								
1974	11,689	3,895	2,827	718	19,129	2,909	217,142	223,808
1976	11,181	4,547	4,075	1,253	21,056	2,961	220,051	244,008
1978	11,428	5,353	4,800	1,072	22,649	3,044	229,306	254,999
1980	12,804	6,525	6,106	802	26,237	2,902	247,274	276,413
1982	12,714	7,158	7,420	911	28,203	3,046	234,954	266,203
1984	13,044	7,783	9,069	969	30,805	3,342	231,623	265,830

Source: Higher Education General Information Survey (HEGIS). National Center for Education Statistics, 1976, 1978, 1980, 1982, and 1984. Washington D.C. *Peak values are underlined.

TABLE 1.2
Total Enrollment in the United States, 1976–1984
Percent Change by Race/Ethnicity and Degree Level

Degree Level	Black	Hispanic	Asian	Native American	Total Minority	Nonresident Alien	White	Total
All								
1976	942,962	348,236	174,797	66,433	1,532,428	197,997	8,022,833	9,753,258
1984	894,179	429,755	321,371	68,471	1,713,776	348,260	8,328,632	10,390,668
Percent Change	−5.2	+23.4	+83.9	+3.1	+11.8	+75.9	+3.8	+6.5
Undergraduate								
1976	866,455	323,445	152,237	61,293	1,403,430	128,949	6,899,156	8,431,535
1984	830,071	398,716	284,409	63,988	1,577,184	190,088	7,280,449	9,047,721
Percent Change	−4.2	+23.3	+86.8	+4.4	+12.4	+47.4	+5.5	+7.3
Graduate								
1976	65,326	20,244	18,485	3,887	107,942	66,087	903,626	1,077,655
1984	51,064	23,256	27,893	3,514	105,727	154,830	816,560	1,077,117
Percent Change	−21.8	+14.9	+50.9	−9.6	−2.1	+134.3	−9.6	*
Professional								
1976	11,181	4,547	4,075	1,253	21,056	2,961	220,051	244,068
1984	13,044	7,783	9,069	969	30,865	3,342	231,623	265,830
Percent Change	+16.7	+71.2	+122.5	−22.7	+46.6	+12.9	+5.3	+8.9

*Less than .1 percent
Source: HEGIS.

Encouraging as this fact is, not all minority group enrollment rates have been as positive. During this period, Black aggregate enrollment actually declined from 942,962, to 894,179. The 5.2–percent loss in Black enrollment stands in sharp contrast to the increases for other minority groups—Hispanic (23.4 percent), Asian (83.9 percent), and total minority (11.8 percent). The rate of enrollment changes for white (3.8 percent) and Native American (3.1 percent) are also positive. However, during this period, no group experienced as large a rate of increase as did nonresident aliens, whose enrollment increased by 75.9 percent.

The rates of change for undergraduate enrollment in magnitude mirror those for aggregate enrollment for all groups (total), with the exception of nonresident aliens who, as a group, continue to be positive and increased by 47.4 percent, placing them second behind Asians (Table 1.2).

However, the rate of enrollment change for graduate enrollment are substantially different. Overall graduate enrollment has remained nearly steady ranging between 1,077,655 in 1976 and 1,077,117 in 1984—which amounts to no significant change.

White enrollment on the graduate level shows a 9.6–percent decline, at the same rate as Native Americans. The Black rate of decline at 21.8 percent is great—a bit more than five times the decrease in undergraduate enrollment.

A modestly positive rate of change is found for Hispanics (14.9 percent). The Asian increase is less than it was for undergraduate enrollment but is still quite high at 50.9 percent. Nonresident alien enrollment has increased by 134.3 percent, the highest rate observed for any group at all degree levels. This fact provides some evidence on how nonresidents are becoming more disproportionate in the nation's graduate programs.

Due to the inclusive nature of the professional enrollment category, a positive increase is found for all groups except Native Americans. An examination of rates of change in enrollment across groups and categories designates Blacks as the losers and Asians and nonresident aliens as the decided winners.

Over and Underrepresentation

The direction and magnitude of change in enrollment for the nation's minority groups is now known. The next issue to be addressed is whether minority enrollment in higher education for 1976 and 1984 are representative relative to their population base. By comparing what percentage each minority represents in the national population with what percentage they represent in graduate enrollment, it is possible to address this issue.

For example, if the enrollment percentage for a minority group exceeds that of the group's percentage in the population then the group is over-represented in enrollment. Underrepresentation exists when the group's percentage in enrollment is less than it is in the population.

In this case, 1980 population is used as a basis to determine the degree to which minority groups are over and underrepresented since it falls halfway between the dates of the two sets of enrollment and degree-attainment data being examined.

No surprises are revealed here (Table 1.3). Blacks and Hispanics are underrepresented in enrollment for both years and on all enrollment levels in contrast to Asians who are overrepresented in all categories. Native American enrollment is underrepresented on all levels. Other data show that whites are overrepresented in enrollment with the exception of 1984, where they are underrepresented on the graduate level at a time when the non-resident aliens share of graduate enrollment reached +14.4 percent.

TABLE 1.3

Percentage of Over or Underrepresentation of Minority Enrollment in the United States for 1976 and 1984 by Level of Enrollment Based on 1980 Population

Level of Enrollment and Year	*Black Percent*	*Hispanic Percent*	*Asian Percent*	*Native American Percent*	*Total Minority Percent*
Percentage of U.S. Population	(11.7)	(5.7)	(1.6)	(.7)	(19.7)
All					
1976	−2.0*	−2.1	+ .2	0.0	− 3.9
1984	−3.1	−1.6	+1.5	0.0	− 3.2
Undergraduate					
1976	−1.4	−1.9	+ .2	0.0	− 3.1
1984	−2.5	−1.3	+1.5	0.0	− 2.3
Graduate					
1976	−5.7	−3.8	+ .1	− .3	− 9.7
1984	−7.0	−3.5	+1.0	− .4	− 9.9
Professional					
1976	−7.1	−3.9	+ .1	− .2	−11.1
1984	−6.8	−2.8	+1.8	− .3	−18.0

Over or underrepresentation is calculated by the difference between the proportion of race/ethnicity in the United States population and the percentage that race/ethnicity represents in higher education enrollment.

( )=Proportion of total United States population that race/ethnic group represents.

* The number that appears is the difference between the population percentage and the enrollment for each group.

DEGREES EARNED

It is obvious that enrollment trends, since they are the starting point in the process of attaining a college degree, are extremely important because they establish the baseline for future degree attainment which is the end product of the educational pipeline. Declines in enrollment will, undoubtedly, negatively affect future degree outcomes for some minority groups and will positively increase such outcomes for others. With this consideration in mind, it is worthwhile to assess the changes in earned degrees for the groups being considered between the years 1975–76 and 1984–85. Eight earned-degree categories are examined: associate (A.A.), baccalaureate (B.A.), master's (M.A.), doctorate (Ph.D.), medical (M.D.), law (L.L.B./J.D.), dentistry (D.D.A./D.M.D.), and the residual category comprised of all other first-time professional degrees (OPD), excluding those already mentioned.

Rates of Change

In 1984, there were 1,876,211 degrees conferred in higher education, which represents a negligible increase (Table 1.4). Increases in earned degrees are reported for all groups during the period except for Blacks and whites, the only groups to show a decline in degree attainment during this nine-year period. Black losses in earned degrees amounted to 8.4 percent while Asians increased their share of earned degrees by 81.7 percent and nonresident aliens dramatically increased by 351.0 percent.

Rates of change in earned Associate of Arts degrees, two-year degrees attained at junior or community colleges, are decidedly different from the aggregate earned-degree acquisition pattern (Table 1.4). On this level, Blacks gained by 2.6 percent, Asians by 24.9 percent and nonresident aliens by 1,408.4 percent. Decreases are shown for all other groups as it does for total A.A. degrees which declined by 7.3 percent during this time span.

Baccalaureate degrees earned between 1975–76 and 1984–85 increased for all groups except two. Blacks experienced a 7.4–percent decline, and whites decreased by 1.9 percent. The increase in B.A. degrees earned were led in order by nonresident aliens (387.1 percent), Asians (110.4 percent), and Hispanics (33.4 percent). Overall, B.A. degrees increased by 6.3 percent.

On the master's level, the first graduate degree, there is an overall loss of 7.9 percent, dropping from 309,264 to 284,985 during the nine-year period examined (Table 1.4). Increases in earned M.A. degrees were enjoyed by only four groups, led by nonresident aliens with a 122 percent increase, followed by Asians (80.7 percent), Native Americans, and Hispanics.

Losses are observed for whites where the number of degree recipients declined from 262,772 to 221,957, which represents a 15.5–percent decrease. The most distressing losses occurred in number of M.A.s earned by Blacks (a loss of 35.7 percent) which amounts to 17,273 fewer M.A. degrees being conferred to Blacks in 1984–85 than in 1975–1976.

The overall number of Ph.D. degrees granted also declined by 2.4 percent. White Ph.D. attainment dropped and heads the loss column with a drop of 17.9–percent followed by Native Americans (11.8 percent), and Blacks, where a 10.9–percent decline took place. The big gainers in Ph.D. degree acquisition are nonresident aliens, Asians, and Hispanics with respective increases in percentages of degrees awarded of 88.2, 75.6 and 56.1.

Medical degrees earned by Blacks during this nine-year time span moderately increased by 1.4 percent, the lowest increase experienced by all groups (Table 1.4). Asian and Hispanic increases in M.D. degrees earned both exceeded 120 percent, while white gains rose by 15.9 percent, which is close to the overall increase of 18.8 percent for this degree category.

Positive changes in the number of law degrees earned were found for all but one category, lead by nonresident aliens and followed by Asians, Hispanics, and Native Americans. Only in the case of Blacks was there a decline. Their rate of loss was 7.4 percent.

Overall, dentistry degrees conferred increased by 4.4 percent. Whites and Native American degree recipients increased by 8.2 and 83.3 percent respectively. The losses are led by Asians (43.5 percent) and Blacks (30.2 percent).

The residual category of other professional degrees (OPD) recorded positive change in number of degrees earned for all groups. Even though the Black change of 7.6 percent is positive, the rate of change is lower than that for all others, which totals 20.6 percent.

Overall, Blacks are losing ground in degrees earned and, considering the losses in enrollment already discussed, future degrees attained will decline further as fewer Black students move through the pipeline. Black degree attainment is negative in all but three degree categories (Table 1.4). It is positive in the A.A. degree category, the one which has least transferability in the educational attainment degree hierarchy. Positive rates for Blacks are also found in the other professional degree (OPD) category which is the catch-all for professional degrees other than M.D., L.L.B./J.D. and D.D.A./D.M.D. degrees.

It is important to note that the rate of Black losses in degree attainment on the graduate level are appallingly high. There is a 35.7–percent loss at the M.A. level and a 10.9–percent loss at the Ph.D. level. Such losses drastically reduce the number of Blacks with this prestigious degree, further reducing the availability of Blacks prepared for important leadership roles.

TABLE 1.4
Total Degrees Earned 1975–1976 and 1984–1985
Percent of Change by Race/Ethnicity and Degree Level

Degree Level	Black	Hispanics	Asian	Native American	Total Minority	Nonresident Alien	White	Total
All								
1975–76	126,707	44,812	22,978	7,201	201,598	40,147	1,617,388	1,859,213
1984–85	116,054	50,439	41,746	7,774	215,948	181,076	1,479,187	1,876,811
Percent Change	−8.4	+12.6	+81.7	+8.0	+7.1	+351.0	−8.5	+.9
AA								
1975–76	40,925	19,171	5,462	2,522	68,080	3,651	412,918	484,649
1984–85	41,979	16,558	6,823	2,400	67,760	55,072	326,339	449,171
Percent Change	+2.6	−13.6	+24.9	−4.8	−.5	+1,408.4	−20.9	−7.3
BA								
1975–76	59,122	17,964	11,193	3,498	91,777	15,012	811,600	918,389
1984–85	54,766	23,967	23,553	3,832	106,118	73,116	794,460	975,694
Percent Change	−7.4	+33.4	+110.4	+9.5	+15.6	+387.1	−1.9	+6.3
MA								
1975–76	20,345	5,299	3,991	783	30,418	16,074	262,772	309,264
1984–85	13,072	5,981	7,212	1,034	27,299	35,720	221,957	284,985
Percent Change	−35.7	+12.9	+80.7	+32.1	−10.3	+122.3	−15.5	−7.9

Ph.D

1975–76	1,213	396	583	93	2,285	4,068	27,434	33,787
1984–85	1,080	618	1,024	82	2,804	7,655	22,522	32,981
Percent Change	−10.9	+56.1	+75.6	−11.8	+22.7	+88.2	−17.9	−2.4

MD

1975–76	708	203	227	36	1,174	208	11,911	13,373
1984–85	718	455	565	53	1,791	193	13,905	15,889
Percent Change	+1.4	+124.1	+148.9	+47.2	+52.5	−7.2	+15.9	+18.8

LLB/JD

1975–76	1,519	616	312	75	2,522	199	29,520	32,241
1984–85	1,406	980	571	101	3,058	2,682	31,752	37,492
Percent Change	−7.4	+59.1	+83.0	+34.1	+21.3	+1,247.7	+7.6	+16.3

DDS/DMD

1975–76	181	84	148	5	418	106	4,901	5,425
1984–85	139	121	262	30	552	115	4,530	5,197
Percent Change	−30.2	−3.6	−43.5	+83.3	−24.3	−7.8	+8.2	+4.4

OPD

1975–76	2,694	1,079	962	189	4,924	829	56,332	62,085
1984–85	2,899	1,759	1,756	242	6,566	6,514	61,722	74,802
Percent Change	+7.6	+63.0	+82.5	+28.0	+33.3	+685.8	+9.6	+20.6

Source: HEGIS

Some have attempted to explain Black losses by suggesting that those Blacks who would have normally entered graduate programs are lost to enrollment in medical and law programs. The rates of increase and absolute numbers of degree attainment in law and medicine are contrary to that position, and the data do not support this explanation.

Whites, on the other hand, are experiencing increases in medical, law, and other professional degree attainment, but show losses in all undergraduate and graduate earned-degree categories. These losses are particularly extreme at M.A. and Ph.D. levels. Perhaps, in the case of whites, decreases in M.A. and Ph.D. degrees earned are offset by the high rate of increase in medical degree attainment.

Therefore, the argument posed to explain Black declines in M.A. and Ph.D. degree programs may better serve to explain the white decline in Ph.D. degree attainment. It is possible that whites are opting for professional degrees rather than Ph.D.s. The rate of change and the absolute numbers suggest this possibility.

The change in degrees earned for the remaining minority groups and nonresident aliens are positive (Table 1.4), with nonresident aliens showing the highest rates of increase at each degree level—followed in order by Asians, Hispanics, and Native Americans. Nonresident alien increases in degree attainment are exceptionally high at the M.A. and Ph.D. level. There is also the possibility that white declines in these categories are also being impacted and replaced by nonresident alien increases.

Over and Underrepresentation

For all degree levels, black earned degree percentages were below their proportion of total population (Table 1.5). This finding is not surprising since Blacks were underrepresented on all levels of enrollment in higher education which is the basis for future degree attainment. Blacks were nearest to the 11.7 percent which they represent in the population in 1984 at the Associate of Arts degree level where 9.3 percent of the degrees earned went to Black recipients. Considering the character of and limited transferability of these degrees in the educational pipeline, this high level of representation in A.A. degrees received is not as important as it appears because, in most instances, the degree is terminal and has little value for continuing study in higher education.

On the other hand, the percentage of Blacks receiving Ph.D. degrees in 1984 is one of the least representative (3.2 percent) relative to their percentage in the population and is just behind dentistry degrees (Table 1.5). The reduction in Black Ph.D. recipients is significant, and the potential impact that these reduced numbers will have on the future positioning of Blacks in leadership of our society is not promising.

TABLE 1.5
Percentage of Over or Underrepresentation
of Minority-Earned Degrees in the United States
for 1975–76 and 1984–85 by Degree Level
Based on 1980 Population

Degree Level	Year	Black Percent	Hispanic Percent	Asian Percent	Native American Percent	Total Minority Percent
Percentage of U.S. Population		(11.7)	(5.7)	(1.6)	(.7)	(19.7)
All	1975–76	−4.9*	−3.3	− .4	− .3	− 8.9
	1984–85	−5.5	−3.0	+ .7	− .3	− 8.1
AA	1975–76	−3.3	−1.7	− .5	− .2	− 5.7
	1984–85	−2.4	−2.0	− .1	− .2	− 4.7
BA	1975–76	−5.3	−3.7	− .4	− .3	− 9.7
	1984–85	−6.1	−3.2	+ .8	− .3	− 8.8
MA	1975–76	−5.2	−4.0	− .3	− .4	− 9.9
	1984–85	−7.1	−3.6	+ .9	− .3	−10.1
Ph.D	1975–76	−8.1	−4.5	+ .1	− .4	−12.9
	1984–85	−8.5	−3.8	+1.5	− .5	−11.2
MD	1974–75	−6.4	−4.2	+ .1	− .4	−10.9
	1984–85	−7.2	−2.8	+2.0	− .4	− 8.4
LLB/JD	1974–75	−7.0	−3.8	− .6	− .5	−11.9
	1984–85	−7.9	−3.1	− .1	− .3	−11.5
DDS/DMD	1974–75	−8.3	−4.2	+1.1	− .6	−12.0
	1984–85	−9.1	−3.4	+3.4	− .1	− 9.2
OPD	1975–76	−7.4	−4.0	− .1	− .4	−11.8
	1984–85	−7.8	−3.4	+ .7	− .4	− 8.1

Over or underrepresentation is calculated by the difference between the proportion of race/ ethnicity in the United States population and the percentage that race/ethnicity represents of higher-education enrollment.
* The number that appears is the difference between the population percentage and enrollment percentage for each group.

Native Americans and Hispanics are also underrepresented when the percentages of degrees earned by these groups on all levels are compared with the percentage they represent in the total population (Table 1.5). It is only in the case of Asians that a minority group's percentage of degrees earned exceeds their percentage in the population. However, Asians continue to be underrepresented on the undergraduate level, particularly at the A.A. degree level. In 1984–85 they are overrepresented in B.A. and M.A. degrees received, a considerable change from their underrepresentation in both degree categories nine years earlier. The degree of overrepresentation of Asians in Ph.D., M.D. and D.D.A./D.M.D. degrees over the ten-year period is indeed impressive. Asians have consistently earned higher percentages of degrees in these categories relative to their representation in the population, nicely positioning members of the group to assume important leadership roles in the future.

Obviously, whites continue to be overrepresented in degrees earned at all levels, regardless of year (Table 1.5). Where whites are found to be slightly underrepresented is probably due to the effects associated with the enormous increases in nonresident aliens' degree attainment, particularly at the M.A. and Ph.D. levels.

Outcomes

Drastic reductions in the number of Ph.D. degree recipients will make it nearly impossible for African Americans to adequately fill leadership roles and to serve as role models for others to follow, especially among the underclass ranks. According to William Julius Wilson (1987), the lack of Black leadership only serves to perpetuate the social dislocation found in our inner cities. The diminishing number of Black Ph.D.s will also reduce America's chances of moving toward a more diverse and pluralistic society through increased Black participation.

Many of the nation's universities have attempted to achieve greater cultural, ethical, and racial diversity as one means to address the problem of a shortage in Black leadership. Among the various policies and initiatives undertaken has been an emphasis on increasing Black faculty presence on campuses. Although vigorous recruitment has resulted, many institutions attribute their lack of success in this effort to the fact of an extreme shortage of Blacks available for such posts. The observed sharp declines in Blacks with earned Ph.D. degrees establishes indisputably that the pool is shrinking.

Ironically, universities which initiate minority faculty recruitment are the training grounds for Ph.D.s. As they lament the reduced Black pool, it should be noted that universities have exclusive control over the entire Ph.D. educational process, from admissions through training to degree confirmation. Thus, these institutions should take the necessary steps at all relevant points in the process beginning with high school graduation to ensure that sufficient Blacks are in the pipeline to produce sufficient numbers of Blacks graduating with the Ph.D. degree.

The reduction in the number of Blacks enrolled in graduate education is clearly established, and the rates of outcomes in Black Ph.D. production was, in fact, set nearly a decade earlier. The lesson to be learned here is that, if enrollment figures like those examined earlier are seriously taken into account, the overproduction of Asians in Ph.D., M.D., and D.D.A./ D.M.D. degrees, as impressive as they are, is predictable. Asians have earned a much higher percentage of degrees in these categories relative to their percentages in the population and in contrast to Blacks. Similarly, if a serious examination of Black enrollment patterns a decade earlier had been undertaken, today's outcome could have been easily forecasted (Deskins 1984). As a result of early enrollment, Black decreases in advanced degree attainment is also predictable. Blacks are clearly the losers in the long run as Asians are the designated long-term winners.

REGIONAL VARIATION

Minority populations are not distributed evenly across the United States, nor are the educational institutions which they attend, although the distribution of these institutions follows the distribution of the total population. National enrollment and degree-attainment patterns have been examined, and the knowledge of which groups have made gains in enrollment and earned degrees as well as those that registered losses is well established. Now, a selective exploration of regional enrollment and earned-degree trends for minority groups is made to determine the degree of variance that may occur. An attempt is also made to explain these differences when possible.

Enrollment

National trends in enrollment for Blacks show a decline of 4.2 percent. However on the regional level there is considerable variation. Three of the four regions—Northeast, Northwest, and West—all show that Blacks have declined with the sharpest decline of 24.2 percent recorded in the West. Black undergraduate enrollment is increasing in the South where slightly more than half of the nation's Black undergraduate enrollment is found, although the increase is only 7.1 percent. Hispanic enrollment on the other hand, is expanding in three regions and decreasing in just one, the Northeast by 3.5 percent. Hispanic gains in the Midwest and South exceed their national rate of 23.3 percent, whereas in the West, the rate of increase for this group is only 8.7 percent, in contrast to the national norm.

Asian increases in undergraduate enrollment are positive in all regions. The lowest rate of increase 64.0 percent is found in the West where the highest absolute number of Asian population resides. In the Midwest and South, Asians experienced an enormous increase in enrollment, 148.4 and

211.1 percent respectively. This increase has occurred in a region where the Asian population is quite small. Rates of increase for whites and nonresident aliens across all regions are positive and converge around the national rates.

On the graduate level, Black enrollment is declining in all regions, even in the South where a 16.4–percent loss has occurred in contrast to the Asian rates of increase, where growth is positive in all regions and extremely strong in the South and West. Although Hispanic enrollment is positive regionally, there is considerable variation. Almost no change is observed in the Northeast and West, but increases in the Midwest reached 22.2 percent and, in the South, 38.8 percent. Native Americans, like Blacks, are losing in graduate enrollment in all regions, as are whites except in the West. Nonresident aliens' graduate enrollment is increasing in all regions, and by as much as 378.9 percent in the South. Regionally, the rates of increase for nonresident aliens on the average exceed those for Asians.

Regional variations in enrollment in professional programs is mostly positive for all groups. The regional rates of change do not, in most instances, greatly deviate from the national rates. It is difficult to determine which groups are beneficiaries or losers in this category of enrollment because the rates are positive for all.

Degree Attainment

White acquisition of associate degrees decreased in all regions, the greatest losses occurred in the West and South, where the rates of loss in each region is about 30 percent or approximately three times the rate of loss in the Northeast and Midwest. Hispanic A.A. degree recipients also lost ground in three of four regions. A slight reduction in the West of 4.6 percent and losses of 41.4 percent in the Northeast and 25.2 percent in the South stands in sharp contrast to a 32.7–percent gain in the Midwest. On the other hand, Blacks experienced growth in earned A.A. degrees in the Northeast and West. In the South they lost ground.

There are enormous rates of increase in A.A. degrees earned by Asians in three regions—Northeast, Midwest, and South—that range between 116.7 and 231.9 percent. The drop in A.A. degrees earned by Asians is in the West where their base population is largest. A quarter fewer Asians received A.A. degrees in the West by the end of the nine-year period being examined. The Native American degree recipient regional pattern followed that for Asians, but the magnitude of the increase is much lower. Like Asians, Native American A.A. degree acquisition also declined in the West. Increases in degree acquisition by nonresident aliens are positive in all regions. The least growth is experienced in the South (25.3 percent) and the largest growth occurs in the West (144.3 percent), which is in contrast to a tenfold increase for nonresident aliens in the remaining regions—Northeast and Northwest—where the increase exceeds 1,400 percent.

Changes in rates for earned B.A. degrees—the prerequisite degree for graduate and professional studies—is important to discuss because it is the first step on the academic ladder leading to higher academic and professional credentials. All minority groups except Blacks are increasing their acquisition of these degrees. Regionally, the rate at which Blacks are attaining B.A. degrees is negative. In the Northeast, the .4–percent decrease is insignificant. In the South, where the largest number of B.A. degrees are earned by Blacks, the rate of loss was 4.1 percent.

Much more drastic declines are found in the West where B.A.s conferred to Blacks decreased by 26.0 percent, compared to a loss of 15.7 percent in the Midwest. The only group to record losses in earned B.A.s in three of four regions is whites, although their rate of loss is much less than that for Blacks. B.A. degrees acquired by all the remaining minority groups and nonresident aliens is positive for all regions with the exception of Native Americans in the South where they decreased by 1.1 percent. The rates of increase of nonresident aliens exceeds 250.0 percent in all regions. For Asians it ranges between a low of 80.5 percent in the West to a high of 239.0 percent in the South, while in the Northeast and Midwest, the rates of change are just over 125.0 percent in each region. Native Americans had the greatest increase (34.8 percent) in B.A. degrees earned in the Northeast.

Nationally the total number of M.A. degrees earned decreased by 24,279 between 1975–76 and 1984–85 for a loss of 7.9 percent. Native Americans, Blacks, and whites shared in this loss, while the number of Master's degrees received by nonresident aliens, Asians, and Hispanics increased. Blacks, again, showed the sharpest decline of all groups. Their overall drop in M.A. degrees earned fell by more than a third. The greatest losses for Blacks occurred in the West (60.6 percent). Among other comparison groups, only whites experienced a decline in M.A. degrees conferred for this same period and region. The number of M.A.s awarded to Blacks decreased by about 36.0 percent in both the Midwest and South. No other group experienced similar declines in M.A. degrees earned. Asians and nonresident aliens experienced the highest growth rates in all regions for earned M.A. degrees— as high as 164.2 percent.

On the Ph.D. level, the overall number of degrees awarded declined by 2.4 percent. Whites nationally experienced the greatest decline—17.9 percent—followed by Blacks and Native Americans with losses of 10.9 and 11.8 percent respectively. Blacks lose significant ground in Ph.D. degrees received in the Midwest (33.6 percent) and in the West (41.7 percent). It is only in the South that Blacks made gains of 18.5 percent in earned Ph.D. degrees. Hispanics, Asians, and nonresident aliens, on the other hand, showed increases in Ph.D.s received in all regions. Hispanic gains are especially strong in the Northeast (118.8 Percent). However, Hispanics experienced the lowest rate of increase in the South where their population base is regionally strong, and particularly in the western reaches of the region. Asian rates of increase in doctoral degrees are generally higher than those for Hispanics. An increase of 133.9 percent—the highest for Asians—occurred in the Midwest, with the lowest regional increase of 46.7 percent found in the West. Nonresident aliens increased their share of Ph.D. degrees by the highest rate—186.5 percent in the South and 178.0 percent in the West. Again at the Ph.D. level, as before, the winners are nonresident aliens and Asians, and the losers are Blacks.

Collectively, the number of professional degrees earned increased by about 20 percent. Nested within this category are medical, law, and dentistry degrees. Increases are observed for each of these degrees for all groups. Although nationally, Blacks received M.D.s at an increasing rate, the rate of Black increase for this degree category is only 1.4 percent. The largest regional increases in M.D. degrees for Blacks occurred in the South and in the West. Only in the Midwest was there a decrease in the number of medical degrees awarded to Blacks.

Whites, Asians, and Hispanics all increased their numbers in M.D. degree acquisition. Hispanics enjoyed the largest gains in the Midwest (214.8 percent) and the least (17.7 percent) in the West. Asian M.D. degree recipients were strong in all regions with growth ranging from (43.2 percent) in the West to the highest (414.8 percent) in the South. Largest increases for whites were also in the South, followed by the West and Midwest in order.

Law degrees also increased overall, as did other degrees in the professional degree category. Again, Blacks were the only group registering a decline in number of law degrees received over the nine-year period ending in 1984. Regionally, Black losses were once more largest in the Midwest (50.5 percent) followed by a 15.8–percent loss in the West. However, substantial growth in Black L.L.B./J.D. degrees received occurred in the Northeast with 26.8 percent and in the South with 19.5 percent. Nearly half of the groups considered experienced large increases in the number of law degrees earned in the Northeast (whites, Asians, and Blacks). Hispanic L.L.B./J.D. growth in degree acquisition was highest in the South (164.6 percent) and lowest (6.1 percent) in the West. Native Americans and nonresident aliens had the highest rate of increase in the Midwest, and Asian increases were strongest in the Northeast.

The total number of dental degrees received did not change much between 1975–76 and 1984–85. Although there was a decrease in absolute numbers from 5,425 to 5,197 (a loss of 4.2 percent), the change is quite small, particularly so when regional trends are examined. Blacks had the greatest losses in D.D.S./D.M.D. degrees awarded, with the sharpest decline of 43.8 percent occurring in the Midwest and with small decreases occurring in the South (13.1 percent). The greatest increase for Hispanics occurred in the Midwest where the increases in dental degrees exceeded 400.0 percent. Losses for Hispanics registered 37.5 percent in the Northeast and 2.9 percent in the West. Asian dental degree recipients increased in all regions. The numbers are so small for Native Americans. Nationally, they earned five dental degrees in 1975–76 and only thirty in 1984–85. Whites lost the most in the Northeast (14.5 percent) and about half of that in the Midwest and South. The gain of 1.8 percent in the West is not very significant.

Overall for the residual category, professional degree recipients (OPD) increased by 20 percent with all groups showing increases. Regional losses were recorded only for Blacks, with 35.1 percent in the Midwest and 6.4 percent in the West. The only other group for which loss was recorded is Native Americans in the Midwest by 13.6 percent.

Overview

By now, it is apparent that African Americans have recorded the greatest losses in enrollment and degrees earned—more than any other group, and followed by Native Americans and Hispanics. Asian, on the other hand, recorded the greatest increases. When Blacks' increases are observed, they were primarily found in the South, followed by the Northeast and West in that order. However, consistent declines for Blacks in degree attainment were found in the Midwest. The concentration of losses for Blacks in this region clearly delineate it from other regions.

Native American losses are regionally concentrated in the South followed by the Midwest and the West. The greatest growth experienced by Native Americans took place in the Northeast. Asian growth took place in all regions, making strong inroads in all regions except the West, where gains are not of the same magnitude. The Midwest is the region where increases were most favorable for Hispanics, followed closely by the South and then the Northeast where some losses occurred. The least growth for this group occurred in the West.

WINNERS AND LOSERS

By examining enrollment and degree acquisition over time, winners and losers among the nation's minority groups are well documented. Education has long been recognized as an important—if not *the most* important—

vehicle through which status attainment and upward mobility is achieved. From this examination, it is clear that African Americans, one of the nation's most underrepresented minority groups in higher education, are clearly the losers in enrollment and degree acquisition across all categories. Black losses in higher education over the nine-year period examined have been catastrophic. Black enrollment declines occurred much earlier in time and in the educational pipeline than the declines experienced by other minority groups. Consequently, earned degrees for Blacks continued to decrease over the nine-year period and as the educational degree hierarchy was ascended. In other words, Blacks' losses in degree attainment at both graduate and professional levels exceed those for the levels below. It is only at the bottom of the degree hierarchy that Blacks show some growth—in the associate degree category—growth in a degree category that has limited transferability and utility in ascending the education ladder.

Possible explanation of this dismal pattern of African American enrollment and degree acquisition may be attributed to several national economic and political conditions. It is obvious that between 1975–1985, the period considered here, our nation experienced a political transformation which resulted in the dismantling of affirmative action. Previously, national commitment to equal opportunity and affirmative action programs provided the legal and moral justification for increased Black participation in higher education.

Since 1976, with changes in the political climate (Gamson and Modigliani 1987), support for "remedial action"—which once was dominant—lost ground to "no preferential treatment," evolved into "undeserving advantage," and finally culminated in the doctrine of "reverse discrimination." Throughout this progression the plight of Blacks in higher education has worsened. Further dismantling of affirmative action policies and practices by recent Supreme Court decisions is verification of this national change and provides a legal interpretation supportive of the Reagan administration's doctrine calling for a "color-blind society."

The university community has not been totally isolated from this national attitudinal change. Paralleling this period of political transformation, universities, after earlier admitting the largest number of African American students in history in a concentrated quest for diversity, shifted their concern to the maintenance of quality and are placing an increasing emphasis on "excellence." In essence, academia began to follow the color-blind doctrine of the Reagan administration and, in the process, dismantled equal-opportunity and affirmative-action programs. As a result of this change in stance, Black representation in the university, starting at the top with graduate enrollment, dropped precipitously from 1976 and has since then similarly affected Black enrollments and consequently degree attainment at all levels. Not only has the new policy deemphasizing affirmative action been implemented, but it apparently has been implemented first and most widely at the nation's best institutions where the decline in Black representation has been greatest.

Justification for the shift in emphasis from diversity to "excellence" can be found in the *Closing of the American Mind* (Bloom 1987) and *Cultural Literacy* (Hirsch 1987), books that encourage universities to preserve their mission of knowledge creation above all others and to remove themselves from direct involvement with the nation's social agenda. Each of these works encourages universities to restrict their activities only to academic issues, a position clearly supporting elitist ideas and not inclusive of underrepresented minorities.

In addition to the political transformation that has undermined affirmative action, and the philosophy of elitism that has recently been fully reinstituted at universities, the cost of education is increasing. These increases in cost, alongside declining Black employment and earnings, place a substantial financial burden on Blacks who now seek higher education. During this period of increasing college tuitions, federal funding of education—particularly student aid—has declined, significantly so under the leadership of William Bennett, the former Secretary of Education. These economic factors alone have negatively affected Black participation in higher education to the degree that present negative trends may prove irreversible.

The conditions for Black enrollment, retention, and graduation in higher education have worsened. Nevertheless, opponents of affirmative action who are, at the same time, proponents of elitism, have identified Asians as the model minority group in higher education. These voices hold Asians up as an example for other minority groups to follow as they seek status attainment through education.

The Asian presence in higher education and degree attainment has increased, but not solely as a result of the political transformation previously discussed. The Asian increase is not so much the result of present political conditions and social doctrine, but is attributable more to their increasing numbers in the population and to their success in the acquisition of wealth. Although this groups' success is often used as a ploy in the argument against increasing the Black presence on our campuses, Asians are also beginning to encounter problems in the academy. Problems which have some racial overtones, such as the notion of restricting Asian admission, have ironically reared their ugly heads.

Hispanics, like Blacks, are also greatly underrepresented in American higher education. Their enrollment pattern and degree attainment is positive although not as strong as is observed for Asians. The Hispanic group is steadily gaining ground, However, the progress they are making should be viewed with caution. As indicated earlier, after years of progress in undergraduate enrollment, Black enrollment started to decline after 1980 (and on the graduate level after 1976)—a decline which has continued to have a disastrous effect on recent Black degree production. An examination of enrollment data for Hispanics shows that their undergraduate enrollment has declined since 1982, and that Hispanic graduate enrollment began to decline two years earlier. The pattern is identical to that observed for Blacks. Thus, a similar negative impact on future degree acquisition among Hispanics can be expected. Unfortunately, not much attention is currently being paid to Hispanic progress in education. The group is not at the center of contemporary discussions in higher education, as are Blacks and Asians who represent polar opposites in rates of enrollment and degree attainment.

Regionally, Blacks are doing better in degree attainment in the South and making the least progress in the Midwest. Although they are sustaining losses in the South, the rates of loss are much less than those found in the remaining regions. This is particularly true in contrast to the Midwest. Obviously, the Midwest has suffered severe economic decline relative to other regions and has undergone dramatic restructuring of its industrial base (U.S. Department of Commerce 1962, 1970, 1980, and 1986). It is also obvious that the Midwest has sustained short-range losses in high school graduation, with a decline of 10.6 percent between 1986–87 and 1990–91 (Western Interstate Commission for Higher Education 1988). However, these declines are not sufficient to explain the severe drop in Black participation in the region's institutions of higher education. Perhaps Blacks' losses in the Midwest, which exceed those for other regions, can best be explained by the regional universities' explicit and implicit acceptance of the Bloom/Hirsch and Reagan doctrines mentioned earlier.

The picture in the South is quite different. It is not surprising that Blacks are doing relatively better there in both enrollment and degree attainment and as compared to other regions, since more than half of the nation's African American population resides there. There is another plausible explanation for the higher rate of Black participation in the South in contrast to the losses experienced in other regions. There is no doubt that Black institutions, most of which are located in the South, are committed to increasing education opportunities for Blacks and improving the quality of that education. It is for this reason that Black institutions in the South continue to be as attractive to Black students as they have traditionally been.

Since enrollment patterns are established first, these serve as reasonably good predictors of future outcomes. With this in mind, the educational future for Blacks and Hispanics looks quite dim. According to past enrollment numbers, which continue to decline, fewer will be receiving degrees in the future—thus reducing their chances to become full participants in all aspects of our society. Enrollment figures clearly show that Asian ascendancy in earned degrees will continue, as will that for nonresident aliens, a group which has made considerable inroads in enrollment and degree acquisition in recent years, particularly at the graduate and professional levels.

In light of these trends, the real loser may be larger American society, unless there is a drastic change in the next few years resulting in increasing African American and Hispanic enrollment in higher education. If these patterns do not change soon, a significant growing segment of our national human resource base will remain untrained, underutilized and unproductive. In light of the stringent global economic competition and challenges which this nation faces, we can ill afford the failure of extending full educational opportunities to underrepresented minorities whose base population collectively continues to grow and is forecasted to challenge the white population's majority status by the midpoint of the twenty-first century (Wattenberg 1987). Otherwise, the route for nearly a third of our current population to productive citizenship is blocked . . . with potentially devastating consequences for the society's overall and long-range well-being.

WILLIAM T. TRENT

Chapter Two

Focus on Equity: Race and Gender Differences in Degree Attainment, 1975–76; 1980–81

Inequality in higher educational attainment among different race and ethnic groups and between sexes continues to be a critical problem for American education. The rapid escalation of change in the nature of work along with continuing discrimination further disadvantages minorities lacking sufficient credentials and accentuates disparities between males and females in the labor force. Recent evidence reporting educational, economic, and political gains for minorities and women notwithstanding, substantial race and sex differences remain in the educational pipeline transitions and occupational attainment (Freeman 1976).

It is now apparent that population demographics provide still another source of concern about the responsiveness of higher education to race and gender differences in higher education attainment. A recent report by the National Institute of Independent Colleges and Universities presents a challenging scenario for education in the 1990s (Hodgkinson 1983). Posing the question of "Guess Who's Coming to College . . . ,'' The report gives a portrait of the current student population for the next decade which *should* entail substantial numbers of minority and female students at the postsecondary level. In the words of the report:

> The conclusion for higher education is inescapable. There is no alternative but to accept the fact that American public schools are now very heavily

41

enrolled with minority students, large numbers of whom will be college eligible. Private elementary and secondary schools do not enroll enough students (mostly white) to alter this trend. Previous policies like "benign neglect" seemed reasonable to some when the percentage of minorities was 10 to 12 percent, but what state can neglect 40 to 45 percent of its youth?

Thus, out of sheer self-interest, it behooves the higher education community to do everything to make sure that the largest possible number of minority students do well in public schools and thus become college eligible. If this is not done . . . the potential decline in the college cohort would not be 24 percent for the nation in 1990, but could be twice that.

If, as the report suggests, it is important to examine the educational careers of various groups, we will see the questionable record of higher education's response to minority and female matriculation. Often identified as "educational pipeline" concerns, underpreparation, differential access, and attrition continue to constrain educational opportunities. Even when access and persistence are achieved, there remains a further problem of minority and female representation across the different major fields at each degree level.

Finally, the report suggests that pressure from newly emerging middle-management role models for women (and parenthetically for Blacks, particularly males) will be a source of encouragement for these population segments to increase their numbers in occupations heretofore severely restricted or closed to them. This necessarily means postsecondary credentials in the appropriate fields. Succinctly stated, existing research on higher education with respect to minorities and women does not suggest a receptive response to the emerging college student pool, and recent patterns of attainment by race, ethnicity, and gender provide mixed evidence for expectations of rapid change.

This paper examines bachelor's, master's, and doctorate degree attainment for Blacks, Hispanics, and whites for 1975–76 and 1980–81 by gender. In addition to comparing general distributions for race and gender groups at each time point, special attention is given to major field distributions and concentrations at each timepoint by race and gender. Finally, the paper looks at degrees awarded by predominantly Black and predominantly white colleges to assess their relative roles, especially as this pertains to Black degree attainment.

These descriptive data will contribute to the discussion of higher education's recent record of performance with regard to equity in race, ethnic, and gender differences in degree attainment and suggest areas where policy attention is needed if the existing and emerging challenges are to be successfully met.

DATA AND METHODS

This paper reports tabulations from the national surveys of degrees conferred which are collected every two years by race from all colleges in the nation as part of the federal government's Higher Education General Information Survey (HEGIS). The tabulations reported are for 1975–76 and 1980–81 covering the bachelor's, master's and doctorate degrees.

In addition to reporting degrees conferred for each major field for race and sex groups, the HEGIS files also contain data on institutional characteristics including the predominant race of the student body, region, control, and level. For the following analyses, the predominant race of the student body is reported only for those that are Black (PBCs) and those that are white (PWCs). The analysis uses the 1980–91 institutional report of the predominant race of the student body for both the 1980–81 and the 1970–75 degrees conferred in order to maintain consistency across the two time-points.

Assessing equity in attainment depends fundamentally on parity between minorities and whites or representation equal to some base at all levels of education. The U.S. Census Bureau's *Current Population Reports* (1973 A; 1973 B; 1981), which list the social and economic characteristics of students, have been used to develop two separate measures of a base from which we can assess progress toward parity for minorities and females at the bachelor's degree level.

The first is a population age cohort identifying the number of persons in the population of college age (eighteen to twenty-four) by race and sex who could be bachelor's degree recipients in 1975–76 and 1980–81. This cohort base was identified for 1974 and for 1979, the years immediately preceeding the awarding of bachelor's degrees reported here.

The second measure is of the availability pool—those persons aged fourteen to twenty-four who had completed four years of high school by March 1972 and March 1977 respectively and would, therefore, be eligible for college graduation in 1975–76 and 1980–81.

The debate over the appropriateness of either measure is critical and hinges on the fact that minorities continue to graduate from high school at a lower rate than whites (Institute for the Study of Educational Policy 1981). As a result, the contention is that the availability pool measure has a built-in racial bias which, if ignored, would argue for parity on a smaller proportion of minorities and could lead to an overstatement of progress towards parity (Institute for the Study of Educational Policy 1981). In effect, this view suggests that Black-white parity based on the high-school graduate availability pool proportions could be achieved, but that it still might not be equitable. We examine the use of both measures and assess the differences in their implications.

The basis for parity at the doctoral level is somewhat less precise. We use an availability pool measure based on the percentage of twenty- to thirty-four-year-olds in the population who had completed at least four years of college in 1970 and 1976—five years prior to 1975–76 and 1980–81 respectively—in order to determine an expected proportion of Black doctoral recipients in those latter two years. These bases are presented only for Blacks and whites.

Finally, in addition to the data on Blacks, Hispanics, and whites, overall summary data is presented for "other minorities," a category made up of nonresident aliens, Asians, and Pacific islanders and native Americans.

RESULTS

Table 2.1 presents an overall summary for each degree by race and gender for each time point. A number of broad patterns are shown in Table 2.1.

First, only at the bachelor's degree level was there an increase in the total number of degrees awarded overall. Compared to five years earlier, 12,654 more degrees (one percent) were awarded at the bachelor's level in 1980–81. By contrast, a net decrease occurred at the master's and doctorate degree levels. For the master's degree, 14, 945 (five percent) fewer degrees were awarded in 1980–81. The corresponding decrease at the doctoral level was 393 degrees or approximately 1 percent.

A second general trend is the broad-based improvement in degree attainment among females. Nearly all of the increase in degrees awarded at the bachelor's degree level is attributable to increases for females, irrespective of race group. At the doctoral level, all categories of females increased their degree totals, nearly offsetting the across-the-board decrease in earned doctorates for males. Females increased their shares at each degree level by no less than four percent in 1980–81 compared to 1975–76. Only at the master's degree level, and mainly for Black females, was there a departure from this general pattern of increase in degrees earned by females from 1975–76 to 1980–81. Black females experienced a decrease of 1,326 M.A. degrees or eleven percent of their 1975–76 total. Despite the general improvements for females, approximating 50 percent at the bachelor's and master's levels, the share disparity at the doctoral level remains two to one (66 percent to 33 percent) favoring males, even after a 37 percent increase for females in 1980–81 over 1975–76 totals. Given the bachelor's and master's levels, gender comparability, the disparity appears even greater at the doctoral level.

TABLE 2.1
Race and Sex Percentage Distribution of BAs, MAs, and Ph.D.s
Awarded in 1975–76 and 1980–81

	1975–76						1980–81					
	BA		MA		Ph.D		BA		MA		Ph.D	
Race	M	F	M	F	M	F	M	F	M	F	M	F
Black	5.0% 25,301	7.9% 32,952	4.6% 7,611	8.5% 12,301	2.8% 743	5.2% 426	5.2% 24,511	7.8% 36,162	4.2% 6,158	7.5% 10,975	3.1% 694	5.1% 571
Hispanic	2.0 10,114	1.8 7,721	1.7 2,791	1.6 2,368	1.1 279	1.3 104	2.3 10,810	2.4 11,023	2.1 3,085	2.3 3,376	1.2 277	1.6 179
White	87.7 441,191	86.3 361,608	81.8 136,366	83.6 120,375	77.7 20,281	77.3 6,363	86.4 406,185	86.2 401,149	78.6 115,562	84.5 125,654	76.4 17,310	76.2 8,578
Other	6.0 26,648	4.0 16,972	11.9 19,881	6.2 8,995	18.4 4,796	16.3 1,342	6.0 28,392	4.9 22,822	15.1 22,241	5.8 8,692	19.3 4,370	17.2 1,942
	100% 503,254	100% 419,253	100% 166,649	100% 144,039	100% 26,099	100% 8,253	100% 469,898	100% 465,263	100% 147,046	100% 148,697	100% 22,651	100% 11,290

The patterns of change for each race group shown in Table 2.1 are interesting but require careful interpretation, especially when gender is considered and when viewed in the larger context of overall change. To begin with, both Blacks and Hispanics slightly increased their share of bachelor's degrees in 1980–81 over their 1975–76 totals. Whites, although increasing their actual bachelor's degree count by 4,535, received a slightly smaller share of all degrees. Only Hispanics and other minorities increased their actual degree count and percentage share of earned degrees at each of the three degree levels.

Blacks received a lower actual count and share of master's degrees in 1980–81 compared to five years earlier—2,779 fewer degrees, a 14 percent decrease and a smaller share of all earned master's degrees (.6 percent). This is in sharp contrast to the overall 5 percent decrease in earned master's degrees. Among Blacks, the decrease was more precipitous for males in actual count (1,453 versus 1,326) and in percentage, 19 percent versus 11 percent. Whatever the factors causing the greater reductions for all Blacks at the master's level, they are somewhat more deleterious for the educational careers of Black males.

The pattern of gender differences among Blacks continues at the doctoral level. Like all males, Black males received more doctorates than their female counterparts in 1980–81. However, this disparity between Black males and females decreased from 27 percent in 1975–76 to 9.8 in 1980–81. Black females earned 145 more doctorates in 1980–81 (a 34–percent increase) compared to five years earlier, Black males earned forty-nine fewer doctorates, thus the overall increase in earned doctorates by Blacks is attributable to gains by Black females. In fact, Black males earned a smaller share of degrees at each level in 1980–81 when compared to five years earlier.

Hispanics show actual and percentage increases at each degree level, but here also gender differences are apparent with the advantages favoring females. Hispanic males show increases of 7 percent and 11 percent in actual counts at the bachelor's and master's degree levels, and about a 1–percent decrease at the doctoral level. The comparable figures for Hispanic females, all increases, are 43, 43 and 72 percent. Despite the small size of the numbers, such increases are encouraging. Here again, however, the advantages that the Hispanic females have at the earlier degree levels are dramatically reversed at the doctorate. Despite the 72–percent increase in earned doctorates in 1980–81 compared to 1975–76, Hispanic females earned just 39 percent of all doctorates earned by Hispanics for a 21–percent gap.

The pattern of change in earned degrees among whites is far more straightforward, and the gender differences clear and consistent: white females increased their actual count and share of earned degrees at each level, while the reverse was true for white males. The actual count improvements for white females were 39,541 (11 percent), 5,279 (4 percent), and 2,235 (35 percent) for the bachelor's, master's, and doctorate degrees respectively. Nonetheless, in 1980–81, white males still received 50 percent of white bachelor's degrees, 48 percent of white master's degrees, and 66.8 percent of white doctorates. Thus, significant increases on the part of white females, combined with substantial declines for white males, produced apparent comparability in 1980–81 at the earlier degree levels with a substantial gap remaining at the doctoral level.

Finally, Table 2.1 presents the degree attainment of other minorities. This category consists of nonresident aliens, Asian, and Pacific islanders, Native American and Alaskan Indians. With the exception of earned doctorates by males in this category and earned master's degrees by females in this category, there were increases in actual counts and percentage shares for other minorities at each degree level. Despite the decreases reported above, the summary panel shows that other minorities increased their share of all degrees in 1980–81 as compared to five years earlier. The most substantial increase occurred at the master's level, from a 9–percent share to 11–percent share and is attributable solely to the greater number (2,360) of other minority males earning degrees at the master's level in 1980–81.

Also, it is very instructive to note the nearly doubling share of degrees earned by other minorities as we proceed from the bachelor's degree level to the doctorate. Indeed, at the doctoral level, this category received more than three times the comparable share of bachelor's degrees earned in either year. While it may not be appropriate to assume that other minorities are a fixed group from one degree to the next, these figures may show a remarkable degree of persistence for some substantial numbers of students. Equally interesting are the implications that these figures suggest regarding the consumption of our more advanced educational resources. While about 13 percent of educational resources are consumed by minorities at the bachelor's degree level, a total of about 24 percent of such resources are consumed by minorities at the doctoral level. However, no more than 5 percent of those resources at the doctoral level are consumed by Blacks and Hispanics, the two groups constituting the overwhelming share of the nation's minority population and for whom considerable educational attainment needs exist, especially at the more advanced degree levels.

These specific changes in degree attainment are informative, but a more complete assessment of progress toward equity depends upon parity between minorities and whites or representation equal to some base at all levels of education. The Census Bureau's *Current Population Reports*, Series P–20, have been used to develop two separate measures of parity for

Blacks and whites at the bachelor's degree level, and one at the doctoral level. Persons of Spanish origin may be of either race in the census data, and hence are not treated as a percentage of the overall or gender group totals. The first measure uses a population age cohort—the number of persons in the population of college age (eighteen to twenty-four) by race and sex who could be bachelor's degree recipients. This cohort base was identified for 1974 and for 1979, the years immediately preceeding the awarding of degrees. Using this base, parity is defined as a percentage of bachelor's degrees awarded to Blacks that equals the percentage of Blacks in the general population.

The second measure is of the availability pool, those persons aged fourteen to twenty-four who had completed four years of high school by March 1972 and March 1977 respectively, and would therefore be eligible for college graduation in 1975–76 and 1980–81. Using this base, parity is defined as a percentage of bachelor's degrees awarded to Blacks that equals the percentage of Blacks who have the prerequisite credentials—that is, Blacks who have graduated from high school. A similar measure of the availability pool is used at the doctoral level based on persons aged twenty to thirty-four who had completed at least four years of college as of March 1970 and March 1976, five years prior to doctorates awarded in 1975–76 and 1980–81, respectively.

Table 2.2 shows that Blacks fail to approach parity on either measure at the bachelor's degree level, and this is especially clear for Black males. However, Black females have made gains toward parity between the earlier and later time points.

Overall, the Black population age cohort (middle panel) was 12.1 percent in 1974 and 12.6 percent in 1979, but Blacks received only 6.3 percent of bachelor's degrees awarded in 1975–76 and 6.5 percent in 1980–81. Actually, the difference between the population cohort percentage and the degree attainment percentage widened during the five-year period. The increase in Black cohort representation (.126 less .121, or .005) was greater than the increase in degree attainment (.067 less .065, or .002), a net decrease in progress toward parity or representation in degree attainment.

By contrast, the Black proportion of the availability pool was 10.9 percent in 1974 and 11.0 percent in 1979, thus the increase in the availability pool (.001) was less than the increase in degree attainment (.002), indicating that a slightly larger percentage of those Blacks who finished high school in 1977 also completed college in 1980–81, compared to their 1972 and 1975–76 counterparts.

Blacks are a demographically younger population than whites, with high concentrations in this age range. Although the Black-white gap in high-school completion rates is closing it continues to be substantial. But

TABLE 2.2
Comparison of BA and PHD Degrees
on Proportions of College Age and Available Pool by Race and Gender

Race	College Age (18–24) in 1000s				Available Pool (HS grads 19–24) in 1000s				BA Degrees Awarded			
	1974		1979		1972		1977		1975–76		1980–81	
	M	F	M	F	M	F	M	F	M	F	M	F
Black	5.4%	6.7	5.6	6.9	4.5	6.4	5.0	6.0	2.7	3.6	2.6	3.9
	1,396	1,709	1,577	1,934	515	722	634	764	25,301	32,952	24,511	36,162
Total	12.1%		12.6		10.9		11.0		6.3		6.5	
	3,105		3,511		1,237		1,398		58,253		60,673	
White	41.8	44.5	41.9	43.5	38.6	49.4	41.2	46.2	47.8	38.2	43.4	42.3
	10,772	11,419	11,721	12,174	4,388	5,611	5,233	5,862	441,191	361,616	406,185	395,256
Total	86.3%		85.4		88.1		87.3		87.0		85.7	
	22,141		23,895		9,999		11,095		802,807		801,441	

Race	College Age (20–34) in 1000s				Available Pool (Completed 4 yrs. College) in 1000s				PHD Degrees Awarded			
	1970		1976		1970		1976		1975–76		1980–81	
	M	F	M	F	M	F	M	F	M	F	M	F
Black	5.2%	5.9	4.8	6.0	2.2	3.0	2.2	3.5	2.2	1.2	2.0	1.7
	2,092	2,385	2,413	3,012	81	107	132	214	743	426	69	571
White	42.3	45.4	43.2	43.9	47.8	44.5	47.6	42.6	59.1	18.5	51.0	25.3
	17,103	18,372	21,583	21,925	1,725	1,606	2,893	2,590	20,281	6,363	17,310	8,598

completion of high school is a prerequisite credential for college entry, and, until that gap closes or, in fact, until Blacks graduate from high school and college at a greater rate than whites, there can be little progress in closing the total population parity gap.

In addition to between-race differences, there are also within-sex differences (Top panel). Among males, the parity issue is most severe for Blacks. Although Black males increased as a percentage of both bases (by .2 and .5 respectively), they decreased as a proportion of degree recipients (by .1) over the five-year period. White males also increased somewhat as a proportion of either base and also declined as a percentage of degree recipients. However, unlike Black males, white males continue to receive a larger share of all degrees than either their population or availability pool proportions would predict.

Table 2.2 shows that Black and white females, however, are progressing toward parity. Females constitute more than half of both the population age cohort and the availability pool and, over the five-year period covered by these data, have narrowed the gap between these base proportions and their degree shares. In 1974, females were 52 percent of the fourteen-to-twenty-four age cohort and received 45 percent of the degrees awarded from July 1975 to June 1976. By 1979, females were one-half percent fewer of the fourteen-to-twenty-four age group but received a 4.3 percent greater share of degrees awarded in 1980–81 (49.6 percent of all degrees). The availability pool comparison shows even greater increases in bachelor's degree attainment for females.

At the doctoral level, the equity patterns are quite different but some similarities remain. First, Black and white females have made progress toward parity, but the gap remains large. Females were a slightly smaller proportion of the population aged twenty to thirty-four and a slightly smaller proportion of the availability pool in 1980–81 when compared to five years earlier, but they were a larger share of all doctorates in 1980–81. Nonetheless, the parity gap remains for both the population and availability pool measures.

For Blacks, the parity issue at the doctoral level is quite complex. Compared to the population base, Blacks made very small progress toward equity with a .3–percent gain in degree shares compared to a .2–percent reduction as a portion of the population. Compared to the availability pool, however, Blacks did not keep pace. They were a .5–percent greater share of the 1976 pool but only a 3–percent greater share of 1980–81 doctorates for a net decrease in parity of .2 percent. Moreover, the situation is very different for males and females. Black males are closer to parity using the population base than are Black females at either time point, and are at or near parity using the availability pool base. Black females, however, are at less than 50 percent of parity using the availability pool base as of 1980–

81, despite an increased share of doctorates. These comparisons yield two major implications: first, sexism is dramatic at the doctoral level, irrespective of race; and second, if Blacks, and Black males in particular, were closer toward parity earlier in the pipeline (bachelor's and master's degrees) substantial increases in equity could occur given the Black doctoral level parity comparisons, especially for Black males.

One unexpected result of using these census data population and availability pool measures to assess Black-white parity is the relative distribution of postsecondary education between Black males and females. Examining the population base, we note that, at each timepoint, Black males are a smaller proportion of Blacks in the twenty to thirty-four age group. And, when we compare this base with the availability pool base for the same time points, Black males are an even smaller share of the availability pool. Even more disturbing is the apparent trends in Black males' shares of college credentials which show substantial decreases. In 1970, Black males were a 43–percent share of Blacks with at least four years of college, and by 1976, only a 38–percent share, a 5–percent decrease compared to a 2–percent decrease in population percentage. When we consider that bachelor's degrees awarded to Blacks for 1975–76 and 1980–81 show a larger proportion going to Black females, this evidence suggests that, at least at the early degree stages, the largest share of educational credentials is increasingly held by Black females. Thus, while the main problem is the constraints on the acquisition of educational credentials for all Blacks, there are apparently either more intense effects on Black males or still other processes constraining the early postsecondary educational careers of Black males.

Our second question focuses on race and sex similarities in major field distributions. Tables 2.3, 2.4, and 2.5 present the 1975–76 and 1980–81 distributions by race, sex, and major field for bachelor's, master's, and doctoral degrees respectively.

In general, males continue to dominate the sciences and technical fields—business and engineering, for example—while females continue to show an advantage in education and the health professions. Second, minorities and women show shifts out of social sciences and education into more math- and science-related fields. The general patterns of shifts show some small increase in the comparability across the race and sex groups, but the concentrations in specific major fields are more informative. Table 2.5 compares the participation of white and minority males and females in 1975–76 and 1980–81 in the major fields that ranked highest for white male degree recipients in 1975–76 at each degree level.

The five fields listed in Table 2.5 accounted for over 60 percent of the bachelor's degrees received by all males in 1975–76 and 1980–81. For females, however, only Black females received more than 50 percent of their

TABLE 2.3
Percentage of Fields by Race and Gender for Degrees Received in 1975–1976*

Major Field	Black Male BA	Black Male MA	Black Male Ph.D	Black Female BA	Black Female MA	Black Female Ph.D	Hispanic Male BA	Hispanic Male MA	Hispanic Male Ph.D	Hispanic Female BA	Hispanic Female MA	Hispanic Female Ph.D	White Male BA	White Male MA	White Male Ph.D	White Female BA	White Female MA	White Female Ph.D
Business	23.0	15.8	2.2	10.9	2.5	0	19.7	15.2	2.9	6.0	2.3	0	23.0	23.0	3.3	6.2	3.3	0.8
Social Science	22.2	6.2	10.6	15.6	3.1	7.7	19.1	7.0	12.5	13.8	3.5	3.8	15.2	6.4	12.4	10.9	3.4	11.9
Health Professions	1.0	2.2	1.5	6.9	3.6	1.2	2.4	2.6	1.4	8.9	4.1	0.9	2.3	2.6	1.5	10.4	5.9	2.3
Engineering	5.0	2.5	2.4	0.2	0.2	0	8.0	7.6	5.7	0.4	0.3	0.9	8.6	7.9	7.8	0.3	0.3	0.8
Education	15.0	47.6	51.3	31.7	70.3	66.4	9.3	35.6	31.5	24.3	59.0	46.2	8.2	28.4	21.1	27.1	57.3	32.9
Biological Sciences	4.0	1.4	4.3	3.4	0.8	2.8	5.4	1.4	5.7	4.0	0.6	4.8	7.2	2.9	10.8	4.5	1.4	9.0
Public Affairs	5.9	8.5	2.4	5.5	7.6	2.3	5.0	8.4	2.5	3.8	7.9	5.8	3.7	5.7	0.8	3.2	4.9	1.2
Psychology	4.5	2.5	5.9	6.1	1.8	4.0	6.3	3.9	10.7	7.9	3.1	8.7	4.5	2.7	7.6	6.4	2.6	11.5
Physical Science	1.7	1.2	3.9	0.6	0.3	0.7	2.2	1.4	7.5	0.9	0.6	5.8	3.6	2.7	11.8	1.0	0.5	3.3
Agriculture	1.0	0.9	2.2	0.1	0.04	0.5	1.3	0.8	1.8	0.4	0.2	0	3.4	1.6	2.8	0.9	0.3	0.5
Other	7.7	11.2	13.3	19.0	9.76	14.4	21.3	16.1	17.8	30.0	18.4	23.1	20.3	16.1	20.1	29.1	20.1	25.82
Percent	100	100	100	100	100	100	100	100	100	100	100	100	100	100	100	100	100	100
Totals	2	7	7	3	1	4	1	2	2	7	2	1	4	1	2	3	2	6
	5	6	4	5	0	2	0	7	7	7	3	0	4	3	0	6	0	3
	3	1	3	9	9	6	1	9	9	2	6	4	1	6	2	1	3	6
	0	1		5	7		1	1		1	6		1	3	8	6	7	3
	1			2	5		4				8		9		1	0	5	
																8		

*Note: Bachelor's Degree totals in this table are for institutions located in the fifty states and the District of Columbia only.

TABLE 2.4
Percentage of Fields by Race and Gender
for Degrees Received in 1980–1981*

Major Field	Black Male			Black Female			Hispanic Male			Hispanic Female			White Male			White Female		
	BA	MA	Ph.D	BA	MA	Ph.D	BA	MA	Ph.D	BA	MA	Ph.D	BA	MA	Ph.D	BA	MA	Ph.D
Business	26.5	25.2	3.7	19.0	7.3	1.1	23.7	21.9	0.3	14.1	5.7	0.6	27.6	30.6	3.0	15.4	9.6	1.2
Social Science	15.0	5.1	9.5	12.3	2.8	6.0	14.3	5.9	13.4	12.1	2.9	8.4	11.9	4.8	10.1	9.2	2.8	8.3
Health Professions	1.8	3.2	1.3	8.8	6.3	3.0	2.4	2.8	1.1	8.1	4.9	2.8	2.3	3.0	2.2	11.8	8.5	3.6
Engineering	8.2	3.6	3.3	1.2	0.3	0.2	12.0	8.1	7.9	1.2	0.8	0.6	13.4	7.9	7.5	1.6	0.8	0.7
Education	10.6	33.5	41.6	19.1	60.0	56.9	7.0	28.2	23.8	19.0	58.1	41.3	5.6	20.2	19.1	17.7	47.3	36.0
Biological Sciences	3.9	1.3	5.2	3.6	0.8	4.9	5.9	1.2	10.8	4.5	1.0	5.6	5.2	2.8	13.2	4.0	1.6	10.3
Public Affairs	7.0	11.6	2.7	8.7	10.8	5.8	5.5	10.0	2.2	5.3	9.4	2.2	3.1	6.2	1.2	4.2	7.3	1.5
Psychology	4.2	2.7	8.9	6.3	2.4	9.5	4.5	2.5	12.3	7.4	3.0	17.3	3.0	2.5	8.6	5.6	3.2	13.4
Physical Science	2.5	1.3	4.0	0.8	0.3	0.7	2.7	1.5	7.6	1.0	.03	1.1	4.0	2.8	12.4	1.3	0.7	3.4
Agriculture	1.1	0.9	2.0	0.3	0.2	0.2	1.7	1.6	5.0	0.6	0.4	0	3.4	2.0	3.3	1.6	0.6	1.0
Other	19.2	11.6	17.8	19.9	8.8	11.7	20.3	16.3	15.6	26.7	13.5	20.1	20.5	17.2	19.4	27.6	17.6	20.6
Percent	100	100	100	100	100	100	100	100	100	100	100	100	100	100	100	100	100	100
Totals	2	6	6	3	1	5	1	3	2	1	3	1	4	1	1	3	1	1
	4	1	9	6	0	7	0	0	7	1	3	7	0	1	7	9	2	7
	5	5	4	1	9	1	8	8	7	0	7	9	6	5	3	5	5	3
	1	8		6	7		1	5		2	6		1	5	1	2	6	1
	1			2	5		0			3			8	6	0	5	5	0
													5	2		6	4	

*Note: Bachelor's Degree totals in this table are for institutions located in the fifty states and the District of Columbia only.

Table 2.5
A comparison and Contrast of the Top Five Major Fields for
Degree Recipients in 1975–1976 and 1980–1981 by Race and Sex
Group: 1975–1976 White Male Degree Fields Are Used as the Base.

		Bachelor's Degrees Percent Distribution and Rank					
1975–76 Top Five White Male Major Fields		*WM*	*BM*	*HM*	*WF*	*BF*	*HF*
Business	1975–76	23.0(1)	23.0(1)	19.7(1)	6.2(6)	11.0(3)	6.0(6)
	1980–81	27.6(1)	26.5(1)	23.7(1)	15.7(2)	19.0(2)	14.1(1)
Social Science	1975–76	15.2(2)	22.0(2)	19.1(2)	10.8(2)	16.0(2)	13.8(2)
	1980–81	11.9(3)	15.0(2)	14.3(2)	9.0(4)	12.3(3)	12.2(2)
Engineering	1975–76	8.6(3)	5.0(5)	8.0(4)	0.3(17)	0.2(13)	0.4(15)
	1980–81	13.4(2)	8.2(4)	12.0(3)	1.6(13)	1.0(14)	1.2(14)
Education	1975–76	8.2(4)	14.5(3)	9.3(3)	27.1(1)	31.7(1)	24.3(1)
	1980–81	5.6(4)	10.5(3)	7.0(4)	17.9(1)	19.1(1)	10.9(3)
Biological Science	1975–76	7.2(5)	4.0(6)	5.4(5)	4.5(7)	3.5(7)	4.0(9)
	1980–81	5.2(5)	3.8(9)	5.9(5)	4.1(9)	3.5(8)	4.5(9)

		Master's Degrees					
		WM	*BM*	*HM*	*WF*	*BF*	*HF*
Education	1975–76	28.4(1)	47.6(1)	35.6(1)	57.3(1)	70.3(1)	59.0(1)
	1980–81	20.2(2)	33.5(1)	28.2(1)	47.3(1)	60.0(1)	58.1(1)
Business	1975–76	23.0(2)	15.8(2)	15.2(2)	3.3(7)	2.5(6)	2.3(9)
	1980–81	30.6(1)	25.2(2)	21.9(2)	9.6(2)	7.3(3)	5.7(3)
Engineering	1975–76	7.9(3)	2.5(5)	7.6(4)	0.3(19)	0.2(18)	0.3(16)
	1980–81	7.9(3)	3.6(5)	8.1(4)	0.8(16)	0.3(15)	0.8(12)
Social Science	1975–76	6.4(4)	6.2(4)	7.0(5)	3.4(6)	3.1(4)	3.5(6)
	1980–81	4.8(5)	5.1(4)	5.9(5)	2.8(9)	2.8(5)	2.9(7)
Public Affairs	1975–76	5.7(5)	8.5(3)	8.4(3)	4.9(3)	7.6(2)	7.9(2)
	1980–81	6.2(4)	11.6(3)	10.0(3)	7.3(4)	10.8(2)	9.4(2)

		Doctoral Degrees					
		WM	*BM*	*HM*	*WF*	*BF*	*HF*
Education	1975–76	21.1(1)	51.3(1)	31.5(1)	32.9(1)	66.4(1)	46.2(1)
	1980–81	19.1(1)	41.6(1)	23.8(1)	36.0(1)	56.9(1)	41.3(1)
Social Science	1975–76	12.4(2)	10.6(2)	12.5(2)	11.9(2)	7.7(2)	3.8(6)
	1980–81	10.1(4)	9.5(2)	13.4(2)	8.3(4)	6.0(3)	8.4(4)
Physical Science	1975–76	11.8(3)	3.9(6)	10.7(3)	3.3(7)	0.7(10)	5.8(2)
	1980–81	12.4(3)	4.0(6)	7.6(6)	3.4(7)	0.7(11)	1.1(9)
Biology	1975–76	10.8(4)	4.3(4)	5.7(5)	9.0(5)	2.8(5)	4.8(5)
	1980–81	13.2(2)	5.2(5)	10.8(4)	10.3(3)	4.9(6)	5.6(5)
Engineering	1975–76	7.8(5)	2.4(8)	5.7(5)	0.8(13)	0.0	0.9(8)
	1980–81	7.5(6)	3.3(8)	7.9(5)	0.7(17)	0.2(13)	0.6(10)

*Key: WM=White male; BM=Black Male; HM=Hispanic Male; WF=White Female; BF=Black Female; HF=Hispanic Female
( )=Degree field's rank order

degrees in these same fields in either year. This clearly shows the sex differences in major-field concentrations. The specific race and sex group comparisons show other important differences.

At the baccalaureate level, focusing first on white males and minority males, Black male rankings are similar to white male rankings except that biological sciences was their sixth-ranked and ninth-ranked degree field in 1975–76 and 1980–81 respectively. For Hispanic and white males, the same degree fields constitute the top five but the relative ranks are different. For 1975–76, education and engineering ranked third and fourth for Hispanic males while the ranks were reversed for white males. In 1980–81, social science and engineering were second and third for Hispanic males and the reverse was true for white males. Moreover, the Hispanic male distribution in percentages is more similar to that of white males than is the distribution of Black males, especially in engineering, education, and biology. Thus, both the ordering and the levels within major fields are more comparable for white and Hispanic males in contrast to Black males. This underscores the importance of not treating minorities as a homogeneous group, but rather recognizing potentially important race-ethnic patterns.

Table 2.5, also shows that males, irrespective of race/ethnicity or degree level, have more similar distributions to one another than they do to their same-race female counterparts. In neither year were more than three of the top five degree fields for males also within the top five degree fields for any female group. Most importantly, neither engineering nor the biological sciences were within the top five for females, and engineering did not rank among the top ten for any females in either year.

Engineering and education show both the male and the female advantages and minority and female shifts. From 1975 to 1980, all males increased the percentage of their degrees in engineering (Table 2.5). So, too, did females, and at much greater rates, except at the doctoral level. Yet there are still gaps (as great as ten-to-one) favoring males. For education, all groups reduced their share of degrees at each level, but females still have at least a two-to-one advantage overall up through the master's level, although there are within-race ratios that are lower.

Special mention should be made of distinct patterns at the master's and doctoral level. First, at the master's level, the male advantages in business are nearly as great as they are in engineering, and this holds despite the near tripling of business degrees at the master's level for females from 1975–76 to 1980–81 (Table 2.5). In an occupational structure dominated by high status/economic reward positions requiring these credentials, there is small wonder why there are such gross disparities in male-female earnings. Moreover, with education at the master's level accounting for no fewer than

47 percent of any female-race group degrees, there can be little confusion about the likely separate career paths available to females and males.

At the doctoral level, the distributions are somewhat less disparate in education but the sciences (physical and biological) and engineering remain distinctly male (Table 2.5). A further problem at the doctoral level is the two-to-one numerical advantages to males that is not available to them at the bachelor's or master's degree levels (see Table 2.1). This male advantage, however, is driven mainly by white and other minority males, *not* by Black and Hispanic males. Thus, at the doctoral level, females are doubly disadvantaged: in access to that degree status, *and* in access to key fields within that degree level.

Minority males are also more different from majority males at the doctoral level when compared to the earlier degree levels (Table 2.5). Education doctorates are especially large for Black males—more than double the percentage of white males and less than half of the white male concentrations in physical science, biology, and engineering. In physical science, the white-Black ration is three-to-one. Here again, the consequences for earnings parity and occupational representation comparing Black and white males are clear: for the same level of educational credential, Black males will likely earn less and will disproportionately follow different career paths as compared to white males or compared to Hispanic males whose major-field concentrations at the doctoral level more closely approximates those of white males.

The third issue this paper addresses is the predominant race of the student body at colleges from which Blacks receive their degrees. There are two points to be examined here: (1) the relative Black degree productivity of predominantly Black (PBC) and predominantly white colleges (PWC); and (2) within major-field degree distribution for predominantly Black and predominantly white colleges.

Table 2.6 addresses these degree productivity questions. Here the issue is the extent to which PBCs and PWCs are underrepresented or overrepresented in certain fields, given the overall percentage of degrees awarded by each. For these HEGIS data, PBCs comprise about 9 percent of the nation's B.A.-granting schools. Yet these institutions account for more than 30 percent of all bachelor's degrees awarded to Blacks. In certain fields where Black access has traditionally been difficult, PBCs have dominated in degree productivity for Blacks. Table 2.6 shows the extent of representation of PBCs for selected majors for males and females respectively at the bachelor's and master's degree levels and makes clear the changes over the five years.

The first four columns of Table 2.6 give the within-field share of selected bachelor's degrees awarded to Black males and females respectively in 1975–76 and 1980–81. For Black males, PBCs accounted for 37 percent

TABLE 2.6
Percentage of BA and MA Degrees Earned in
Predominantly Black Colleges by Year and Gender

| | BA Degrees | | | | MA Degrees | | | |
| | 1975–76 | | 1980—81 | | 1975–76 | | 1980–81 | |
Major Field	M	F	M	F	M	F	M	F
Business	44%	56%	37%	41%	10%	19%	14%	21%
	(5858)	(3604)	(6503)	(6897)	(1201)	(310)	(1554)	(805)
Social Science	35%	39%	29%	3%	19%	23%	15%	15%
	(5611)	(5144)	(3696)	(4433)	(474)	(384)	(311)	(304)
Health Professions	27%	22%	27%	27%	5%	4%	3%	2%
	(378)	(2268)	(436)	(3167)	(106)	(444)	(197)	(692)
Engineering	35%	45%	36%	29%	1%	0%	10%	3%
	(1268)	(62)	(2020)	(429)	(188)	(21)	(222)	(38)
Education	54%	55%	49%	48%	30%	30%	29%	24%
	(3669)	(10440)	(2587)	(6907)	(3622)	(8646)	(2061)	(6584)
Biological Sciences	42%	46%	42%	40%	23%	38%	34%	42%
	(1120)	(1115)	(954)	(1315)	(106)	(100)	(82)	(89)
Public Affairs	23%	34%	23%	29%	12%	15%	13%	16%
	(1495)	(1797)	(1726)	(3143)	(646)	(932)	(713)	(1180)
Psychology	23%	27%	23%	26%	10%	13%	17%	11%
	(1128)	(2007)	(1040)	(2268)	(193)	(218)	(104)	(260)
Physical Science	38%	50%	40%	46%	28%	30%	35%	50%
	(440)	(197)	(613)	(293)	(93)	(33)	(79)	(28)
Agriculture	57%	54%	57%	57%	54%	33%	21%	10%
	(230)	(37)	(259)	(121)	(71)	(6)	(53)	(20)
Total Percentage	37%	43%	33%	35%	21%	23%	19%	21%
Total Number	25,301	32,952	24,511	36,162	7,611	12,301	6,158	10,975

of their 1975–76 bachelor's degrees but in agriculture, biology, business, education, math and the physical sciences, they awarded no fewer than 38 percent of all degrees in those fields. By 1980–81, PBCs awarded just 33 percent of all bachelor's degrees to Black males but were overrepresented in the above named fields and in engineering. It is especially interesting to note that in math, where the total number of degrees declined, the share awarded by PBCs increased.

PBCs accounted for a greater share of the bachelor degrees awarded to Black females during each time period (43 percent and 35 percent respectively), and, as was true for males, a pattern of representation is apparent in agriculture, biology, business, education, math, and physical sciences. Also for Black females, PBCs are overrepresented in the fields of computer science and health professions. Interestingly, however, in engineering, where Black females increased their degree count by a factor of seven (from

62 to 429), the percentage awarded by PBCs declined substantially, from 45 percent to 29 percent.

The pattern of degrees awarded by PBCs at the master's level depicted in Table 2.5 and 2.6 is quite similar to the above results for both males and females. For males, PBCs accounted for 21 percent and 19 percent of all master's degrees in 1975–76 and 1980–81 respectively. For Black females the comparable figures are 23 percent and 21 percent. Again, however, in biology and physical sciences, especially, PBCs account for a substantial portion of Black master's degrees. In 1980–81, PBCs accounted for nearly twice the proportion of degrees one would expect based on their overall degree representation.

These figures make clear the essential role of PBCs, but it is important to focus on two aspects of this role. First, PBCs account for approximately 9 percent of all four-year colleges and universities but awarded at least three times that percentage of degrees. Second, both access to and within higher education and the enhancement of PBCs are national goals. These data continue to show the critical role of PBCs in providing access to and within higher education. To a lesser extent, these data may represent some amount of enhancement of PBCs as they improve their range and level of offerings at the bachelor's and master's levels. Nonetheless, they continue to award degrees to Blacks at a rate which suggests that access to and within PWCs continues to be restricted.

Finally, although not shown in Table 2.6, PBCs accounted for thirty-five or 3 percent of all doctorates earned by Blacks and twenty of those were in education. In 1980–81, PBCs accounted for sixty-nine or 5.5 percent of all doctorates earned by Blacks but only eight were in education and twenty-one were in biology. That latter figure was nearly half of the forty-three doctorates earned by Blacks in biology during 1980–81.

The implications here are quite clear: predominantly Black colleges continue to contribute substantially to both the quantity and diversity of Blacks with postsecondary credentials. Especially with regard to diversity of major fields, and particularly in the sciences, PBCs are vital educational resources. It is critically important that we examine the fairness of about three PBCs producing as many Black biology doctorates as the one hundred or more PWCs with doctoral programs in biology.

CONCLUSIONS

Several conclusions can be drawn from these results with important policy implications. First, the results show that degree-attainment patterns and progress towards equity may be race and/or gender specific and should be treated with that kind of detailed consideration. Simple summary reports—especially those not giving a parity measure or those that report increments without specifying the overall context of change—may be very misleading. Given the complexity, we should expect that intervention strategies for minorities will be group specific and gender specific.

Special attention needs to be focused on the educational careers of Blacks in general, and Black males in particular. Funding policies that constrict education overall are clearly more perverse for Blacks and most severe for Black males at the early degree levels. Also with regard to Blacks, we must carefully observe the gender-different degree rates. It appears in these data that something fast approaching the feminization of education among Blacks may be occurring at the bachelor's and master's degree levels. The ramifications of such a trend has implications for mate selection and community structure as well as occupational distribution implications given the interaction of racism and sexism in employment.

Females generally have made progress both in parity and in the transition into science, math, business, and engineering, but mainly at the bachelor's and master's degree levels. Even with improvements at the doctoral level, both the access and distributional problems are great. In business, for example, beginning at the master's level, the gaps are almost as great as in engineering. The doctoral level male-female disparities in biology, physical sciences, and engineering suggests that, for the near future, there will be little change in the earnings or occupations gaps. Intervention strategies in educational programs early on are vital, and structural affirmative efforts at the university level may prove beneficial.

Finally, predominantly Black colleges continue to be a primary source of degrees for Blacks, and, in some major fields, they produce more than would be expected. While degrees earned by Blacks from predominantly white colleges are continuing to increase, a substantial amount of that increase is due to a shifting of students from predominantly Black to predominantly white colleges at the B.A. level. This produces a smaller net gain in Black degree attainment than would occur if the number of Black degrees from predominantly Black colleges remained constant or increased. For this reason, the increase in Black B.A.s from predominantly white colleges must be cautiously interpreted. Particular attention should be paid to changes in degrees earned from such colleges in the sciences and technical fields in which Black access and retention has traditionally been more difficult to achieve. A positive change in these areas would be meaningful progress.

GAIL E. THOMAS

Chapter Three

Assessing the College Major Selection Process for Black Students

INTRODUCTION

Making well-informed decisions about college majors, career choices, and educational investments is extremely important given the rising cost of higher education and an increasingly competitive labor market. Such decisions are especially important for African Americans on at least two counts. First, despite their high educational and career aspirations, Black students continue to experience a large disparity between their aspirations and actual attainments (Portes and Wilson 1976; and Thomas 1980). Second, Blacks remain highly underrepresented in college majors and careers that offer the greatest opportunity for future job access and earnings.

The record shows (Table 3.1) that baccalaureate (B.A.) recipients in selected fields obtain higher income and employment opportunities than do B.A.s with majors in the humanities and the social sciences. Recent studies also show that Black students, in comparison to whites, are highly underrepresented in the natural and technical sciences (Thomas 1983, 1984; and Vetter and Babco 1986) among college majors, college graduates, and employed workers. A substantial portion of the income differential between Blacks and whites has been attributed to differences in major-field and career choices (Angle and Wissman 1981; Herzog, 1982; and Rosenfeld 1980).

Given the importance of major-field choice for career attainment, attempts must be made to clarify the major-field choice process for African

61

TABLE 3.1
Recent Starting Salary and Unemployment Data
by Major Field for BA Degree Recipients

Major Fields	1978 Salary	1982 Salary	Unemployment
Humanities	$9,000	$15,396	10.7
Education	9,500	N/A	4.1
Biological Sciences	9,800	16,500	10.5
Social Work	10,000	N/A	6.0
Chemistry	10,800	21,012	3.0
Social Sciences	10,875	15,432	9.3
Mathematics	11,400	21,324	0.0
Physical and Earth Sciences	11,500	23,760	2.7
Nursing*	12,600	17,568	2.6
Engineering	15,500	25,128	5.0
Economics	13,200	18,516	8.8
Business/Management	13,300	17,724	3.2
Accounting	13,700	18,540	2.5
Computer Science	N/A	22,896	N/A

*1982 Salary data for nurses from *National Survey of Hospital and Medical School Salaries*, University of Texas Medical Branch.
Sources: 1978 Data from *Labor Force Status of Recent College Graduates*. NCES. 1982 Data from *College Placement Council Salary Survey* 1982–1983.

Americans. This paper will describe theories and hypotheses that may be useful in understanding Black students' major-field choices. In addition, it will employ multivariate analyses to examine the influence of selected variables on the enrollment of African American students in the natural and technical sciences versus other majors.

PREVIOUS RESEARCH ON STUDENTS' MAJOR-FIELD CHOICES AND CAREER ASPIRATION

Past studies of students' major-field choices and career aspirations have been primarily descriptive and based on whites. Some of these studies have employed economic arguments in explaining students' college-major choices. For example, Koch (1972) argued that students select undergraduate majors that offer them the highest economic returns for their educational investments. Koch compared cross-sectional data on income by student enrollments in various major fields for 1970 and 1971. He found that students' major-field choices were significantly related to the labor-market-value associated with various majors. Accounting, mathematics, and economics had higher economic rates of return for graduates. As a consequence, these fields also had higher student enrollments than did education, the fine arts, and the social sciences.

Cebula and Lopes (1981) retested Koch's (1972) economic incentive argument and extended it by noting that, apart from the monetary value of various college majors, the jobs prospects of the major and students' GRE scores were also important in determining major field choice. The results from this study indicate that earning differentials among fields and differences in the rate of change in earnings among fields were the two most important factors affecting students' major-field choices.

A study by Davis (1966) applied sociological theory to examine other nonmonetary factors that might explain students' major-field choices and career aspirations. Davis (1966) argued that, by the time of college entry, students' career aspirations are fairly crystallized and do not change substantially because of previous family and school socialization. His results showed that early career expectations and aspirations—and being male— were positive and significant determinants of students' career aspirations.

My investigation (Thomas 1981) was based on a sample of Black and white high-school seniors who participated in a 1972 National Longitudinal Survey. My findings confirmed Davis' (1966) observations regarding the importance of students' early career aspirations. The results showed that gender and early expectations of pursuing a specific major were the two most important determinants of major-field choices. Specifically, being male and having the intent and expectations of pursuing a college major in the natural and technical sciences were positively related to actually selecting a college major in these fields.

ADDITIONAL FINDINGS AND HYPOTHESES ABOUT STUDENTS' MAJOR-FIELD CHOICES

Additional hypotheses have been formulated about students' major-field choices and vocational aspirations, but, for the most part, have not been tested. This is especially true regarding Blacks. Therefore, I developed and conducted a survey to assess the importance of various factors and theories in explaining the college-major choice process for Black students. Some of these variables and previous findings concerning them are:

Family Socioeconomic Status

Werts (1966) and Davis (1966) observed a strong positive relationship between students' family socioeconomic status and their choices of a mathematics- or science-based major. Students whose parents have college or subsequent higher eduction are more often enrolled in these majors than students with less-educated parents. The family background measures employed in this study are mother's and father's education. On a six-category item (ranging from less than high-school graduation to graduate or professional education) respondents indicated the highest level of education obtained by their parents (or guardians).

Advanced High-School Mathematics and Science Preparation

The amount and type of high-school mathematics and science that students take also influence their major-field choices. Data consistently show that Black students take fewer mathematics and science courses than do whites, and receive lower grades in these courses (Fox 1976; and Berryman 1983). Sells (1976) reported that 50 percent of the Black college students in her study were barred from natural and technical science majors due to inadequate high school grades and courses. In summarizing the consequences of inadequate mathematics preparation for major-field choice, Sells stated that:

> Students whose arithmetic skills are too far below level in high school are effectively barred from access to the first year of high school algebra, which is the minimal mathematics preparation required by most colleges and universities. Students who have had three-and-a-half to four years of high-school mathematics are immediately eligible for the standard freshman calculus sequence at any college or university in the country. Until very recently, those students who had not pursued second-year algebra and trigonometry in high school had no way of catching up before entering as freshmen, to qualify for the standard calculus sequence which is required for undergraduate majors in every field except education, criminology, the social sciences, and the humanities. These fields have almost no current job related potential for persons with a bachelor's degree (Sells 1976).

Respondents were asked to indicate from a list of subjects the high-school science and mathematics courses that they had taken. Separate high-school science and math indices were constructed from their responses. A coding of 1 on each of these indices indicated that respondents had taken such courses and a coding of 0 meant that they had not taken these courses.

High-School Math and Science Grades

The high-school mathematics and science grades that Black students receive are also indicators of their high-school academic preparation in these fields. Respondents were therefore asked to indicate on separate items the letter grade that best described their high-school mathematics and science grade performances. The response categories ranged from mostly A (coded 5) to mostly E or F (coded 1).

Educational and Occupational Expectations

Race differences in major-field choices and career aspirations have also been attributed to differences in the educational and occupational expectations between Blacks. In general it has been found that Black students are more interested in service-oriented and humanitarian type careers than are whites (Holland 1966; Gottfredson 1978; and Braddock 1981). Students who choose majors in the natural and technical sciences also have been found to have higher educational and occupational expectations than non-science majors (Davis 1966; and Werts 1966). Studies have also shown that Blacks have relatively high educational and occupational aspirations (Portes and Wilson 1976; and Allen 1981). However, the relationship between their educational and career aspirations to major-field choices has not been examined.

The influence of educational and occupational expectations on Black students' major-field choices will be examined in this study. On a four-category item, respondents indicated the highest level of education they expected to obtain (ranging from "do not expect to graduate from college" to "expect to obtain an advanced graduate or professional degree"). On the occupational expectation measure, respondents indicated from a list of occupations the job that they expected to obtain after completing their educations. This information was coded into Duncan Socioeconomic Index (SEI) scores, ranging from the lowest occupational prestige (1) to the highest (100).

College Characteristics

The type and characteristics of the college attended also affect students' access to various majors. For example, students who attend four-year colleges more often pursue majors in the natural and technical sciences than do students who attend two-year and junior colleges (Olivas 1979; and Willingham 1970). In addition, Black students in predominantly Black colleges generally have higher enrollments in the natural and technical sciences than do Black students in predominantly white colleges (Thomas 1980; and Trent 1983). In this study, the impact of attending a predominantly white college (coded 1) versus a predominantly Black college (coded 0) on students' college-major choices will be examined.

College Major

The major dependent variable in this study, major-field choice, is based on an item that asked respondents to indicate their present majors from a list of major fields. Because respondents were selected based on their enrollment in certain college majors, most students were majoring in one of thirteen fields: mathematics, chemistry, physics, biology, accounting, economics, engineering, social work, psychology, sociology, nursing, education, and business management.

CONTEST AND MERIT VERSUS SPONSORSHIP AND SELECTION IN THE COLLEGE MAJOR PROCESS

The variables that have been identified as affecting Black students' major-field and career choices suggest that this process can be viewed in terms of Ralph Turner's (1960) typology of "contest" (i.e. open competition) versus "sponsorship" mobility. Turner used this typology to describe the American versus the English system of educational access and mobility. He maintained that a type of "contest" mobility characterized the U.S. educational system whereby opportunity for access and mobility is relatively open and primarily based on the aspirants' own choices, motivations, efforts, and abilities. Therefore, to the extent that this study indicates Black students' high-school grades and their high-school math and science preparation to be the most significant determinant of their college major, then Turner's typology of contest mobility will have been supported.

"Sponsorship mobility" was Turner's alternative ideal-type construct. He applied this typology to the English system of educational access and mobility. Under the sponsorship system, individuals gain access to the educational system primarily through sponsors or referral networks and selective recruitment for access to a private club where "particularistic" rather than "universalistic" criteria are of prime importance. Under the sponsorship type system, students' family background, support from referral networks, and other particularistic attributes, were of prime importance in determining educational access and mobility. Therefore, to the extent that Black students' gender, parents' education, and the type of college they attend significantly influence major-field choices among Black students, it can be concluded that Turner's typology of sponsorship is most applicable in explaining Black students' college majors.

DATA AND METHODS OF STUDY

The data for this analysis are from a sample of four-year college students who participated in a survey conducted primarily in the Southern Atlantic states. The survey involved some 2,046 Blacks and whites who were officially classified as junior and seniors in the spring of 1982 in eight four-year colleges and universities. Forty-four percent of the survey respondents were Black students (N=927), and 56 percent were white students (N=1,119). Sixty-four percent (N=1,328) of the respondents were females, and 36 percent were males. Five of the institutions were public, and three were private. Students who participated in the survey were officially majoring in one of thirteen selected major fields: mathematics, chemistry, physics, biology, accounting, economics, engineering, social work, psychology, sociology, nursing, education, and business management.

Students were asked to complete a questionnaire that was designed to test various hypotheses regarding their major-field choices and career aspirations. The survey inquired about students' early childhood, family, and elementary and secondary schooling experiences (such as study habits, academic performance, mathematics and science preparation, and extracurricular activities), students' educational and occupational values and expectations, their major-field choices, changes in those choices, and the reason why they chose their present college majors.

Two types of data collection methods were employed based on the preference of participating schools. In one instance, the surveys were distributed on campus, and students completed it inside or outside of class. The second survey procedure entailed mailing the questionnaire to students. These students received two follow-up mailings. The overall response rate to the survey was 43 percent (N=2,046).

FINDINGS

Multiple regression analysis was employed to assess the impact of various independent variables on Black students' college-major choices. Associated with this procedure is a casual model involving a set of additive linear relations and residual terms that are assumed to be uncorrelated among themselves and with variables in the model (Kerlinger and Pedhazer 1974). The primary dependent variable—college-major choice—originally consisted of thirteen fields. For purposes of regression analyses, these fields were collapsed into two categories: the natural and technical sciences (coded 1) versus the remaining fields (coded 0).[1]

Table 3.2 presents that standardized regression results for the total sample when various independent variables are entered in the regression in a step wise fashion (see Appendix for interitem correlations, means, and standards deviations).

The first equation in Table 3.2, with sex and parental education, permits a test of Turner's (1960) "sponsorship" typology which stresses the importance of ascriptive variables (for example, sex, family background,

TABLE 3.2

Regression Model of Black Students' College

Major Choice—Total Sample[a]

Independent Variables	College Major	College Major	College Major	College Major	College Major
Sex	.290[b]	.268	.224	.222	.213
Father's Education	.126	.095	.063	.066	.069
Mother's Education	.003*	−.018*	−.031*	−.033*	−.036*
Advanced Science		.050	.045*	.054	.056
Advanced Math		.119	.112	.126	.125
High-school Math Grades		.157	.127	.119	.135
High-school Science Grades		.106	.099	.111	.124
Education Expectations			−.151	−.152	−.132
Occupation Expectations			.321	.328	.341
College Control				−.047*	−.058*
College Race				−.112	−.122
R^2	.106	.203	.289	.300	.308

[a]Analysis is based on SPSS subprogram regression option Pairwise Deletion. The number of cases (N=915) is based on the N for the major dependent variable—major-field choice.

[b]Coefficients are standardized regression coefficients.

*Coefficients are less than twice their standard error.

and the like) and particularistic criteria. These variables account for 10 percent of the variance in Black students' choice of a major in the natural and technical sciences. In addition, being male and having a father with high education credentials are significant assets for majoring in these fields. It might, therefore, be initially argued that ascription and sponsorship (sex, being male, and parental education) are important in gaining access to natural and technical science majors. However, the second equation in Table 3.2 shows that the percent of variance explained (R^2) is nearly doubled when Black students' high-school performance in math and science course preparation are added to the list of predictors. The explanatory power of the model increases by nearly 9 percent when student educational and occupational expectations are added as predictors.

The finding that high-school preparation, academic performance, and educational and occupational expectations account for an additional 9 percent of explained variance in Black students' major-field choices is significant. The finding suggests that, although background factors (sex and parental educational) are important, ''contest'' or meritocratic factors (academic performance and expectations) more strongly influence Black students' choices of a major in mathematics or science.

It is also interesting to note that college racial composition has a significant negative influence on Black students' access to majors in the natural and technical sciences. Specifically, attending a predominantly white college is negatively related to Black students' choices of these fields. This observation is consistent with Trent's (1983) finding that Black students who attend predominantly Black, as opposed to predominantly white, colleges are more likely to major in the natural and technical sciences. Tables 3.3 and 3.4 show the results from separate analyses of the regression equation in Table 3.1 for Black males and females, and for Blacks in three different types of college environments, (namely predominantly white, predominantly Black public, and predominantly Black private colleges).[2] The corresponding interitem correlations, means, and standards deviations for these subgroups are reported in the Appendix. Separate regression equations were constructed for these groups because "contextual effects" or differences among Black students by sex, college race, and college control (such as public or private) have been previously demonstrated (Thomas, Alexander, and Eckland 1979; Thomas 1980; and Allen 1986). In addition, previous analyses of these data reported elsewhere (Thomas 1984)

TABLE 3.3
Regression Model of Black Males' and
Black Females' College-Major Choices[a]

	Black Males	Black Females
Father's Education	.006[b]	.021
	.030*	.083
Mother's Education	−.025	−.002
	−.121*	−.009*
Advanced Science	.118	.062
	.111	.048*
Advanced Math	.113	.202
	.094*	.129
High-school Math Grades	.021	.105
	.042*	.178
High-school Science Grades	.068	.094
	.115*	.143
Occupation Expectations	.007	.014
	.196	.390
Education Expectations	−.097	−.091
	−.175	−.137
College Control	−.074	−.044
	−.085*	−.044*
College Race	−.137	−.181
	−.112*	−.124
R^2	.112	.309

[a]Analysis is based on SPSS subprogram regression option Pairwise Deletion. The number of cases for Black males ranged from 217 to 258 and for Black females from 526 to 668.
[b]The top coefficients are the unstandardized values, and the bottom coefficients are the standardized (beta) coefficients.
*Coefficients are less than 1.5 times their standard error.

revealed distinct patterns between Black males and females, and between Black students enrolled at predominantly Black versus white institutions.

Beginning with Table 3.3, the most striking observation is that the independent variables are almost three times less effective in explaining college majors for Black males ($R^2 = .112$) than for Black females ($R^2 = .309$). The two most important—and in fact, *only* significant variables influencing the college-major choices of Black males—are occupational and educational expectations. High occupational expectations have a positive effect ($B = .196$) on Black males' selection of a natural and technical science major, while high educational expectations have a negative effect ($B = -.175$). The significance of this finding is to suggest that Turner's typology of "contest" mobility, which stresses the importance of individual efforts and motivation, may be most applicable to Black males, choices of college majors. However, the low percent of variance explained in Black males' college-major choices suggests that other factors associated with "contest" mobility, and possibly "sponsorship," not included in the present model may be more important. For example, the type of high-school curriculum that Black males pursue and the influence of "significant others" on their educational and occupational expectations might be relevant factors.

For Black females, high occupational expectations and high grades in high-school mathematics exert the greatest influences on their choice of natural or technical science majors (Table 3.3). Also, high-school courses in advanced mathematics and high grades in high-school science are positively and significantly related to Black females' selection of these "nontraditional" majors. Educational expectations and college racial composition (for example, attending a predominantly white college) significantly impact Black females' selection of college majors. However, both variables are negatively related to the selection of a natural or technical science major. With the exception of college racial composition, the remaining significant variables in Table 3.3 suggest that, like Black males, factors of "contest" (such as merit) are more significant in determining Black females' choices of natural or technical science majors than are factors of "sponsorship."

The final table, Table 3.4, attempts to determine the extent to which the major-field selection process varies for Black students in predominantly white colleges versus Black students in private and public predominantly Black colleges. These results reveal interesting differences.

For example, the independent variables are less effective in predicting the choice of a natural and technical science major for Black students in predominantly Black public colleges ($R^2 = .283$) than for Blacks in predominantly Black private ($R^2 = .352$) and predominantly white colleges ($R^2 = .348$). The means on the dependent variable show that about 50 per-

TABLE 3.4
Regression Model of Black Students' College-Major Choices
in Predominantly White Colleges, Predominantly Black Private, and Black Public Colleges[a]

	Blacks in White Colleges	Blacks in Private Black Colleges	Blacks in Public Black Colleges
Sex	.323[b]	.144	.309
	.299	.133	.274
Father's Education	−.016	.020	.036
	−.065*	.083*	.126
Mother's Education	.028	−.032	.005
	.107*	−.137	.017*
Advanced Science	.003	.110	.041
	.002*	.084	.031*
Advanced Math	.057	.167	.236
	.037*	.108	.128
High-school Math Grade	.218	.056	.090
	.377	.099	.146
High-school Science Grade	.010	.100	.082
	.014*	.153	.116
Education Expectations	−.112	−.133	−.053
	−.175	−.184	−.080
Occupation Expectations	.010	.016	.009
	.252	.443	.222
College Control	−.024	−.010	−.008
	−.014*	−.011	−.002
R^2	.348	.352	.283

[a]Analysis is based on SPSS subprogram regression option Pairwise Deletion. The number of cases for Blacks in white colleges ranged from 98 to 126; and for Blacks in private Black colleges, 296–367; and for Blacks in Black public colleges, 332–434.
[b]The top coefficients are the unstandardized values, and the bottom coefficients are the standardized (beta) coefficients.

cent of the Blacks in Black public colleges selected such majors versus 60 percent in Black private colleges and 42 percent in predominantly white colleges.

The data in Table 3.4 further suggest that there are differences in the importance of variables influencing the selection of a natural or technical science major for Blacks in Black versus white colleges. This is indicated by both the rank ordering of the independent variables and the magnitude of their effects.

For example, being male is the most important determinant for majoring in the natural and technical sciences for Blacks who attend public predominantly Black colleges. In addition, fathers' education is a significant and positive determinant of natural or technical science majors for Blacks in public predominantly Black colleges. However, occupational expectations are more important than sex for Black in Black private colleges; and high-school math grades are more important than sex for Blacks in predominantly white colleges. Thus, while sponsorship (primarily the ascription of sex) is most influential on the college-major choices for Blacks in Black public colleges, meritocratic and universalistic factors (including high-school grades and expectations) are more important for Black students in Black private and predominantly white colleges. Thus, Turner's (1960) "contest" typology, which stresses open competition and meritocracy is relatively more important for major choices on Black private and predominantly white campuses.

SUMMARY AND CONCLUSIONS

The data in this study permitted an assessment of factors that explain African American college students' choices of majors in the natural and technical sciences. In addition, these data provided an opportunity to examine the relevancy of Turner's (1960) typology of "contest" versus "sponsorship" educational access and mobility to the process of Black students' major-field choices. The results for Black males and Black females suggest that factors of merit and motivation (among them high-school mathematics preparation, and educational and occupational expectations) associated with Turner's "contest" types are more important influences.

The data also showed that a higher percentage of Black males than Black females were natural and technical science majors. The nature of this advantage for Black males—and whether it might be attributed to the greater access of Black males to important support networks and other sponsorship mechanisms—cannot be determined from these data. However, findings based on these data and presented elsewhere showed that a greater percentage of Black males than females indicated that they received encouragement from "significant others" to pursue natural and technical science majors (Thomas 1984). In addition, these data indicated that during childhood Black females were less likely than Black males to express an interest in hobbies and careers related to mathematics and science and to have participated in high-school science clubs. Thus, a lack of support and sponsorship from "significant others," as well as the possible effects of traditional sex-role socialization and values, may be important factors explaining the higher representation of Black males in natural and technical science majors.

The present results also showed that African American students who attended predominantly white colleges were less likely to be natural and technical science majors than those who attended predominantly Black colleges. Again, the reason for this effect of college racial composition cannot be fully determined from the present data. However, an examination of the college-major choice process as depicted by the analytical model in this study suggested that Black students' personal and academic attributes, as well as levels of expectations in Black and white colleges, differentially affect the college-major selection process. For example, the collective impact of the independent variables on college-major choices in the natural and technical sciences was greater for Blacks in Black private and predominantly white colleges than for those attending Black public colleges. In addition, the female disadvantage in the natural and technical science college-major choice is far less on Black private college campuses than for Black students in public and predominantly white colleges.

The descriptive data presented elsewhere showed that Black females in private Black colleges expressed a greater affinity from high-school science and more often pursued a high-school academic curriculum than lack females in Black public colleges and in predominantly white colleges (Thomas 1984). Thus, apart from the college environment itself, the preferences and experiences that Black females (and males) bring with them also influence their access to various majors.

To conclude, the findings from this study are informative but are also limited to some extent. Thus, additional research is needed to extend their generalizability and to clarify their meanings. For example, the low degree of variance explained in college-major choices, for Blacks—especially for Black males—clearly indicates that other variables and explanations must be sought. It has been suggested that the greater interest of Blacks in service-oriented careers, their interest in more substantive issues regarding the general welfare of Blacks, and their preference for majors and careers where there is a "critical mass" or adequate representation of other Blacks are important factors (Blackwell 1981; Gottfredson 1978; Gurin and Epps 1975).

Second, knowledge about the manner in which the independent variables in this study influence the college-major selection process should be useful. This is especially true concerning the formation and development of students' educational and occupational expectations, and the effects of various college and high-school environments on Black students' educational and occupational ambitions and attainment. Finally, other measures of sponsorship, and structural and institutional factors external to Black students need to be considered if we are to more adequately test the applicability of Turner's (1960) typology (especially the "sponsorship construct") to the college-major selection process for Black students. These variables are often difficult to measure and incorporate in multivariate models

(Kerckoff and Campbell 1977). However, until these variable can be successfully measured and incorporated, the question of the extent to which the college-major choice process for Black students (and for students in general) more closely involves individual merit and choice versus sponsorship and early selection and channeling—or some combination of both—cannot be adequately assessed.

MICHAEL T. NETTLES

Chapter Four

Racial Similarities and Differences in the Predictors of College Student Achievement

Observers of important trends in higher education have noticed a decline in the number of African American students attending college in the 1980s as compared to the late 1960s and 1970s. Clearly, most of the legal and public policy emphasis has been placed upon increasing access and retention of minority students. While access and retention are important elements of the educational equity, the disproportionate attention given these two components of equity has been at the expense of attention devoted to equality in student performance. Student performance is also an important equality goal in that it is in need of greater attention by educators, policy makers, and the federal courts which are concerned with genuine equality.

This paper focuses on performance aspects of equity in higher education by examining the differences between Black and white students' college performance and the effects of student, faculty, and institutional characteristics on their performances. The aims of this chapter are:

1. To discover whether there are differences in the college performance of Black and white college students;
2. To identify the factors related to performance of Black and white students; and
3. To determine if there are key differences between Black and white students on the significant factors.

By increasing the knowledge and understanding of the factors related to performance and the differences thereof, educators will be able to develop strategies to eliminate some of the barriers to equality.

Several factors have been found to contribute to students' academic performance in college. Researchers generally conclude that the major determinants of academic performance are the characteristics that students develop before entering college—mainly, their high-school preparation, socioeconomic status, and admissions test scores. Recently, researchers have found that students' college experiences and the attributes of their college or university are also contributing factors. Most, however, agree that both precollege and college experiences, along with personal characteristics and university support services, operate in concert to affect performance. It has not been determined, however, whether (1) the same variables are predictors of both Black and white students' academic performances, or (2) there are differences in Black and white students' academic and personal characteristics that result in racially differentiated academic achievement.

The literature comparing African American students' college performances reveals varying results. In a study comparing Black and white students' grades and attrition rates at the University of Georgia, White and Suddick (1981) found no significant race differences in students' grade-point averages or in attrition rates. They attributed the absence of significant race differences to the selective admissions criteria of that university in which students of both races were equally prepared for college. This suggests that the selectivity of a university can virtually eliminate the effects of differences in the students' noncognitive and cognitive college experiences.

These findings by White and Suddick (1981) confirm the results of earlier studies which found no racial differences in the actual predictors of college performance (Scott 1933; and Stanley and Porter 1967) after controlling for academic admissions criteria. On the other hand, some researchers have concluded that biographic characteristics, motivational characteristics, and social characteristics have a greater effect upon the performance of Black students than white students (Anastasi, Meade, and Schneiders 1960; Clark and Plotkin 1964; Aiken 1964; Sedlacek, Brooks, and Mindus 1973; and Beasley and Sease 1974).

The present study examines the differences in Black and white student performance by applying a broader range of student, faculty, and institutional variables than have been applied in previous studies. In addition to the demographic background/character variables, the variables in this study include college/environmental factors and student/faculty interaction which have been found to be significant predictors of students' college performance (Astin 1964; Pascarella and Terenzini 1980), but have not compared Black and white students.

METHODOLOGY

The research presented is designed to determine the differences between Black and white students' college performance, and to identify the differences in the factors associated with their performances. This section describes the sampling procedures and the sample, the procedures used for collecting the data, and the statistical procedures and methods for analyzing the data.

DESCRIPTION OF SURVEY INSTRUMENTS

The Student Opinion Survey (SOS) is a machine-readable questionnaire booklet containing 109 items which elicit information about students' performances, behaviors, and attitudes. The majority of items are in Likert format with five optional response categories. Three require the respondents to write in numerical responses, and the rest have from two to eleven optional categories from which the respondents are to choose the one that best describes themselves. Substantive areas covered by the SOS include demographic characteristics, study habits, attitudes about higher education in general and the individual respondent's institution in particular, feelings of student/institutional "fit" or congruence, socioeconomic status, peer relationships, student/faculty relations, personal problems, social activities, educational and career goals, feelings of racial discrimination, length of enrollment in college, number of credit hours earned, academic ability and preparation, and academic performance while in college.

The second questionnaire, entitled the Faculty Opinion Survey (FOS), was designed to elicit information from faculty members concerning their behaviors and attitudes toward their students and their institutions. The FOS contains 84 items, most of which are in Likert format with five optional response categories. Substantive areas covered by the FOS include demographic characteristics, professional status, teaching style, contact with students outside the classroom, concern with students' personal and emotional development, comparisons of Black and white students' college performances, satisfaction with the institution and other faculty members, opinions on whether the institution is racially discriminatory, and whether or not the institution teaches Black history.

DESCRIPTION OF THE SAMPLE

The sample includes 4,094 students and 706 faculty from thirty colleges and universities in ten Southern and mid–Atlantic states. The thirty universities include six each of the following five types: large predominantly white public (flagship), Black public, regional predominantly white public, white large private, and Black private. The institutions within each of the .five categories are similar not only in the type of governance, but in terms of size, racial composition of enrollment, and type of degree programs offered.

The sample of 4,094 students consists of 2,218 Black students and 1,876 white students. The sample was stratified by race and randomly selected from the thirty colleges and universities. The sampling procedure required the selection of 150 Black students, fifty each from the sophomore by race and randomly selected from the thirty colleges and universities. The sampling procedure required the selection of 150 Black students, fifty each from the sophomore, junior, and senior classes at each university. In cases where universities did not have fifty minority students in its enrollment, the entire population of students from that class was included in the sample. This procedure yielded a total of 7,428 students. The 4,904 student respondents represent 65.8 percent of the students who received the SOS.

The faculty sample was also randomly selected from the thirty colleges and universities. Thirty faculty members were selected from each university stratified such that twenty were selected from the racial majority on campus and ten from the minority racial group. This procedure produced an original sample size of nine hundred faculty. The 706 faculty members who completed and returned the FOS represent 79 percent of the those originally sampled.

In order to control for oversampling minority students, the following weighting procedure was used to weight individual responses of students:

$$\text{Weight} = \frac{\begin{array}{l}\text{percentage of students at} \\ \text{the institution who are} \\ \text{of respondent's race}\end{array}}{\begin{array}{l}\text{percentage of} \\ \text{institutional sample who} \\ \text{are of respondent's race}\end{array}} \times \frac{\begin{array}{l}\text{percentage of total students'} \\ \text{population who} \\ \text{attend respondent's institution}\end{array}}{\begin{array}{l}\text{percentage of total sample who} \\ \text{attend respondent's institution}\end{array}} \times \frac{N}{En}$$

This computerized weighting procedure does not affect degrees of freedom. Therefore, tests of significance are based upon the actual number of cases rather than the weighted number and are unaffected by the weighting scheme.

THE DEPENDENT VARIABLES

The dependent variables in this study are students' college performance as measured by their progression rates and the cumulative grade-point average. Progression rate is a measure of efficiency in the college experience, and grade-point average is a measure of academic achievement. Students' college progression rate is defined as the average number of credit hours which students successfully complete per term of enrollment. This variable is obtained by dividing students' total credit hours completed by the number of terms enrolled in college.

Students' college grade-point averages are cumulative. Students were asked on the SOS to choose the letter grade equivalent to their numerical grade-point average. The following nine choices were provided as options: A, A−, B+, B−, C+, C, C−, and D. Both the progression rates and cumulative college grade-point averages are self-reported on the SOS.

THE INDEPENDENT VARIABLES

The following personal, demographic, academic, and student and faculty attitudinal/behavioral characteristics are the predictor variables in this study:

1. Composite SAT score
2. Socioeconomic status
3. Sex
4. Age
5. High-school grade-point average
6. Marital status
7. Type of high school attended
8. Number of hours spent working on a job
9. Where lived while in school
10. Racial minority status
11. Whether a transfer student
12. Number of miles between college and permanent home
13. Fit between racial composition of high school and college
14. Fit between racial composition of home neighborhood and racial composition of college
15. Highest expected degree
16. Whether works while in college
17. Academic integration scale
18. Financial need
19. Commitment to institution scale
20. Academic motivation scale
21. Feelings of discrimination scale

22. Social integration scale
23. Interfering problems scale

FACULTY CHARACTERISTICS

1. Significant contact with students outside the classroom scale
2. Satisfaction with the institution scale
3. Conservative teaching styles scale
4. Feelings that the institution is discriminatory scale
5. Concern for student development scale

INSTITUTIONAL CHARACTERISTICS

1. Total enrollment

The six student attitudinal/behavioral characteristics—academic integration, commitment to the institution, academic motivation, feelings of discrimination, social integration, and interfering problems—are factor scales that were produced through a principal factor analysis of seventy-seven items from the SOS. The five faculty factors were produced using the same factor analysis procedure on FOS responses.

DATA ANALYSIS AND METHODOLOGY

Four sets of analyses are presented in this study to determine differences between Black and white students' performances, to demonstrate significant predictors of their performances, and to determine actual racial differences on the significant predictors.

First, comparisons are made of Black and white students' overall progression rates and college grade-point averages, using the T-test to determine if the differences are significant.

Second, multiple regression analyses are used to illustrate the significant predictors of students' progression rates and college grade-point averages. Separate regression analyses are performed for Black and white students, and both models include all independent variables. In these regression analyses, the entire set of independent variables are entered into the analyses concurrently; therefore, the partial regression coefficients and T-values represent the independent contribution of each variable, while all the other variables are statistically controlled.

Third, chi-square analyses are used to compare Black and white students and demonstrate significant differences among the categorical variables.

Finally, T-tests are utilized to compare Black and white students on the interval-level independent variables that were used in the regression analyses. T-tests are also used to compare the faculty attitudinal/behavior characteristics for faculty of Black and white students. The chi-square analyses and T-tests illustrate the racial differences of students on the significant variables, pointing out some factors which need to be addressed in efforts to achieve equality in the performance of Black and white college students.

FINDINGS

Racial Differences in Student Performances

Comparisons of overall progression rates and cumulative college grade-point averages (GPA) for Black and white students reveals that white students have both faster progression rates and higher GPAs than Black students. White students progress at an average rate of 15.3 credit hours per term, compared to 14.4 for Black students T < .001). White students have GPA of B (mean=4.2), compared to a GPA between B− to C+ (mean=5.5) for Black students (T < .001). One major question to be addressed in his paper is: what are the probable causes for the slower progression rates and lower GPAs of Black students that can be addressed by policy makers and university officials to bring about racial equality in students' performances?

Table 4.1 illustrates separate regression analyses of the student, faculty, and institutional characteristics predicting Black and white students' progression rates. Table 4.2 summarizes the regression analysis for the sample's college GPAs. In addition to showing the significant predictors of grades and progression rates of the differences between Blacks and whites, the two tables reveal some differences in the predictors of progression rates as compared to GPAs.

For both Black and white students (Table 4.1), progression rates are fastest for students who are younger; who attend larger universities; who attend college a relatively far distance from home; who have higher high school grades; who are in the racial majority on their campuses; who have low financial need; and who have low commitment to their universities

The following characteristics contribute to faster progression rates for Black students but not for white students: having a faculty with nontradi tional teaching style, being married, having high academic motivation, working a low number of hours on a job, living in on-campus housing, having low feelings of discrimination and not being a transfer student.

The following characteristics contribute to faster progression rates for white students but not for Black students: having a faculty with a high

TABLE 4.1
Regression of Students' Progression Rate on Student, Faculty, and Institutional Characteristics

Independent Variables	Black Students B[1]	Black Students Beta[2]	White Students B[1]	White Students Beta[2]
Student Characteristics				
SAT Score	.001	.038	.002	.076**
Socioeconomic Status	−.058	−.013	−.22	−.046
Sex (0=Female, 1=Male)	.055	.006	.030	.029
Age	−.551	−.247**	−.467	−.199**
High School Grade Point Average	.368	.139**	.252	.099**
Marital Status				
(0=Single, 1=Married or Living Together)	1.85	.120**	.424	.029
Type of High School Attended				
(0=Public, 1=Private)	.346	.025	.062	.005
Hours Spent Working on a Job	−.310	−.116**	−.218	.075
Where Lived				
(0=Private Home or Apartment,				
1=On-campus Housing)	.800	.095**	.410	.052
Racial Minority Status				
(0=Majority Status, 1= Minority Status)	1.22	−.135**	−.652	−.586
Transfer Student (0=Yes, 1=No)	.469	.093*	.133	.017
Miles from Permanent Home	.439	.160**	.316	.101**
Fit Between Racial Composition				
of High School and College				
(0=Different, 1=Alike)	.287	.034	.666	.057
Fit Between Racial Composition				
of Home Neighborhood				
(0=Different, 1=Alike)	.270	.031	−.068	−.005
Highest Expected Degree				
(0=Bachelor's or Less,				
1=Master's or More)	.168	.016	.435	.052*
Whether Works While in School				
(0=Yes, 1= No)	−.125	−.014	−.021	−.002
Academic Integration	.055	.014	.081	.019
Financial Need	−.491	−.086	−.389	−.083
Commitment to Institution	−.376	−.084**	−.588	−.129**
Academic Motivation	.588	.118*	.207	.048
Feelings of Discrimination	.312	.087	−.109	−.022
Social Integration	.021	.004	.421	.093**
Interfering Problems	−.151	−.031	−.273	−.058*
Faculty Characteristics				
Significant Contact with Students	−.246	−.035	−1.23	−.077
Satisfaction with Institution	−.186	−.021	−1.05	.136**
Conservative Teaching Style	1.87	.140**	1.01	.056
Feeling that Institution is Discriminatory	−.575	−.039	−.176	−.013
Concern for Student Development	.781	.074	2.41	.225**
Institutional Characteristics				
Total Enrollment	.00004	.113**	.00006	.289**
Constant	15.39		12.89	
F (Equation)	14.02		11.66	
R[2]	.240		.216	

[1]Unstandardized regression coefficient.
[2]Standardized regression coefficient.
*Significant at .05 level (two-tailed).
**Significant at .01 level (two-tailed).

concern for student development, having faculty with low satisfaction for their university, having high social integration, having high SAT scores, having a lack of interfering problems, and having high degree aspirations.

The total model explains 24.0 percent of the variance in Black students' progression rates, and 21.6 percent of the variance in white students' progression rates.

Most of the significant predictors of college GPA are the same for both Black and white students, but there are some differences. Table 4.2 shows that both Black and white students who have relatively high grades, who are highly motivated and highly integrated into the academic environment, also have a low commitment to their university. They also have high SAT scores, a high degree of contact with faculty outside the classroom, faculty with nontraditional teaching styles, and they have low financial need. These students receive relatively high college grades.

The characteristics of Blacks students with higher grades, that are not significant for white students are: being married, having a highly satisfied faculty, attending a college with racial composition similar to their high schools, and being a nontransfer student.

The characteristics of white students with relatively high college GPAs which in contrast, are not significant for Black students are: having few interfering problems, high discrimination on the campus, low social integration, living in on-campus housing, having higher degree aspirations, being in the racial majority on campus, being female, attending a private high school, and attending college a relatively far distance from home.

The regression model used is better suited for predicting white students' GPAs, thus explaining 42 percent of the variance as compared to 35 percent for Black students.

Racial Comparisons on Significant Variables

The regression analyses revealed important factors related to Black and white students' performances that can be useful to educators in their efforts to eliminate racial differences. In order to determine the areas in which to focus university efforts, however, comparisons of Black and white students on the predictor variables are needed. In other words, Black students may already be equal or even superior to white students on some important variables, thereby requiring no special attention in such areas.

Tables 4.3 and 4.4 provide comparisons of Black and white students on all the student characteristics included in the regression analyses, as well as comparisons by student race of faculty attitudinal/behavioral characteristics. Table 4.3 provides results of chi-square analyses on the categorical variables. Table 4.4 provides comparisons of Black and white students on the

TABLE 4.2
Regression of Students' Grade-Point Averages on Student, Faculty,
and Institutional Characteristics

Independent Variables	Black Students B^1	Black Students $Beta^2$	White Students B^1	White Students $Beta^2$
Student Characteristics				
SAT Score	.001	.140**	.002	.193**
Socioeconomic Status	.023	.013	.001	.000
Sex (0=Female, 1=Male)	−.038	−.010	−.246	.064**
Age	.012	.013	.037	.033
High-School Grade-Point Average	.296	.265**	.340	.275**
Marital Status				
(0=Single, 1=Married or Living Together)	.659	.101**	.203	.029
Type of High School Attended				
(0=Public, 1=Private)	.231	.040	.332	.059**
Hours Spent Working on a Job	−.004	−.004	−.025	−.018
Where Lived				
(0=Private Home or Apartment,				
1=On-campus Housing)	.172	.048	−2.53	−.065**
Racial Minority Status				
(0=Majority Status, 1=Minority Status)	.323	.084	1.162	.069
Transfer Student (0=Yes, 1=No)	.235	.063**	.162	.041
Miles from Permanent Home	.036	.032	.088	.058*
Fit Between Racial Composition				
of High School and College				
(0=Different, 1=Alike)	.227	.063**	.120	.021
Fit Between Racial Composition				
of Home Neighborhood				
(0=Different, 1=Alike)	.157	.043	−.291	−.046
Highest Expected Degree				
(0=Bachelor's or Less,				
1=Master's or More)	.125	.029	.284	−.070**
Whether Works While in School				
(0=Yes, 1=No)	−.024	−.006	−.153	−.039
Academic Integration	.435	.252**	.436	.210**
Financial Need	−.184	−.076	−.146	−.063**
Commitment to Institution	−.372	−.198**	−.400	−.179**
Academic Motivation	.565	.268**	−.724	−.341**
Feelings of Discrimination	−.071	.046	.242	.098**
Social Integration	−.041	−.021	−.200	−.090**
Interfering Problems	.044	.022	−.260	−.113**
Faculty Characteristics				
Significant Contact with Students	.556	.188**	.766	.098**
Satisfaction with Institution	.317	.084*	.138	.037
Conservative Teaching Style	−.604	−1.06	−.566	−.064*
Feeling that Institution is Discriminatory	.018	.002	.234	.035
Concern for Student Development	−.159	−.036	−.149	−.029
Institutional Characteristics				
Total Enrollment	−.002	−.019	−.006	.06
Constant	6.31		6.37	
F (Equation)	23.59		31.15	
R^2	.347		.424	

[1]Unstandardized regression coefficient.
[2]Standardized regression coefficient.
*Significant at .05 level (two-tailed).
**Significant at .01 level (two-tailed).

interval-level attitudinal/behavioral characteristics and on some interval-level precollege characteristics.

Table 4.3 presents chi-square comparisons of Black and white students' racial minority/majority status distribution, gender distribution, distribution by type of high school attended, distribution by degree aspiration, distribution by where they live while attending college, and whether they work on or off campus while in college. Each of these factors had some significant predictive effect for either students' progression rates, grade-point average, or both. We see that Black and white students are significantly different on each of the categorical variables.

In general, white college students are overwhelmingly more likely to be in the racial majority. White students have a more equal (50:50) sex distribution, whereas Black females are nearly twice as numerous as Black males (63:37). A significantly larger percentage of white than Black

TABLE 4.3
Chi-Square Analyses Comparing Black and White Students

Dependent Variable	Percentage for Black Students	Percentage for White Students
Racial Status		
Majority group	45.3 (1005)	87.7 (1646)
Minority Group	54.7 (1213)	12.3 (230)*
Sex		
Female	62.7 (1368)	49.7 (919)
Male	37.3 (813)	50.3 (930)**
Type of High School		
Public	89.8 (1972)	83.4 (1544)
Private	10.2 (233)	16.6 (307)**
Degree Aspirations		
Baccalaureate or less	21.6 (473)	34.8 (647)
More than Baccalaureate	78.3 (1712)	65.2 (1211)**
Where They Live		
Campus student housing	65.9 (1444)	54.0 (1005)
Private housing	34.1 (748)	46.0 (846)**
Work		
On campus	41.4 (897)	25.8 (469)
Off campus	24.3 (526)	31.3 (568)
Do not work	34.3 (742)	42.8 (777)**
Transfer Status		
Never taken courses elsewhere	64.5 (1413)	54.9 (1021)**
Taken courses elsewhere	35.5 (777)	45.1 (840)
Marital Status		
Single	93.6 (2044)	85.0 (1556)**
Married or living together	6.4 (140)	15.0 (275)

**Chi-Square significant at the .001 level.
*Chi-Square significant at the .01 level.

students attend private high schools (16 percent compared to 10 percent). A significantly larger percentage of Black students have degree aspirations beyond a baccalaureate (78 percent compared to 65 percent). A larger percentage of Black students work while attending college (66 percent compared to 57 percent); and the largest percentage of Black students who do work, work on campus while the largest percentage of working white students work off campus. A significantly larger percentage of white than Black students are transfer students (45 percent compared to 35 percent); and a significantly larger percentage of white students are married (15 percent compared to 6 percent).

Five of the seven categorical variables are significant predictors of Black students' progression rates, and two are significant predictors of their GPAs. On three significant variables—working while attending college, being in the racial minority group, and being single—Black students appear to be negatively affected in (Table 4.3). The remaining two significant variables—living in campus housing and being a nontransfer student—are variables upon which Black students compare favorably, and would appear from the regression analyses to be supportive of their progression rates and college GPA.

For white students, none of the categorical variables are significant predictors of progression rates (Table 4.3), but three are strongly associated with higher GPAs—living in campus housing, being in the majority racial group, and being female. The greater tendency of white students to be in the majority racial group may provide a clear advantage for their academic performances. On the other hand, the lesser tendency of white students, as compared to Black students, to live on campus and to be female would appear to detract from the overall GPA advantage observed above.

The findings suggest that the major differences in the performance of Black and white students are more likely to be explained by differences in their attitudinal/behavioral characteristics and their precollege characteristics.

In Table 4.4, T-tests were used to compare Black and white students' attitudinal/behavioral characteristics, revealing some important racial differences in the variables shown earlier to be significant predictors of progression rates and college GPAs. These analyses are especially important since all the variables in Table 4.4, with the exception of socioeconomic status, are significant predictors of progression rates and college grade-point averages.

Table 4.4 illustrates that white students are better integrated academically, have higher high-school grades, and have higher SAT scores than do Black students. All of these factors contribute favorably and significantly to white students' college grade-point averages. White students are also found

TABLE 4.4
T-Tests Comparing Black and White College Students

Dependent Variable	Mean for White Students	standard deviation	Mean for Black Students	standard deviation	degrees of freedom
Academic Integration	.163	.943	.021	1.044**	2822
Financial Need	−.120	.801	.289	.757**	2807
Commitment to the Institution	−.142	.950	−.386	.922**	2833
Academic Motivation	.042	.923	.028	.875	2808
Feelings of Discrimination	.015	.861	.647	1.275**	2546
Social Integration	.032	.884	.295	.920**	2833
Interfering Problems	−.015	.806	.203	.901**	2819
High-School Grade-Point Average	2.91 (B+)	1.7	3.51 (B to B+)	1.6*	3882
SES	.064	.845	−.897	1.0**	2788
Age	4.11 (21)	2.0	4.01 (21)	1.8	3826
Composite SAT Score	1056.8	178.6	853.2	156.6**	3760

**Significant at .001 level of significance using two-tailed students' T-test.
*Significant at .01 level of significance using two-tailed students' T-test.
[1]Numbers refer to the mean *category* numbers. The value represented by those categories (as rounded off) are enclosed in parenthesis.

to have greater commitment to their universities and higher socioeconomic status. However, commitment to the university has a negative impact on both progression rates and college grade-point average, while socioeconomic status is not related to students' progression rates or grade-point averages. White students are shown to have lower financial need, lower social integration, and fewer interfering problems—all of which contribute significantly to their college performances.

Table 4.4 shows that Black students have significantly greater financial need, stronger feelings of discrimination, lower academic integration, more interfering problems, lower SAT scores, and lower high-school grade-point averages—all of which impact negatively upon their performances. Black students also have lower commitment to their universities and lower socioeconomic status. For Black students, lower commitment is positively related to college performance, while socioeconomic status has no significant influence.

Comparisons of age and academic motivation reveal no significant differences between Black students and white students (Table 4.4). Younger students have significantly faster progression rates regardless of race. High academic motivation, is a significant predictor of both Black students' progression rates and college grades, but only for white students' college GPAs. Since there are no significant racial differences in age and academic motivation, Black students would not appear to be disadvantaged regarding their college performance because of age or academic motivation.

Faculty Influence upon Students' Performances

Thus far, several racial differences in student characteristics have been identified and examined. These race differences explain, in part, the slower progression rates and lower college GPAs of Black students. Faculty attitudinal and behavioral characteristics were also shown to play an important role in students' performances (Table 4.5). White students are more likely to have faculty who report greater student contact, greater satisfaction with their universities, more conservative teaching styles, and stronger feelings of discrimination. Black students are more likely to have faculty who report more concern for student development.

Faculty teaching style is the only faculty factor that is a significant predictor of Black student progression rates, with nonconservative teaching styles contributing to faster progression rates of white students. Since Black students were more likely to encounter faculty with nontraditional approaches, teaching styles are not likely to explain the slower progression rates of the Black students in this sample.

Similarly, for white students, high concern for student development and low faculty satisfaction contribute to faster progression rates. Yet, Table 4.5 shows that white students are less likely to experience faculty with high satisfaction. Thus, these faculty factors do not explain the faster progression rates of white students.

Three of the faculty attitudinal/behavioral characteristics are significant predictors of Black students' college grade-point averages, and two are sig-

TABLE 4.5
T-Tests Comparing the Faculty Attitudes of
Black and White College Students

Faculty Attitudes	*Mean for Faculty Black Students*	*standard deviation*	*Mean for Faculty White Students*	*standard deviation*	*degrees of freedom*
significant contact with students	−.237	.547	.008	.381**	3951
satisfaction with their universities	−.318	.526	−.107	.526**	4005
conservative teaching style	−.201	.335	−.018	.317**	4041
feelings of discrimination	−.063	.289	−.031	.319**	3826
concern for student development	−.198	.406	.061	.414**	3953

**Significant at the .001 level using two-tailed T-test.

nificant predictors of white students' college grade-point averages. For Black students, frequent faculty contact outside the classroom, nonconservative teaching styles, and faculty with a high degree of satisfaction contribute to higher college grade-point averages. Table 4.5 also shows that Black students are less likely than white students to experience faculty in frequent contact with students outside the classroom. They are also less likely to have highly satisfied faculty members.

For white students, having a faculty in more frequent contact with students outside the classroom and nonconservative teaching styles contributes to their grades. White students are more likely than Black students to have faculty with conservative teaching styles. Thus, while the faculty contact is supportive of white students' grade-point averages, conservative teaching style does not appear to explain their relatively high grade-point averages.

DISCUSSION

The slower college progression rates and lower college GPAs of Black students represent important qualitative challenges to equality in higher education. Institutions of higher education are successful in integrating their enrollments only when they have enrolled a sufficient number of minority students to be representative of the racial distribution in their service area *and* when minority student performance is equal to majority student performance.

This chapter identifies several student and faculty characteristics that are significant predictors of the performance of Black and white students. These characteristics appear to offer concerned colleges and universities ways in which to address the racial differences in students' performances. In terms of progression rates, Black students average 14.4 credit hours per term as compared to 15.3 for white students. Universities should be able to close the racial gap in progression rates by directing their efforts at Black students' feelings of discrimination, their racial minority status, their employment patterns while attending the university, and their high-school preparation. Although there are other predictors of Black students' college progression rates, these four represent areas where Black students are discovered to be significantly disadvantaged compared to their white peers.

Generally, universities should explore methods to reduce the negative consequences for Black students of being in the racial minority group on campus and their feelings of discrimination. This is especially significant since the majority of Black college students now attend universities where they are in the racial minority group; and, as a quantitative desegregation progesses, this trend is likely to continue. The sensed discrimination factor includes students' perceptions about their universities which need to be addressed. These include students' feelings that the university's faculty and administration discriminate against minority students, that the university does not make sufficient effort to recruit minority students, and that the university is generally racially discriminatory.

Although it is considered normal behavior for students to work part-time to support their college educations, the greater number of hours worked by Black students appears to have a negative impact on their rate of progress. It was demonstrated that Black students are more frequently required to pay their own college expenses. This indicates the need for university financial-aid programs and academic advising programs to assist Black students in reducing the number of hours worked in order to achieve faster progression rates.

The high-school preparation of Black students is outside the purview of university faculty and staff, except as the faculty prepares students to teach in elementary and secondary school or otherwise interface with faculty and administrators at the precollegiate levels. However, because of the need in the desegregation process to provide better preparation to prospective Black college students, there is a greater need for universities to establish partnerships with elementary and secondary schools, especially with schools that have a high concentration of minority students. Such partnerships may include emphasis upon curriculum development and developing teaching/learning techniques geared toward university preparation. Better preparation of Black high-school students will contribute to the improved overall performance of Black college students.

As for Black students' college GPAs, which are found to be significantly lower than those of white students, several issues are identified that would be beneficial for universities to address in the desegregation process. Specifically, greater attention should be given to the following significant predictors since Black students have weaker high-school preparation, as revealed by their lower high-school GPAs and SAT scores. Black students also have lower academic integration, more limited contact with faculty outside the classroom and more faculty who are dissatisfied with their universities. Black students have greater financial need and are less likely to attend a university with a racial composition similar to that of their high schools. High school preparation, financial assistance, and faculty contact are also found to be important for improving Black students' rates of progress in college.

It is important for universities to understand the effects of faculty satisfaction and the fit between the racial composition of high schools and colleges. Academic integration is a factor which includes students' satisfaction with faculty relationships; their feelings that the faculty of the university is sensitive to the interests, needs, and aspirations of students; the ease with which students feel they can develop close personal relationships with faculty members on campus; the perception of students that their faculty are good teachers; and the students' satisfaction with the quality of instruction at their university. From this view, Black students are less academically integrated than white students.

Faculty satisfaction with the university is influenced by their satisfaction with the caliber of scholarly research on the campus, their satisfaction with campus research resources, the opportunities for personal growth, their satisfaction with opportunities for career advancement, and their rating of the university's academic reputation. Black students are found to have comparatively less-satisfied faculty than do white students. There is reason to believe that greater faculty satisfaction would contribute to higher college GPAs among Black students.

The fit between the racial composition of Black students' high-school and college experiences contributes to their college GPAs; therefore, greater integration at the high-school level is likely to improve the academic performances of Black students attending integrated universities. While this is not a matter to be addressed by universities, it provides them with reasons to support public policy makers and federal courts who push for complete desegregation at the elementary and secondary-school levels.

Part Two

The Undergraduate Years: Empirical Research Findings

In this section papers report empirical findings from studies based on the undergraduate data from the National Study of Black College Students. The authors examine the relationship of undergraduate academic performance to student characteristics and the environment. Allen and Haniff look at three outcomes—grades, racial attitudes, and college satisfaction—as these are related to the gender of the student and also to the composition of race on campus. They attempt to elucidate how student characteristics and campus racial identity influence student interpersonal relationships and, through these, determine student outcomes.

Smith focuses on the constrasting environments of Black and white colleges and the difference they make for Black student characteristics, experiences, and outcomes. Of special concern to him is the relative explanatory power of key predictors of Black students' success *across* different racial contexts.

Jackson and Swan extend the concerns raised by Smith; their paper offers a straightforward comparison of the relative effects of the same factors for Black students attending colleges with a different-racial composition. They believe that the same variables may have very different effects depending on whether Black students are pursuing their education on white versus Black campuses.

Finally, Davis looks at a different aspect of the college experience—social support systems—in his search for salient predictors of Black students' success in college. He suggests that Black students' college satisfaction, academic performance, and occupational aspirations are influenced by social support. In this respect, he expects that Black students on historically Black campuses will experience greater social support with more positive results shown in their levels of adjustment and achievement.

Some of the important factors affecting academic performance for undergraduates are analyzed here. Policy makers interested in factors contributing to attrition and retention among Black undergraduate college students should find this section of particular interest. Faculty, and students themselves, will also be interested to know which factors best predict the success of African American college students during the undergraduate years.

WALTER R. ALLEN
NESHA Z. HANIFF

Chapter Five

Race, Gender, and Academic Performance in U.S. Higher Education*

The year 1990 marked the thirty-sixth anniversary of *Brown v. the Topeka Board of Education* and the twenty-fifth anniversary of the Higher Education Act of 1965. The Supreme Court's epic decision outlawing segregation in public schools and the subsequent decision of the U.S. Congress to support equal opportunity in college education irrevocably changed the higher-education experience for African Americans. The number of Black students currently enrolled in higher education has more than doubled since 1960 and, for the first time in U.S. history, Black students are more likely to matriculate at predominantly white colleges than at traditionally Black institutions.

The dramatic shift in postsecondary education patterns among African Black Americans naturally leads to questions about the influence of campus race of Black students' educational experiences and outcomes. This paper overviews findings from a national survey of 1,600 Black students enrolled in sixteen public universities, eight of them Black and eight white. The report explores the extent to which Black students on white campuses have experiences that are qualitatively different from those of Black students on Black campuses.

CAMPUS RACE AND BLACK STUDENT'S EDUCATIONAL EXPERIENCES

Summary of Previous Research Findings

The published literature provides a partial response to questions concerning the difference which campus race makes in the lives of Black college students. Black students on white campuses have been shown to experience considerable difficulty in making the adjustment to an environment which is culturally different, academically demanding, and socially alienating. As a result, Black students do not experience reasonable levels of academic success and college satisfaction on these campuses. Compared to white students, Black students average higher attrition rates, weaker educational backgrounds, less satisfactory relationships with faculty, lower grade-point averages, lower enrollments in postgraduate programs, and report more dissatisfaction and greater alienation (Allen 1986; Blackwell 1982; and Abramowitz 1976).

By contrast, the literature portrays African American students on historically Black campuses as satisfied, engaged in the campus life, and well adjusted. However, these students come from lower economic backgrounds and score lower on absolute measures of academic achievement (such as standardized test scores) by comparison with their peers of both races on white campuses. They are further disadvantaged, relatively speaking, because of the extreme institutional differences between Black and white colleges on measures of wealth or material environment (physical facilities, faculty credentials, and the like). Nevertheless, Black students on Black campuses. evidence more positive psychosocial adjustments, stronger cultural awareness and commitment, greater relative academic gains during the college years, and higher attainment aspirations (Thomas 1984; Fleming 1984; and Gurin and Epps 1975).

Prior research suggests that campus race influences the college experiences of African American students. Whether a student reports a positive or negative, or a satisfactory or unsatisfactory educational experience is affected by the predominant racial composition of his or her campus. What is it about the comparative characteristics of Black students, their educational experiences, and personal relationships on different-race campuses which produces such striking differences in academic performance, satisfaction with college, and feelings of belonging?

Research Questions

This paper examines a wide range of research questions. These questions are centered around three student outcomes: academic performance, racial attitudes, and college satisfaction. How these characteristics are related to the students' gender and campus race context are of primary concern.

The study is also concerned with three sets of causal factors judged to be antecedent to and explanatory of observed differences in student outcomes. These antecedent factors may be grouped into the following categories: student background factors (such as parents' socioeconomic status, and high-school academic record); student college experiences (involvement in campus life, academic competitiveness of the university, adjustment to college life, and race relations on the campus); and student personality orientation (self-concept and occupational aspirations, for example).

The key research questions addressed in this study follow.

1. How does student academic performance vary in relation to student background, campus experiences, and personality orientation?
2. How do student racial attitudes vary in relation to student background, campus experiences, and personality orientation?
3. How does student satisfaction with college vary in relation to student background, campus experiences, and personality orientation?

Specifically we expect to answer the question of "What is the relative importance of student background factors, campus experiences, and personality orientation in the prediction of academic performance?"

Sample and Data

The data for this article are from the National Study of Black College Students (NSBCS), based at the University of Michigan in Ann Arbor. This study collected several waves of data on the achievements, experiences, attitudes and backgrounds of Black undergraduate students attending selected state-supported universities. All of the institutions participating in the 1981 and 1983 NSBCS were selected on the basis of regional diversity and accessibility. The population for both years of study were currently enrolled Black American undergraduates.

The research design relied on collaborators on each of the participating campuses. Data were collected using mailed questionnaires which students returned directly to the University of Michigan via business reply mail for coding and computer tabulation. The selection of students for participation in the study was random, based on lists of currently enrolled students supplied by the various university registrars' offices. Selected students received the questionnaire and four follow-up reminder mailings.

The 1981 phase of the study collected data from black undergraduates at six predominantly white, public universities (University of Michigan at

Ann Arbor, University of North Carolina in Chapel Hill, University of California at Los Angeles, Arizona State University in Tempe, Memphis State University and the State University of New York at Stony Brook).

In contrast, the 1983 phase of the NSBCS collected data from Black undergraduates at eight predominantly Black public universities (North Carolina Central University in Durham, Southern University in Baton Rouge, La.; Texas Southern University in Houston; Jackson State University in Jackson, Miss.; North Carolina A&T University in Greensboro; Morgan State University in Baltimore, Md.; Central State University in Wilberforce, Ohio and Florida A&M University in Tallahassee).

Both data sets were merged to compare and contrast students at predominantly white versus traditionally Black universities. The final response rate for the 1981 undergraduate study was 27 percent, while the 1983 undergraduate response rate was 35 percent. Together, the data sets include 1,583 students.

Measures

Three measures of student outcomes are used in this report: student academic performance, satisfaction with college, and racial attitudes. Academic performance was measured by the respondent's reported grade-point average. Respondent *racial attitudes* are measured using four different items. The items asked respondents to indicate whether they strongly agreed, agreed, disagreed, or strongly disagreed with each of the following statements:

> There is a need for a national Black political party . . .
> Interracial dating and marriage are equally as acceptable as within-race dating and marriage . . .
> Schools with majority Black student populations should have a majority of Black teachers and administrators . . .
> There is a great deal of unity and sharing among Black students at this university . . .

Conservative racial attitudes are defined as students who reject the national Black political party, who oppose interracial dating or marriage, who oppose majorities of teachers/administrators in Black majority schools, and who judge Black unity and sharing to be low.

Student *satisfaction with college* is measured by four items, the first asked about campus activities:

> How much do you, as a Black student, feel a part of general campus life, insofar as student activities and government are concerned?
> *not at all . . . (1) to considerable . . . (4)*

The second measure of student satisfaction with college—asked whether the student had considered leaving school.

The final two indicators of student satisfaction with college asked the student about the quality of personal relationships with white faculty and white staff at the university:

> How would you characterize *your* relations with whites at this university?
> Faculty?:/excellent . . . (1) to very poor . . . (4)
> Staff people?:/excellent . . . (1) to very poor . . . (4)

The independent or predictor variables used in the multiple regression analyses for this study can be placed into three groups

1. *Background Factors,* including campus race, student sex, mother's education, and high-school grade point average;
2. *Campus Experience Factors,* including feelings of involvement in campus life, level of academic competition at the university, whether the student considered leaving or not, and relations with whites at the university;
3. *Social Psychological Factors,* including respondent self-concept, racial attitude index, and occupational aspirations.

Limitations of the Study

There are important limitations to be considered in attempts to generalize findings from this research. To begin, the study was purposely restricted to state-supported universities, even though there is a sizeable group of African American students who attend private universities or colleges. Thus, some findings from this research may not be applicable to private institutions.

Questions can also be raised about the representativeness of the students who participated in this study. The sixteen universities included in this study were purposely selected to maximize regional diversity and to ensure university and research collaborator cooperation. Thus, this study does not necessarily have a random or representative sample of all the state-supported universities that Black students attend nationally.

Sizeable nonresponse rates pose another possible source of bias in the study. It may well be that our sample is biased by the inclusion of students with special motives to respond, that is those who are most satisfied or most dissatisfied with college.

Possible sources of error also result from the study's methodology. Self-completed questionnaires are often subject to bias arising from misunderstood questions and/or inconsistent answers. It may well be that ethnographic or institutional studies would be more appropriate methodologies. Certainly, these methods would help to supplement and enrich the data presented in this study.

Tests of Bivariate Research Hypotheses

Academic performance was found to vary in relation to student background, campus experiences, and personality orientation. Black students on Black campuses reported significantly higher grade-point averages than was true for their peers on white campuses. Three-quarters of the students in the white campus group, versus two-thirds of students in the Black campus group, reported grade-point averages of less than 3.0 on a four-point scale. Observed gender differences are also true to our expectations, with males reporting significantly higher grade-point averages. These differences are less pronounced, however, than are differences between Black and white campuses. Females are only slightly more likely than males to report grade-point averages below 3.0 (72 percent versus 68 percent).

Neither family income nor mother's educational attainment is a significant predictor of student grade-point averages. Academic performance is, however, significantly related to student satisfaction with and involvement in college life. Grades are significantly higher for students who have not seriously contemplated leaving school and for students who find their interests reflected in campus activities. Grades are also significantly higher for students who favorably reported their relationships with faculty and staff, another dimension of college satisfaction.

To our surprise, academic performance is not associated with high or low self-esteem or high occupational aspirations. On the other hand, high educational aspirations are significantly more common among students with higher grades.

Student racial attitudes do, in fact, vary by student background, campus experiences, and personality orientation. Using the indicators of attitudes toward interracial dating and evaluation of unity among Black students on the campus, we find that, as anticipated, females voiced more conservative racial attitudes than males. A sizeable 62 percent of the women, versus 54 percent of males, considered interracial dating to be unacceptable. This difference is statistically significant. Females are also significantly less likely to see a high degree of unity among Black students on their campuses: 52 percent of women versus 57 percent men reported a great deal of unity among Black students. Comparison of these same racial-attitude items across campus racial context provides support for our expectation of greater conservatism on white campuses. Black students on white campuses are significantly more likely to describe unity among Black students on the campus negatively: 62 versus 44 percent judged Black student-unity to be very low. Black students on the different-race campuses seemed equally likely to consider interracial dating acceptable. In both settings, 41 percent of students approve.

Students' racial attitudes are significantly related to economic background in only one instance (Table 5.1): students from higher income families are more accepting of interracial dating. Student assessment of the degree of unity among Black students on campus is strongly related to having more positive feelings about the greater involvement with campus life. Students reporting positive relations with white faculty and staff, and those who find their interests reflected in campus activities are significantly more likely to report the Black student community on campus as beset with disunity. By the same token, students who had not considered leaving school are significantly more likely to see disunity and discord among Blacks on the campus.

Student satisfaction with college, like the other outcome variables, shows important differences by student gender and campus race. Looking first at the extent to which students felt campus activities reflected their interests, there are important, though not striking, interests by gender. Males are much more likely to report campus activities as "somewhat" or "considerably representative" of their interests: 56 versus 52 percent. On Black campuses, two-thirds of the students reported campus activities as being "somewhat" or "considerably representative" of their interests. On white campuses, the comparable figure is 38 percent.

Comparison of the extreme categories reveals great disparities by campus race in Black student satisfaction with college. While 26 percent of students on Black campuses reported campus activities to "considerably" represent their interests, only 8 percent of Black students on white campuses were so positive. At the other extreme, twice as many students on white campuses reported campus activities as not at all representing their interests (19 percent), versus the students on Black campuses who expressed dissatisfaction with campus activities (10 percent).

Results from correlational analyses show that mothers' education and family income—our measures of student economic background—are not statistically related with whether or not a student had considered leaving college (Table 5.1). There are no clear consistent patterns by family income. Student relations with staff are significantly less favorable where family income is highest. The same is true for relations with white faculty, although not significantly so. This finding is clarified when we remember

TABLE 5.1
Correlation Matrix of Variables in the Study: Means and Standard Deviations

N = 809 DF = 807 R @ 0.0500–0.0689 R @ 0.0100–0.905

Variable	MALE	WHTCOL	MEDUC	FAMINC	HSGPA	UGPA	LEAVE	CAMPUSL	COMPETE	RELUNIVX	STFACREL	STSTAFFR	STSTUREL	RATTINDX	BKPRTY	MIXDATE	BCNTRL	UNITY	FUTOCC	SELFEST	HOWFARSC	WHNSUCC
MALE	1.0000																					
WHTCOL	-.057	1.000																				
MEDUC	-.012	.026	1.000																			
FAMINC	.011	.088	.059	1.000																		
HSGPA	-.150	.339	.064	.059	1.000																	
UGPA	.057	-.188	.051	.052	.166	1.000																
LEAVE	.006	-.044	-.020	-.037	-.122	-.175	1.000															
CAMPUSL	.059	-.332	.090	.015	-.073	.176	-.098	1.000														
COMPETE	.000	.273	.059	.076	.105	-.035	-.113	-.090	1.000													
RELUNIVX	-.074	.104	-.074	-.079	.019	-.113	.095	-.211	.047	1.000												
STFACREL	-.070	.147	-.036	-.049	.055	-.153	.099	-.217	.054	.859	1.000											
STSTAFFR	-.048	.095	-.067	-.085	.014	-.103	.093	-.174	.039	.873	.669	1.000										
STSTUREL	-.071	.020	-.085	-.067	-.023	-.028	.046	-.144	.027	.797	.502	.527	1.000									
RATTINDX	-.029	-.046	-.044	-.128	-.014	-.008	-.073	.027	.055	.068	.073	.055	.043	1.000								
BKPRTY	-.032	-.102	-.072	-.078	-.081	-.038	.065	-.031	.025	.083	.081	.051	.078	.453	1.000							
MIXDATE	-.099	.049	-.012	-.099	-.015	.001	-.029	-.067	.044	.126	.119	.098	.101	.519	.542	1.000						
BCNTRL	.028	.192	-.009	-.042	.077	-.030	-.035	-.036	.020	.037	.045	.051	.051	.542	.052	.048	1.000					
UNITY	.041	-.224	-.005	-.044	.097	.043	-.034	-.017	.058	.023	-.085	-.017	-.022	.542	.007	-.007	.046	1.000				
FUTOCC	.069	.093	.124	.107	.072	.014	-.017	.001	.044	-.033	-.021	-.030	-.019	-.040	-.066	.013	.019	-.051	1.000			
SELFEST	.045	.089	.054	.089	.089	.034	-.035	.017	.011	-.021	-.030	-.021	-.012	-.025	.018	.012	-.024	-.054	-.014	1.000		
HOWFARSC	.027	.041	.110	.086	.066	.181	-.035	.105	-.001	-.012	-.019	-.004	-.039	-.011	.002	.004	.012	-.037	.267	.119	1.000	
WHNSUCC	.086	.037	.006	.056	.034	.048	-.025	-.002	.048	-.024	-.028	-.039	-.029	-.002	.008	-.008	.023	-.024	.018	.099	.128	1.000

TABLE 5.1 (continued)

Variable		N	Minimum	Maximum	Mean	Std Dev
MALE	Sex	1580	0	1.0000	0.39747	0.48953
WHTCOL	Campus Race	1583	0	1.0000	0.43904	0.49643
MEDUC	Mother's Education	1511	4.5000	20.000	12.205	3.7929
FAMINC	Family Income	1462	1.0000	17.000	5.8625	3.8286
HSGPA	High-School Grade-Point Average	1376	1.0000	4.0000	3.1212	0.54691
UGPA	College Grade-point Average	1497	1.0000	4.0000	2.6746	0.48994
LEAVE	Consider Leaving the University	1560	0	1.0000	0.36731	0.48223
CAMPUSL	Feel Part of Campus Life	1571	1.0000	4.0000	2.5729	0.93971
COMPETE	Academic Competition on Campus	1574	1.0000	4.0000	3.3170	0.74575
RELUNIVX	Relations with Whites Index	1547	1.0000	12.000	5.4454	1.8717
STFACREL	Relations with White Faculty	1494	1.0000	4.0000	1.9418	0.63178
STSTAFFR	Relations with White Staff	1378	1.0000	4.0000	2.0334	0.65705
STSTUREL	Relations with White Students	1436	1.0000	4.0000	1.8948	0.64073
RATTINDX	Racial Attitudes Index	1564	0	4.0000	2.5627	0.87403
BKPRTY	National Black Political Party	1536	0	1.0000	0.77148	0.42001
MIXDATE	Interracial Dating	1542	0	1.0000	0.58885	0.49220
BCNTRL	Black Controlled Schools	1542	0	1.0000	0.70039	0.45824
UNITY	Black Student Unity	1544	0	1.0000	0.54080	0.49849
FUTOCC	Occupational Aspirations	1499	1.0000	96.020	70.594	16.125
SELFEST	Self-Esteem	1550	1.0000	4.0000	3.0619	0.69679
HOWFARSC	Educational Aspirations	1498	1.0000	4.0000	2.1195	1.0009
WHNSUCC	Career Striving	1507	1.00	5.0000	4.2236	1.1395

that Black students' family incomes are highest on white campuses—the very settings where relations with white faculty and staff have been shown to be most negative. The pattern of high family-socioeconomic status and poor relations with white faculty and staff is repeated for mothers' education, where the general (but not statistically significant) trend is toward more negative relations for students with highly educated mothers.

Student gender and campus race effects are a major focus of this study. Therefore, we turn to an assessment of how these two sets of factors are related to other variables of interest in this study. Males are more likely to claim excellent relations, significantly so in the case of white staff. Twenty-four percent of male students (versus 19 percent of females) claimed to be on excellent terms with white faculty at their universities, while 20 percent of the men (compared to 15 percent of women) reported excellent relations with white staff.

Differences by campus race in relations with white faculty and staff are striking. Students on Black campuses are significantly more likely to report positive relations. The proportion of Black students on Black campuses claiming excellent relations with white faculty (26 versus 15 percent) and with white staff (22 versus 12 percent) nearly exceeds by twice the proportions on white campuses. For whatever reason or reasons, Black students are significantly more favorable about their relations with white faculty and white staff when these occurred in a predominantly Black, as opposed to white, environment.

Our comparisons of mothers' education—an important personal background factor—reveals further significant campus race differences. Nearly a third of students on white campuses reported that their mothers graduated from college, and 11 percent hold advanced degrees. By comparison, only 22 percent of mothers of students attending Black schools graduated from college, and 9 percent hold advanced degrees. Comparing the lower end of the educational ladder, a third of mothers with children attending Black colleges (versus a quarter of mothers of students on white campuses) had not graduated from high school. When students are compared by sex, no substantial differences in mothers' educational attainment is revealed.

Significant differences by gender and campus race are apparent when we compare student grades in high school. Females were clearly the better students in high school—well over a third of females, compared to a quarter of males, reported high-school grade-point averages of 3.5 or better on a four-point scale. Just under three-quarters of the females had grade averages of 3.0 or better; the comparable figure for males is 60 percent. The high-school academic superiority of Black students on white campuses versus those on Black campuses is apparent by comparison. Nearly half the students on white campuses (49 percent) compared to 18 percent of students on Black campuses reported averages of 3.5 or better.

When we are reminded of these students' college grade-point averages, the observed declines in academic performance from high school to college are nothing short of spectacular. Females experience the most drastic decrease in academic performance with the move from high school to college. It must be noted in this connection that, with the move from high school to college, the academic environment changes dramatically. College programs tend to be more male-dominated environments than was true of the elementary and secondary schools where these females excelled.

Looking at aspects of the students' current campus experiences, we again see significant differences by gender and campus race. Males and females display significant and traditional differences in college majors, although to a slightly lesser extent than would have been true twenty years ago. Compared with men, women are significantly overrepresented in the social sciences (21 versus 18 percent); the human service professions, such as social work and nursing (14 versus 10 percent); and the humanities (7 versus 4 percent). They are significantly underrepresented in the natural life sciences (8 versus 11 percent); and the entrepreneurial professions, such as business and engineering (48 versus 56 percent).

Race of campus is also a significant differentiating factor in student major-field choices. Seventy-three percent of students on Black campuses, versus half of students on white campuses, chose to major in some profession. The entrepreneurial professions attracted 57 percent of professional majors on Black campuses and 43 percent of majors on white campuses. Fifteen percent of professional majors on Black campuses, versus 8 percent on white campuses, were in the human-service professions. Black students seem no more nor less likely to major in the natural and life sciences dependent on campus race. Black students on white campuses are, however, considerably more likely to major in the social sciences (24 versus 16 percent) and the humanities (9 versus 3 percent).

The students' report of the level of academic competition on the campus is another measure of campus experience in which we see important differences by gender and campus race. Females are more likely to report the level of academic competition on campus by using the highest category—"considerable amount"—with 39 versus 28 percent. The differences by campus race in the sensed level of academic competition on campus was nothing short of profound. Sixty-one percent of students on white campuses used the highest possible category to report the level of academic competition, while 93 percent used one of the top two categories. The comparable figures for Black students on Black campuses were 13 and 64 percent.

Finally, we come to student relationships with faculty—our last measure of campus experiences. It is interesting to note in this connection that the two categories of students who felt the most academic pressure—females and those on white campuses—also reported the least favorable relationships with faculty. Fewer women claimed "excellent" relations with faculty (19 versus 24 percent); the same was true for students on white campuses (15 versus 26 percent).

We now turn our attention to the students' psychological orientation in search of important gender and campus race effects. We note with little surprise the fact that males and females are comparable on their levels of self-esteem. Further, it is not surprising to find the sample characterized by very good self-concept (only 21 percent of the total sample rated themselves average or below). These students are more likely to rate themselves high (32 versus 25 percent) and above average (55 versus 52 percent). The possibility of a compensatory response by students on white campuses in the face of systematic devaluation must be considered.

Students in this study are also differentiated by sex and campus race on our measure of career striving. Males are significantly more likely to strive for the top of their intended professions (63 versus 53 percent). Needless to say, the realities of differences in gender socialization patterns *and* in the respective responsibilities assigned men and women in the family must be factored into our interpretations of these differences. Related to gender, it is also necessary for us to recognize the potentially dampening effects of sparse female representation at the top of most professions on the kinds of occupational goals that younger females set for themselves. The scarcity of female role models in high-ranking professional positions places subtle, yet powerful, limitation on women's ideas of their potentials as they outline their career aspirations.

Black students on white campuses are considerably more likely than Black students on Black campuses to anticipate future occupations in the highest prestige category (such as, judge, corporate executive, or physician), by a margin of 26 to 13 percent. This fact, coupled with the greater intensity of academic competition may explain why Black students on white campuses reported lower occupational eminence strivings. Black students on white campuses may well adjust their eminence striving downward given a clearer understanding of the competitive odds likely to be encountered. Females are significantly less likely to report occupational goals in the highest prestige category (16 versus 22 percent). For females career strivings and career goals are consistently depressed. This pattern gives credence to hypotheses which point to gender discrimination, and subsequent psychological adjustments, as factors restricting the goal-setting and goal-striving behaviors of women. Unlike students on Black campuses, women in this sample do not adjust their eminence upward as they adjust their career goals downward.

Important gender and campus race differences are also apparent in the educational aspirations reported by these students. We see minor, but interesting, differences by gender: women are more likely to indicate the bachelor's degree as their ultimate goal (33 versus 30 percent). It is also interesting to note that roughly a third of the total sample do not plan to go beyond the Bachelor's of Arts (B.A.) degree. Females are less likely than males to aspire to the prestigious medical (M.D.) or jurisprudence (J.D.) degrees (15 versus 19 percent), although they are equally likely to aspire to doctoral (Ph.D.) degrees.

Race of campus is clearly associated with the kind of terminal degree sought by a student. Black students on Black campuses are more likely to set their sights on master's-level (M.A.) degrees (44 versus 32 percent), probably because of the disproportionate enrollment of Black campuses in professional training programs where the terminal degree is in social work, (M.S.W.), business (M.B.A.), or regional planning (M.R.P.). Black students on Black campuses are also more likely than Black students on white campuses to report the Ph.D. degree as their ultimate goal (17 versus 8 percent). On the other hand, Black students attending white universities are significantly more likely than Black students on Black campuses to aspire to prestigious terminal degrees in medicine or law (29 versus 8 percent).

Results from regression analysis of academic performance on student background, campus interpersonal relationships, and psychological orientation predictors using the total sample are summarized in Table 5.2 (see Table 5.1 for variable intercorrelations, means, and standard deviations). Contrary to expectations, Black student relations with whites on the campus are not significantly correlated with academic performance. Happier, more satisfied students do not necessarily have higher college grade-point averages. It is interesting to note how the strong zero-order relationships between college grades and relations with whites on campus is diminished when other variables, such as student background factors, are entered as controls. Whether a student's interests are reflected in campus activities, whether he or she has satisfactory relations with whites, and how he or she perceives academic competition is not strongly predictive of college grades. College grades are correlated, although not significantly so, with whether a student has considered leaving school. Grades were higher for those students who had not seriously considered leaving school.

Students' background factors are strongly related to students' college grades. High-school grade-point average is the strongest predictor of college grades for this sample. Students whose grades were high in high

TABLE 5.2
Regression of Academic Performance
on Predictors' Total Sample

Predictor Variables	Regression Coefficient	Standard Error	Partial Regression Coefficient
Intercept	1.53	.176**	
Mother's Education	−.002	.004	−.013
High-School Grade Average	.227	.027	.246**
Gender	−.058	.029	−.061**
College Race	.206	.033	.187**
Campus Activities	.022	.016	.043
Academic Competition	−.025	.023	−.033
Consider Leaving	.133	.029	.137
Relations with Whites	−.011	.008	−.041
Self-Concept	−.029	.020	−.043
Racial Attitudes	−.003	.014	−.007
Occupational Aspirations	−.001	.001	−.018
Educational Aspirations	.088	.015	.183**

Multiple R= .394
Multiple R-Square= .155*
Standard Error= .450
N=1084

*=Significant at the .05 level.
**=Significant at the .01 level.

school are significantly more likely to have good college grade-point averages. Consistent with our expectation and the preliminary analyses here, both gender of student and race of campus are significant predictors of academic performance in college. College race is the second strongest single predictor of academic performance, while student gender is also strongly predictive of grades. Students on Black campuses and males were significantly more likely to report higher college grades.

For the most part, students' academic performances were not significantly related to personality orientation in these data. This finding came as a surprise. We had expected students with high self-esteem, strong racial consciousness, and high occupational goals to have better grades. The one exception to this pattern is provided by the strong correlation between college grades and student educational aspirations. The grades of students with high educational aspirations were significantly higher. To the extent that students set high educational goals for the future, their current academic performance seemed to be consistent.

Interpretation of Findings

Central in the determination of how individual and institutional characteristics influence Black students' experiences in higher education are students' interpersonal relationships. Interpersonal relationships form the bridge between individual dispositions and institutional tendencies, and together, these factors determine individual student outcomes. The way a student perceives and responds to events in the college setting will differentiate the college experience. What he or she does when confronted with difficult subject matter and how he or she handles the uncertainty of being a freshman will determine whether the experience is positive or negative in its consequences.

Black students' college outcomes can be reasonably viewed as resulting from a two-stage process. Taking the case of academic performance to illustrate this point, along with the theoretical model implicit in this conceptualization, we are led to conclude the following: whether a student successfully completes college and whether that student graduates with "honors" is, no doubt, sizably influenced by individual characteristics.

How bright the student is, the level of background preparation, and the intensity of personal ambition and striving will all influence academic performance outcomes. Beyond these personal traits, however, is a set of more general factors—characteristics which are more situational and interpersonal in nature. Therefore, the student's academic performance will also be affected by the quality of life at the institution, the level of academic competition, university rules/procedure/resources, relationships with faculty, and friend-support networks.

In discussing the aspiration/attainment process nearly twenty years ago, Rehberg and Westby (1967) introduced the vital notion of facilitation. The concept is useful here for its focus on the fact that the attainment process is influenced by a combination of institutional, individual, and interactional factors. The educational goals and activities of Black students are acted out in specific social environments which affect, not only their context, but their possibilities for realization as well. Actors in the setting—indeed the setting itself—can either facilitate or frustrate the efforts of Black students to achieve high academic performance (Allen 1986).

A. WADE SMITH

Chapter Six

Personal Traits, Institutional Prestige, Racial Attitudes, and Black Student Academic Performance in College

The classical models of educational attainment have had so little efficacy for Black students in general, and Black college students in particular, that the enrollment, retention, and graduation experiences of Black students in both predominantly white and predominantly Black universities remains a pressing—if misunderstood—phenomenon (Tinto 1975). As a result, educational administrators' efforts to improve Black students' success often lack even the most rudimentary grounds for the policies and programs implemented. Previous research has demonstrated that certain elements of traditional educational attainment models must be discarded when considering Black students in higher education (Epps 1981; and Gurin and Epps 1975). Appropriate models should contain measures specific to the Black experience and sensitive to the special characteristics associated with the type of college or university which Blacks most often attend.

Specifically, more recent research has shown that among Black students attending predominantly white public universities, levels of occupational aspiration and academic performance vary according to the prestige of the institution (Smith and Allen 1984). Black students at the most prestigious predominantly white four-year public universities out-perform their counterparts at less prestigious schools, even after controlling for socio-economic background, achievement in high school, and other institutional characteristics. In fact, measures of personal attributes (such as the standard Wisconsin-type background variables) have scant association with academic performance, and only a minimal relationship with Black collegians' occupational aspirations. Moreover, in this same context, Black students' racial identification has been found to be unrelated to their academic performances (Smith and Moore 1983). This finding is contrary to previous research on Black collegians attending predominantly Black schools during the late 1960s and early 1970s (Gurin and Epps 1975). Thus, we come to the central question of this paper: are there similarities between traditionally Black and predominantly white four-year public institutions as regards the impact of institutional characteristics (and the lack of significant effects from socioeconomic background) on educational outcomes?

The answer to this question should clarify, especially for Blacks, whether there are different consequences for attending different kinds of predominantly white universities—to wit, all white schools are not equal—and would add new dimensions to the long-running issue of whether college-bound Blacks benefit more from attending traditionally Black or predominantly white institutions. First, even among four-year public institutions, there is reason to expect a wider range of institutional characteristics in predominantly white universities than traditionally Black ones. Among the institutional qualities commonly referenced in the studies cited above are factors such as regional location, student-body size, and institutional prestige. Thus, the mostly southern, relatively small, and generally teaching-oriented traditionally Black universities should lack the diversity of public predominantly white schools.

Second, the distribution of Black university students has changed dramatically over the past twenty years. In 1970, research confirmed the association between racial outlook and academic outcome on Black campuses. Also at that time, 60 percent of Black collegians were enrolled in predominantly Black institutions, and more than half of them attended schools in the South (Mingle 1981). Since 1978, the correspondence between racial outlook and academic outcomes has weakened. Unlike then, approximately two-thirds of all Black collegians now are to be found in predominantly white institutions, and a majority attend school outside the South.

THEORETICAL ORIENTATIONS AND ISSUES

Over time, the general status-attainment model has been refined into a specific model of educational attainment. Essentially, the basic scenario depicts family background characteristics and ability as co-determinants of individuals' scholastic achievement is said to shape the views which "significant others" hold regarding the person's academic potential. These variables are thought to combine to influence educational aspirations. Finally, all of the preceding variables, plus aspirations, determine attainment.

Recent research has modified this view in specific reference to Black collegians, and, in the process, new questions have been raised. The generalized educational attainment scenario of background and ability as co-determinants of educational outcomes neatly encompasses both of Turner's (1960) sponsored and contest alternatives of how education fosters mobility. However, unlike for Turner, this view posits status and ability to be equally associated with educational outcomes. In contrast, Frazier (1957)—writing that when *very* few blacks attended predominantly white universities—argued that in Black colleges, socioeconomic origins were such strong determinants of educational outcome that these schools merely served to transmit elite status from Blacks of one generation to the next. Thus, one of the primary research questions for this paper is whether a student's socioeconomic status affects his or her educational outcomes at traditionally Black universities in the same way that it does at predominantly white schools. A corollary question raised is whether the characteristics of predominantly Black institutions are related to Black students' educational outcomes as they are at predominantly white schools. In short, the null hypotheses are:

> *Hypothesis 1:* Status characteristics have the same relationship to educational outcomes for Black students attending traditionally Black universities and predominantly white institutions, and
> *Hypothesis 2:* The relationship of intellectual ability to educational outcomes is the same among Blacks attending traditionally black and predominantly white universities.

To operationalize this inquiry will first require the acknowledgement that, among Blacks, the student's gender and mother's socioeconomic characteristic (education, occupation, and the like) are the most salient demographic variables (Treiman and Terrell 1975; Porter 1974; and Sewell and Shah 1968). Moreover, Allen (1985) has demonstrated the utility of Black students' high-school performances (average grades and/or rank in graduating class), high-school racial composition, and high-school desegregation experiences as predictors of collegiate educational outcomes. Also, among Blacks at predominantly white universities, institutional prestige, location, and size have been found to be associated with both aspirations and academic performance (Smith and Allen 1984). This leads to the question of whether these types of relationships also hold for Blacks attending Black institutions. Stated in the null:

> *Hypothesis 3:* The institutional characteristics of Black universities affect the outcomes of Black students similarly to the effects of white schools.

Finally, some particular attributes of Black collegians as students have been associated with aspirations, performance, or both (Allen, 1985; Gurin and Epps, 1975). These include the students' campus residence, class/level, marital status, perceptions of discrimination and racism on campus, perceptions of the availability of extra-curricular activities of interest to them, and adjustment to campus life.

Of the attributes particular to Black students, their racial identification or ideology (militancy) is of special interest because of the prominence this characteristic has held in previous research. Gurin and Epps (1975) documented the existence of a very strong negative relationship between Black militancy and educational outcomes among Black collegiate cohorts of the late 1960s and early 1970s. For these Blacks students, both their adjustments to campus life and classroom performances were depressed by strong racial identification. These students also expressed the view that the available campus extra-curricular activities did not reflect their interests. On the basis of this and other such evidence, Tinto (1975) placed Black students' social and structural integration prominently among factors directly affecting their adjustment and performance-based attrition.

Previous research findings of a strong and direct relationship between racial identification and attainment were obtained during a period of heightened racial militancy—especially among Black collegians. For the most part, these data were obtained from Black students attending predominantly Black institutions. Therefore, another question asks whether the demonstrated relationship between racial identification and attainment is group-specific. Moreover, despite the recent expansion in the number of Black students on predominantly white campuses, they may not be present in sufficient numbers to preclude widespread feelings of isolation. Thus:

> *Hypothesis 4:* The effect of racial militancy on Black collegians' educational outcomes will be the same across both predominantly white and predominantly Black institutions.

If a direct relationship between Black students' racial ideology and their adjustment and performance exists in a more contemporary sample drawn from both predominantly Black and predominantly white institutions, then the earlier findings would be generalized beyond the earlier, more restricted sample. The complete absence of such a finding would mean that the racial ideology attainment relationship previously found among Black collegians was due to a period effect; that is, it was specific to the late 1960s. By the same token, if the finding currently holds *only* among Blacks at predominantly Black, but not white, universities, then ideology has a cohort or group effect on educational outcomes. This analysis includes a measure of racial isolation—students' opinions of whether campus activities reflect their interest—in order that (especially on white campuses) race-pride and commitment can be distinguished from the feelings of isolation and/or alienation.

DATA AND METHODS

The Data

To address the issues raised above, I use the 1981 and 1983 undergraduate samples of Black students attending predominantly white and predominantly Black public four-year institutions. Descriptions of the samples, instrumentation and, data collection procedures are covered extensively elsewhere in this book.

For this analysis, the independent demographic and ability variables employed are: respondent's (R) sex (male=1, female=2), R's mother's education and occupational prestige, R's high-school grade-point average and rank in his/her high-school graduating class, the racial composition of the high school from which graduated, and the number of years attended desegregated schools.

The characteristics of the higher educational institutions were categorized according to: region, (South, West, and North), size (small versus large), and academic prestige (high, higher, or highest). Obviously, the distinctions between predominantly white and traditionally Black universities in these regards are substantial. White universities are more diverse regionally (for example, less likely to be located in the South), usually larger, and historically more likely to emphasize research over teaching than do traditionally Black four-year institutions. This general state of affairs is reflected in these samples as well. Because of the extent of these differences, it is impossible to meaningfully categorize white and Black higher education institutions on the same criteria. Either all of the Black or all of the white schools would comprise one category, thus masking any diversity within one or the other group. Therefore, these characteristics were categorized differently for the traditionally Black and predominantly white institutions in the NSBCS sample.[1]

The variables indicating position in the campus structure are: residence (dormitory, other on-campus, and several off-campus categories), class/level (first-year, sophomore, and so on), marital status (single, married, separated, divorced, or widowed), and encounters with discrimination on campus (yes versus no). These analyses also index a student's Black nationalist ideology—commitment to the Black community (low versus high)—using four questions. Students were asked to respond to the following statements, on a four-point scale ranging from "strongly agree" to "strongly disagree":

1. There is a need for a Black political party.[2]
2. Interracial dating and marriage are equally acceptable as within-race dating and marriage.
3. The future looks very promising for educated Black Americans.
4. Middle-class Blacks have more in common with middle-class whites than they do with lower-class Blacks.

This analysis includes the additional psychological attributes of the students' perceptions of adjustment to campus life. Their responses to the question, "How much do you, as a Black student, feel a part of general campus life, insofar as student activities and government are concerned?", ranged from "not at all" to "considerable" and were divided into low versus high categories.

The outcome of the collegiate educational process are measured using self-reported grades and occupational aspirations. Since there is no universally available measure of undergraduate performance (such as a standardized achievement test administered to all undergraduates), the study queried students as to their current grade-point average (GPA). Here, students' GPAs are divided between those of B and above (high) and those less than B (low)—on the grounds that a cumulative 3.0 average significantly enhances a student's potential for admission to graduate or professional school. In recognition of previous research which demonstrated the influence of students' occupational aspirations (ASP) on academic performances, and the influence of aspirations on other aspects of student life, a dichotomized (low/high) measure of aspirations is included. For all variables, the initial (lowest) category is coded 1 with subsequent categories coded 2, 3, and so forth. The descriptive statistics for all variables appear in Table 6.1.

For this sample, the characteristics of respondents attending predominantly white and traditionally Black schools are similar (Table 6.1). Black females outnumber Black males at both types of universities. Interestingly, while there are no differences between the two groups in mothers' education, the mothers of Black students attending predominantly white schools have a higher average occupational prestige than do the mothers of students at traditionally Black schools (Duncan SEI Scores: 38.8 versus 31.9). Black undergraduates at white schools have somewhat better high school grades

TABLE 6.1
Descriptive Statistics of All Independent and Dependent
Variables[a] for White and for Black Public Universities.

Variable	White Schools[b]		Black Schools[c]	
	Mean	*Std. Dev.*	*Mean*	*Std. Dev.*
Student's Gender	1.65	.48	1.56	.50
Mother's Education	3.37	1.53	3.32	1.48
Mother's Occupation	38.8	24.6	31.9	26.2
High School GPA	3.33	.49	2.95	.53
High School Class Rank	2.62	1.40	3.49	1.37
Percent Black High School	3.58	1.73	3.96	1.67
Yrs. in Deseg. Schools	9.41	4.02	8.28	3.74
University Prestige	2.20	.81	1.93	.76
Region of University	1.85	.82	1.85	.85
University Size	1.91	.80	1.74	.81
Campus Residence	2.42	1.97	2.78	2.04
Student's Class/Level	2.48	1.14	3.14	1.41
Marital Status	1.17	.52	1.16	.48
Perception of Racism	1.40	.50	1.81	.40
Black Commitment Index	10.69	2.08	10.70	1.16
Activities of Interest	2.59	.82	2.92	.88
Feelings of Adjustment	2.26	.85	2.82	.93

Occupational Aspirations/University Grade Point Average

	Frequency	*Percent*	*Frequency*	*Percent*
Low ASP/Low GPA	247	40.2	328	40.4
High ASP/Low GPA	220	35.8	202	24.9
Low ASP/High GPA	74	12.1	159	19.6
High ASP/High GPA	73	11.9	122	15.1
Missing Cases		81		77

[a] See text for definitions and ranges.
[b] N for White schools = 695.
[c] N for Black schools = 888

(3.3 versus 2.95 on a four-point scale), and rank lower in the graduating classes. Compared to respondents attending traditionally Black schools, those attending white universities graduated from high schools with a smaller fraction of Black students, and they spent more years in desegregated school environments.

While there are many statistically significant differences between the two groups regarding institutional characteristics (such as prestige, size, and region), the differences between white and Black schools on the boundaries of the categories for these variables must be kept in mind. (See above, as well as endnote 1).

Study respondents from Black institutions were more advanced in their collegiate careers than were those from white schools. However, there are no other apparent differences between the two groups on the other student attributes of interest here. Moreover, the distributions on the dependent variable from the two types of schools are essentially similar, although, by comparison, respondents from predominantly white institutions reported 10 percent fewer members with high grade-point averages.

Methods and Procedures

The development and dissemination of the generalized educational attainment model has also resulted in the identification of path analysis as the methodology most often associated with the study of status attainment. But path analysis methods have three drawbacks which increasingly affect their utility in educational attainment research.

First, as the variables which define attainment become less interval, and more likely to exist in blocks instead of as singular, definitive measures, the basic assumptions of regression analysis are more easily violated.

Second, as more exogenous variable are added to incorporate factors which may differentially affect attainment for groups other than white males, the list of findings lengthen and debates over the causal order of independent variables detract from discussion of the central substantive findings. In the end, more assumptions are required to *control* for the effects of clearly prior variables on subsequent ones. Since many variables of interest exist only at nominal or ordinal levels, the use of dummy variables lengthens the discussion and decreases the clarity of results.

Third, the case base of some population subgroups is often not large enough in many data sets to support meaningful interpretations of findings generated using path analysis methods (Gottfredson 1981). All three of these drawbacks are not always present in previous research, but, most often, at least one is salient.

This research employs discriminant function analysis instead of path analysis. Briefly, the procedure weights and linearly combines a set of characteristics on which groups are expected to differ. The discriminating variables are weighted and combined into an exclusive set, so as to statistically maximize the differences between the groups (Klecka 1980).[3] This method provides a parsimonious set of results, and one which clearly orders the factors influencing the attainment on Black students in white schools. Further, the relevant factors will be associated with those student outcomes (grades or aspirations) over which they have the greatest influence.[4] Finally, since the general heuristic models of educational attainment posit all prior variables to have both direct and indirect effects on attainment, establishing the existence of a relationship is only an initial question. What is ultimately of interest is whether the relationship between categories of factors, (demographic, ability, institutional and student attributes, and educational outcomes) are similar at both predominantly Black and white institutions. Discriminant analyses speaks directly to these issues.[5]

THE FINDINGS

For Predominantly White Schools

Table 6.2 relates students' sociodemographic, institutional, and personal attributes to academic outcomes. In this regard, there are two statistically significant discriminant functions which together account for 29.7 percent of the variance in the educational attainment of Black undergraduates attending predominantly white, four-year, public universities. The relationships of the exogenous variables to the most desirable result of college attendance in Function 1 accounts for more than half (58.8 percent) of the explained variance. In Function 2, slightly more than one-quarter (28.9 percent) of the remaining variance stems from the ability of these independent variables to account for one other aspiration performance combination. (Note that here, the optimal outcome—high aspirations and high performance—engender the most negative centroid values.)

Function 1 differentiates Black students with both high occupational aspirations and high academic performances (optimal group) from all others at predominantly white universities. By far the most important of the predictor variables for academic outcomes are region and gender. Black collegians attending non-Southern white schools are more likely to have both high aspirations and good grades. Males are also more likely than females to have both high aspirations and good grades. (Reminder: the most positive outcome actually has the lowest and the most negative mean value.) After gender, students' experiences of racism on campus and their class standing are roughly equal in importance as contributors to academic outcomes. Black students in the optimal group report more experience of racism than do Black students with a less desirable mix of aspirations and performance. Moreover, the likelihood that Black undergraduates attending white schools will have both high aspirations and high performance decreases the length of their stay in college. Still, the effects of racial tension and class level are only half as important as the regional location of the school.

Black students in the high ASP/high GPA group more often report that campus activities reflect their interests. But to the contrary, attending a prestigious institution—and, to a lesser extent, being part of a larger campus population—all help to decrease the likelihood that Black collegians will obtain optimal results from their experiences at predominantly white universities. Finally, in these data, most of the background and aptitude

TABLE 6.2

Discriminant Function Analysis for Demographic and
Institutional Effects on Black Students' Performance and
Post-Graduate Aspirations.[a]

Independent Variables[b]	Standardized Coefficients			
	White Schools[c]		Black Schools[d]	
	Function 1	Function 2	Function 1	Function 2
Student's Gender	.62	.62	−.32	.65
Mother's Education	−.10	.06	.28	−.16
Mother's Occupation	−.00	−.00	−.00	−.00
High School GPA	.01	.01	.01	.01
High School Class Rank	.16	−.11	.09	.40
Percent Black of H.S.	.13	−.18	−.11	−.03
Yrs. in Deseg. Schools	.01	−.02	.07	−.10
University Prestige	.30	−.76	−.21	−.36
Region of University	−.78	−.01	.12	.08
University Size	.20	.15	.23	.33
Campus Residence	−.02	.02	.02	−.11
Student's Class/Level	.40	.24	−.01	.01
Marital Status	.04	.62	1.67	.80
Perception of Racism	−.42	.99	.12	.74
Black Commitment Index	.06	.02	−.02	−.06
Activities of Interest	−.32	−.05	.02	.26
Feelings of Adjustment	−.10	−.02	.51	.22
Variance Explained	29.7%		26.1%	
Component of Variance	57.76%	28.9%	68.28%	24.90%

Multivariate Centroid Means

	Function 1	Function 2	Function 1	Function 2
Low ASP/Low GPA	−.47	3.49	7.48	5.43
High ASP/Low GPA	−.93	3.14	7.78	5.08
Low ASP/High GPA	−.93	4.20	8.29	5.79
High ASP/High GPA	−1.89	3.51	8.66	5.11

[a]All functions significant @ p < .05.
[b]See text for definitions and ranges.
[c]N for White schools = 695.

measures (except for sex), and more notably the index of Black national-ism, had little influence in distinguishing high-aspiring/high-performing Black collegians attending predominantly white institutions from their colleagues.

Function 2 identifies an unusual group of Black undergraduates attend-ing predominantly white universities: academically capable Black collegians with relatively low occupational aspirations. Clearly the most important ba-rometer of this group is their strong perception and/or experience of racism on campus, followed by their tendency to be enrolled in relatively lower prestige institutions. Females and married students are more likely to belong to this group than males and singles, respectively. (Perhaps married students' aspirations often extend no further than maintaining the jobs they may hold while attending college.) There are some minimal effects which more likely place Black collegians in the low-aspirations/high-performance group: advanced class standing, attending larger institutions, coming from high schools with smaller Black compositions, and (surprisingly) graduating from high school with higher class ranks. However, again, sociodemographic and nationalist ideology influences on educational outcomes are largely absent among Blacks attending predominantly white, four-year, public universities.[6]

For Traditionally Black Schools

Table 6.2 also presents the effects of background, institutional characteristics, and student attributes on the attainment of Black students attending historically Black institutions. While a little over 26 percent of the variance in educational outcomes is explained, Function 1—which clearly distinguishes between high- and low-academic performance among these students—accounts for more than two-thirds of this explanatory power. Then, Function 2 accounts for about a quarter of the variance explained by accentuating the difference between Black students' aspirations.

Function 1 identifies marital status as the most important determinant of membership in high GPA groups among Blacks attending white schools. The "ever married" Black students clearly out-perform "never married" students, and those attending school after marital dissolution (separation, divorce, or widowhood) appear extremely goal-directed in this regard. While significant, feelings of adjustment to college life account for less than half the contribution of marital status to the observed performance-based distinction between married and never-married students. Notably, males out-perform females, and grades are higher for Blacks with better-educated mothers. Although *very* marginal, institutional effects are not completely absent: attending a larger or a less prestigious institution is likely to bolster grades for Blacks attending predominantly Black public, four-year universities. Here again, there are no notable effects from students' Black nationalism.

Function 2 distinguishes between levels of occupational aspirations among Black collegians at historically Black schools. The most positive outcome—high aspirations—has the lowest centroid means. Perceptions of racism and marital status are clearly the most important factors, while students' gender is a close third. When Black students on the campus of a traditionally Black university report experiencing racism, it is associated with lowered aspirations—regardless of their performances; and marital status also tends to be positively associated with relatively low aspirations across performance groups. Females are also more likely to have low aspirations, regardless of performance. High-school class rank and large university size are inversely associated with aspirations. On the other hand, university prestige tends to raise aspirations to approximately the same degree. A student's adjustments and interest in campus activities have about a quarter of the influence on aspirations as does marital status; and there are minimal effects from a mother's education, years of attendance at desegregated schools, and living on campus. Once more, students' Black nationalist sentiments are not significantly related to their occupational aspirations.

Summary of the Findings

When searching these results for consistency between predominantly white and traditionally Black, public, four-year universities, the only universal finding is that Black students' racial attitudes fail to contribute to academic outcomes. To simplify their presentation, the findings are best summarized according to the four null hypotheses generated earlier.

> *Hypothesis 1:* Clearly, the relationship between sociodemographic characteristics and almost all educational outcomes are different for Blacks at white schools than for those attending Black institutions.
> *Hypothesis 2:* For the most part, the measures of previous educational performance used here are not strongly associated with Black students' educational outcomes, at either type of school.
> *Hypothesis 3:* The institutional characteristics of traditionally Black universities affect Black students' educational outcomes very differently than do the characteristics of predominantly white schools.
> *Hypothesis 4:* The racial militancy of Black collegians fails universally to affect educational outcomes.

DISCUSSION

Although, these analyses explain similar amounts of the variance in educational outcomes at both predominantly white and historically Black universities, it is important to note that the analysis in the first function identifies the contributors to *optimal* educational outcomes on White campuses, while, for Black campuses, the first function merely differentiates between levels of academic performance. In addition, the second function for white schools describes Black undergraduates who represent a peculiar educational outcome (low aspirations and high grades), while, among students on Black campuses, the second function more efficiently separates respondents by their overall level of aspirations, irrespective of grades.

Sociodemographically, not much matters at white schools except gender, where males clearly get the best of things. At Black schools, males generally out-performed females in the classroom, and usually also have higher occupational aspirations. There may simply be more sexism at predominantly Black universities. But, while this could explain Black males' classroom advantage, it would not explain the relatively limited aspirations of Black females. Quite possibly, the occupations to which women have historically aspired are given lower rankings in the general status-attainment scenario. Of course, this fact alone would not account for the pronounced sex differences in academic performance.

At Black institutions, students from high economic status backgrounds (according to their mothers' education) obtain better grades. Although higher-economic-status students have somewhat lower aspirations at white schools, there is little association between economic background and educational outcomes. This might be interpreted as confirmation of Frazier's (1957) view that predominantly Black institutions reinforce the class distinctions with which their students matriculate. In this view, lower aspirations result from students' intentions to return to private businesses or service occupations such as those historically exchanged among family members, and/or rooted in the Black community (for example, proprietorship of retail business). Given both the ongoing and anticipated changes in our society—that is, the demise or constriction of the small business sector—questions of whether this state of affairs is in the best interest of Blacks should be placed squarely before the alumni, administrators, faculty, and students of traditionally Black universities.

However, there is an interpretation of Turner's (1960) sponsored-versus-contest mobility typology which may also incorporate these findings. Relationships between background variables and educational outcomes among Black students attending predominantly white schools may be weak because those institutions are sponsoring their Black graduates (as are Black schools) for elite roles and status positions in the larger society. In these institutions' view, sufficient competition among contenders has already taken place for entry into their student body. Therefore, no further distinction is either necessary or appropriate among Blacks who have succeeded in that competition. After all, the Black students who do graduate will bear the stamp of approval from a prestigious, predominantly white, four-year university.

Research-oriented, flagship institutions in state university systems may attempt to more efficiently sponsor their graduates' (including, and perhaps especially, Blacks) entry into the larger society by systematically leveling the evaluation of academic performance. In other words, it could be that generally higher prestige institutions award higher average grades. The effect of this approach would be to confer greater prestige through the graduation *and* placement of more high-achieving students. If so, there would be much less distinction between Black student grades and those of other students at high-prestige institutions, as opposed to the case at less prestigious schools. All of this could argue in favor of drawing a distinction among Black students based on their occupational aspirations rather than on grade-point averages.

Not only could this interpretation explain the weak or absent effects of background and ability variables among Blacks at mostly white schools, but it could account for the influence of institutional prestige on academic performance. Research-oriented, flagship institutions in state university systems tend to place fewer Blacks in the optimal performance category than do less prestigious white institutions. But according to these data, flagship schools also produce more low-aspiration/high-performance Black students. In effect, there are fewer differences between the grades awarded Black students (and perhaps other minorities) and whites at high prestige institutions than is true for less prestigious schools.

However, the aspirations of Black students are depressed by the more intense racism which they encounter at the higher prestige universities. This explains several things: the report from the optimal outcomes group of more experiences of racism; the inverse relationships between high-school class standing and optimal group membership; and the likelihood that, as class standing increases, so too does membership in the low-aspiration/high-performance group. In other words, the greater experience of racism reported by Black students depresses their aspirations, but not their performance. The effect is to create a division among high-performing Black students based on postgraduate career plans.

On another level, these findings clearly demonstrate that, while the educational outcomes of Black students are subject to varied outcomes at both predominantly white and historically Black universities, earlier findings of effects from students' racial attitudes were clearly products of the period in which that research was conducted. Moreover, since the combination of variables which accounts for Black students' educational outcomes differ so remarkably, depending on whether they attend white or Black universities, future research must examine these obviously different settings.

In the final analysis, these findings have implications for researchers, university administrators, and prospective Black collegians. Academicians will need to analyze the experiences of Black students attending traditionally Black and predominantly white institutions separately. Although the focus is restricted to four-year universities, a natural extension of this research would incorporate additional questions about differences between public and private institutions. All other things considered, are there significant differences between public and private predominantly white universities in Black student educational outcomes? Are there differences between private and public traditionally Black institutions in this same regard? Which is the greater difference—between predominantly white and historically Black, or between public and private institutions?

University administrators at both traditionally Black and predominantly white schools must also consider the implications these findings have for their retention of Black students. At Black universities, officials must rectify the fact that female undergraduates clearly do not fare as well as males. (Is this why the white schools in this sample have a higher proportion of Black females?)

Another cause for alarm among Black schools is that prestige—defined here as the percentage of the faculty holding the terminal degree—is inversely related to academic performance. In other words, the Black schools which *should* be the most effective at producing academic performance are not.

Perhaps, given their historical stature, these institutions have been less open to those more recent innovations found to be useful in higher education. Or it may be that their reputation attracts a wider group of students, more diverse in their levels of academic preparation. Predominantly white universities must simply begin to address and correct the racism (and sexism) which Black students face throughout their infrastructures. The findings here imply that, if immediate measures were taken to either develop activities of interest to Blacks and/or to spur Black students' interest in ongoing activities, significant and positive gains in Black students' academic performances could be realized.

For Black students and their parents attempting to decide which type of school to attend—Black campus or white campus—these analyses offer few universal guidelines. There are general findings that Black undergraduates do not fare well at the more southern and the relatively large white schools. But beyond this, what these results mean for Black students depends a great deal on their personal characteristics. Prospective Black female undergraduates face an especially difficult decision. At traditionally Black schools, males clearly fare better than females. But at predominantly white universities, the occupational aspirations of Black females appear to be more susceptible to depression from racism and sexism than do the goals of Black males. Married Black students apparently fare very well in Black institutions. But Blacks from lower socioeconomic origins might well prefer to avoid the class distinctions apparently operating at historically Black universities—if they think they can better cope with the racism of predominantly white institutions.

Finally, although a choice among higher educational institutions depends on the goals of the student, having a definite career objective does not guarantee clarity of institutional choice. Obviously, in competition for entry in the best graduate or professional schools, as well as for the most lucrative starting jobs, attendance and graduation from a highly prestigious, research-oriented, flagship state university confers a tremendous advantage over other four-year institutions, much less the historically Black schools. But Black students may either have different goals and/or lack the qualifications or financial means required to attend the highest prestige state universities. Depending on Black student gender and socioeconomic origins, this research finds no clear advantage to attending a second- or third-tier predominantly white, four-year school, as opposed to enrolling in one of the otherwise similar historically Black, public, four-year institutions.

KENNETH W. JACKSON
L. ALEX SWAN

Chapter Seven

Institutional and Individual Factors Affecting Black Undergraduate Student Performance: Campus Race and Student Gender

In recent years, African American students have begun to enroll in traditionally white institutions in much greater numbers. The result has been increased concern with the viability as well as utility of traditionally Black institutions. The major arguments contend that Black institutions provide a very mediocre educational experience, wastefully duplicate services, and ultimately perpetuate segregation (Fleming 1984). Such arguments necessarily imply that traditionally Black colleges and universities should either be allowed to die or be systematically phased out.

On the other hand, there is evidence that indicates that all is not well for African American students enrolled in white institutions. Fleming (1984) has found that Blacks have an increased tendency to suffer identity problems on white campuses. Such situations, she argues, may subsequently interfere with the students' academic functioning. Similarly, Hedegard and Brown (1969) have found that Black students on white campuses experience a greater sense of social isolation. The authors go on to contend that this has the result of reducing the student's capacity for intimacy and, subsequently, the attainment of social solidarity.

Findings such as these imply that there are certain benefits for African American students who enroll in predominantly Black environments. These benefits, however, tend to be more directly related to the area of social development, rather than academic performance, which many people do not view as a viable educational outcome. Nevertheless, the study of Gurin and Epps (1975), and the more recent study by Fleming (1984), provide strong evidence of more positive academic outcomes to be associated with predominantly Black environments.

Gurin and Epps (1975), for example, found that those factors that contributed most to academic achievement on Black campuses were the very factors often missing on white campuses. This implies that there are specific achievement-related handicaps associated with attending predominantly white environments, assuming that these factors operate in a similar fashion across educational settings. Findings reported by Fleming (1984) support the implications of the Gurin and Epps (1975) study. Her analysis indicated that Black students in Black environments actually exhibited greater gains in cognitive growth than did their counterparts in white institutions.

Although the arguments against the maintenance of Black institutions as well as the evidence relating to their viability are not definitive, one can speculate that Black students in white environments have quite different experiences from those enrolled in Black environments. What these differences are has seemed to be the principle issue raised by previous studies (Thomas, 1981; Astin, 1982). We believe, however, that the issue goes one step beyond this point. A more telling question is, whether the differences, assuming their existence, are relevant in terms of student performance.

We want to test the assumption that factors across educational environments have comparable effects on student performance. If this is so, then the differences in educational context have extreme significance in terms of the educational opportunities of Blacks. On the other hand, if those factors necessary for successful performance are different across educational environments, then observed contextual differences could very well be a moot issue, especially if performance is comparable. What we are postulating here is that a particular factor could make the crucial difference in terms of whether an African American student performs adequately in a traditionally white school while having little or no impact—or even being detrimental— in a traditionally Black environment.

METHODOLOGY

Data for this analysis are from the National Study, of Black College Students (Allen 1982; Allen and Nweke 1985). The total sample consisted of 1,580 Black students. Of that total, 885 (388 males and 497 females) were enrolled in eight traditionally Black institutions, and 695 (240 males and 455 females) were enrolled in six traditionally white institutions.

To test our assumptions, we propose to examine factors that are normally considered to be important for success in a general academic sense. These factors, we might add, are related primarily to Black academic achievement and therefore might differ in some respects from those highlighted in the traditional educational literature which is based on white populations.

As our primary measure of performance, we propose to use students' grade-point averages. This particular factor is measured in the same general fashion as it is normally reported. Grade-point averages range from 1 to 4, with 4 representing an A. We contend that students' grade-point averages are a function of four preceding conceptual dimensions: family background, secondary institutional experiences and/or characteristics, attitudes, and postsecondary experiences and/or characteristics. Family background is represented by six variables: respondent's age; mother's and father's education and occupations; and parental income. Each variable, with the exception of age and occupation, is measured on an ordinal scale. Age is the respondent's actual age, while occupational prestige is represented by Duncan SEI scores (ranging from a low of 1 to a high 100).

The secondary institutional dimension is represented by two variables: high-school grade-point average and percentage of Blacks attending the respondent's high school. High-school GPA was measured on the same scale as college GPA, while high-school racial composition was a categorical variable.

Two different measures of attitudes were employed: the first subset of measures focused on racial attitudes, while the second set focused on self-attitudes.

Three questions were used to tap racial attitudes. The questions asked whether respondents felt the need for a Black political party, what his or her attitudes toward interracial dating were, and whether he or she thought mobility was due more to race than class. Each item was a categorical variable coded so that a high response indicated strong racial consciousness.

Four variables were used to measure self-attitudes. Respondents were asked how they rated themselves in terms of personal/physical well-being, self-confidence, leadership ability, and overall personal traits. Each item was categorical and coded so that a high response indicated a negative self-evaluation.

The postsecondary institutional dimension includes postsecondary experiences and three support systems: financial, social, and academic. Postsecondary experiences were captured by two indicators: perceived intensity of the host institution's academic competition, and the degree to which the respondent felt he or she was a part of campus life. Low scores on the competition measures indicate low intensity, while high scores imply high intensity. For the alienation indicator, low scores indicate extreme alienation from campus life, while high scores imply considerable integration into the campus environment.

The indicators for the financial support system were constructed so as to be useful with our proposed analysis. The original questions asked respondents to identify their main source of funding. Each category was dichotomized to create three indicators representing the respondent's financial support system. The first of these indicators was a dichotomous variable representing respondent's family. A code of "0" was entered if the family was not the respondent's major source of funding, and a code of "1" was entered if it was. The family variable included parents and spouse as its major components. The second indicator of financial support was the respondent, and was coded in the same fashion. The third financial-support indicator was referred to as "institutional support" and included scholarships, loans, grants, and veterans' benefits as its major components.

The postsecondary social support system indicators, like financial support indicators, were constructed from three dichotomous variables: family support, self-support, and institutional support. As components of the family variable, we included spouse, family, and friends. As components of self-support, respondent reports of self-reliance in problem solving were used. For institutional support, we included counselors, professors, and administration as contributors to social support. Two indicators of academic support were used to measure respondent satisfaction with the advising system and with the tutorial service. In each case, high scores imply positive response.

The basic analytic strategy employed is regression analysis. To test for contextual effects, the sample was stratified by gender, and separate equations were calculated for males and females within each institutional setting. We felt that males and females differed in terms of the mechanism by which success was generated. We focused our comparisons primarily on males found in the two contrasting institutions and, then, on females in a similar fashion. Gender comparisons were not a major concern. However, in some instances, such comparisons were used to highlight major institutional differences.

ANALYSIS

Male Distributions

Black males who attended white colleges tend to have parents who are slightly better educated than Black males who attend Black schools

(Table 7.1). It should be noted, however, that this difference is only statistically significant for mothers' education. The major difference in these background factors is with respect to occupation. The parents of students attending white schools have jobs that are considerably more prestigious than do the parents of their peers on Black campuses. Prestige scores are significantly different for fathers' occupation (35.6 for Black schools versus 43.2 for white schools, p < .05) and for mothers' occupation (30.9 versus 39.6, p < .05). Given this fact, it is extremely interesting to note that parental income is the same for both groups (approximately $21,000 annually), receiving a score of 6.1 in both cases.

When we consider racial attitudes, we find that Black males attending Black schools are slightly more race-conscious than those attending white institutions. However, we should point out that the actual score difference never exceeds 7 percent on any of our indicators. We conclude, therefore, that the two groups are comparable in terms of their racial-awareness level.

The same general conclusion can be drawn with respect to personal attitudes. In fact, the only two indicators that exhibited any noticeable difference were the respondent's general feelings toward physical well-being, and the kind of person, in an overall sense, the respondent reported himself or herself to be. These differences favored the students on white campuses, but only to a minor extent. The largest difference was for the kind of person respondents judged themselves to be, with the score for Blacks on white campuses being greater than for students on Black campuses (2.0 versus 1.8).

Males on white campuses had only *slightly* higher occupational aspirations than did males on Black campuses. Scores for all students attending white schools were significantly higher than for students attending Black schools (75 versus 71).

With respect to secondary-school characteristics, males in white colleges had better high-school GPAs and came from schools that were more integrated. Black males' GPAs were 10 percent higher than that for their peers at Black institutions. The proportion of males attending integrated high schools was 11 percent higher for Black males in Black institutions. This latter difference suggests that, even though the Black male students on white campuses were more likely to come from less racially isolated environments, this was not overwhelmingly so.

Perhaps the most significant difference between the two groups is found in the area of postsecondary experiences. We found highly significant differences in student scores on the intensity of academic competition index across these schools (2.4 on Black campuses versus 3.5 on white campuses). Black males in white institutions more often perceived academic competition as extremely intense than did those attending Black schools. In addition, students on Black campuses felt considerably more a part of their

TABLE 7.1

Difference in Means for Men and Women In Traditionally Black (TBI)
Versus Traditionally White Institutions (TWI)

	Males		Females	
Variables	*Black*	*White*	*Black*	*White*
Age	23.5	23.9	22.7	23.8
Fathers' Education	3.1	3.3	3.1*	3.3
Mothers' Education	3.3*	3.7	3.3*	3.5
Fathers' Occupation	35.6	43.2	32.1	43.0
Mothers' Occupation	30.9	39.6	32.7	38.3
Parental Income	6.1	6.1	5.6*	5.9
Black Party	3.2	3.0	3.2*	3.0
Mix Dating	2.6	2.5	2.7	2.7
Class/Race	2.8	2.7	2.8	2.8
Physical Well-Being	1.9	1.8	2.1	2.1
Self-Confidence	1.8	1.8	2.1	2.1
Leadership Ability	2.0	2.0	2.3	2.2
Kind of Person	2.0*	1.8	2.0**	1.9
Occupational Aspiration	71.1	74.6	68.6	70.4
High-School GPA	2.9*	3.2	3.0*	3.4
High-School Race	3.9*	3.5	4.0*	3.6
Intensity	2.4*	3.4	2.4*	3.6
Alienation	2.8*	2.3	2.8*	2.2
Family/Financial	0.3**	0.4	.4*	.7
Self/Financial	0.3**	0.2	.2	.2
Institutional/Financial	0.4**	0.3	.4**	.3
Family/Social	0.3**	0.5	.4*	.7
Self/Social	0.4	0.2	.2	.2
Institutional/Social	0.1*	0.2	.2	.2
Advising/Academic	2.5	2.4	2.5	2.5
Tutor/Academic	2.1*	2.4	2.3	2.3
College GPA	2.7**	2.6	2.7**	2.6

*Indicates two-tailed T-test $p < .05$.
**Indicates $p < .01$.

environments than did those on white campuses. The difference in scores
was relatively sizeable and statistically significant (2.8 on Black campuses
versus 2.3 on white campuses).

When the financial support system is compared, we find that Black
males enrolled in white schools are considerably more likely to rely on their
families for support. On the other hand, Black males attending Black
schools rely more heavily on institutional support. In each case, the difference in scores is statistically significant.

For social support, the scores imply that more Black males in white
schools rely on family and institutional support systems to handle their personal problems than do those in Black schools. Most students on Black

campuses seem to handle their problems alone, drawing little if any support from friends, family, or the institution to aid in coping. Differences in family, self, and institutional social support are all significant at p < .05 level.

In terms of academic support, we find that attitudes with respect to advising are fairly comparable (2.5 versus 2.4). For tutorial services, students in white colleges were more pleased with these services than those in Black colleges. On this particular indicator, white campus scores were higher (2.1 versus 2.4).

When grades were considered, we found that GPA was slightly higher on Black campuses (2.7 versus 2.6, p > .05). Overall, we would have to conclude that grades are comparable across the different-race campuses.

In summary, among African American males, we identified several important differences between traditionally Black and predominantly white campuses with regards to fathers' education, fathers' occupation, mothers' occupation, high-school GPA, intensity of competition, feeling of alienation, and financial and social support systems. Differences tend to favor students on white campuses with the exception of feelings of alienation and the support-system components. With respect to these two, students enrolled in Black schools tend to feel less alienated and more a part of campus life than do their peers at white schools. Financially, Black males on white campuses rely on family assistance to a greater extent, while students on Black campuses rely more on institutional sources. Regarding social support, students who attend white schools rely more on family and institutional supports, while students who attend Black schools rely on themselves to solve their problems.

Female Distributions

When African American females on traditionally Black and predominantly white campuses were compared, we found significant differences in parental educational and occupational levels (Table 7.1). Fathers of Black women on white campuses had prestige scores which were significantly higher than for their peers on Black campuses (32.1 versus 43, p < .05). The difference for mothers' occupation, while not as great (32.7 versus 38.3), was nevertheless statistically significant at the .05 level.

We also found parental income to differ significantly over these two environments. Black females on white campuses reported higher parental incomes (5.6 versus 5.9, p < .05). The finding of significant family-income differences between females on Black and white campuses contrasts markedly with the absence of such differences for males.

In terms of racial attitudes, our results for females were not substantially different from what we observed for males. Female students in white and Black schools were equally aware racially. The only significant difference revealed had to do with whether the respondent felt the need for a Black political party (3.2 versus 3.0, p < .05). Personal attitudes were also found to be comparable on most points, except for general assessment of self. The difference between indicators failed to achieve statistical significance.

Occupational aspirations were also comparable to the pattern revealed for African American males. Females attending white institutions had slightly higher aspirations. However, the difference was not statistically significant. Females' high-school grades were significantly higher on white than on Black campuses (3.0 versus 3.4, p < .05). In addition, women on Black campuses were much more likely to come from racially segregated high schools (4.0 versus 3.6, p < .05).

The extreme discrepancy between white and Black institutions with respect to reported intensity of academic competition is repeated. Females on white campuses were significantly more likely to feel that their schools were intensely competitive (2.4 versus 3.6, p < .05). The reported difference in feelings of alienation was substantial, with females on Black campuses feeling considerably more a part of their environments (2.8 versus 2.2, p < .05).

Among females, the only campus-race difference in financial support concerns institutional support. Females at Black schools were more likely to utilize institutional sources (.4 versus .3, p < .001). Regarding social support, we found that family members play a considerably more important role for female students who attend white colleges (.4 versus .7, p < .05). For the academic support system, the scores are comparable among females on the different-race campuses. When GPA is considered, the pattern for females is similar to that for males. Females at Black schools reported significantly higher GPAs (2.7 versus 2.6, p < .001).

The differences observed for Black females enrolled in predominantly and traditionally Black universities were basically the same as those observed for Black males. Parental occupation stands out among the background factors as the most glaring difference, and the same was true for males. The key difference between males and females in this particular dimension had to do with the higher parental income of females on white campuses as compared to females on Black campuses.

High-school GPAs were higher for white-campus females, and they were less likely than females on Black campuses to come from racially isolated schools. As was the case for males, one of the most profound differences concerned the reported intensity of academic competition and feelings of alienation. White campuses were perceived by these Black females as more competitive. At the same time, those on Black campuses felt themselves to be more a part of campus life.

A major difference present for females, that was not so pronounced for males, had to do with the role of the family as a major source of social support. Females in white institutions relied more upon the family for support than did females in Black institutions. For males, the difference existed, but was not as pronounced.

Estimates of Male Performance

We found some rather significant distributional differences by campus-race and student-gender. The critical issue remaining is to determine whether these differences are important with respect to the generation of successful performance within the respective environments. Overall, only three predictors were significantly related to Black males' college grades across both campus environments: respondent's age, self-confidence and high-school GPA (Table 7.2). What this implies is that the distributional differences observed earlier are unimportant with respect to successful performance on different-race campuses, except in terms of these three factors. What becomes crucial, then, is to determine how successful performance is generated in each context. It is obvious from a cursory review of the regression results that the mechanisms generating academic performance are significantly different on Black and on white campuses.

Student background does not strongly predict academic performance on either Black or white campuses (Table 7.2). It seems that the distributional differences observed earlier for students' backgrounds are irrelevant since none of these factors are important determinants of Black male academic achievement.

Looking at racial attitudes, we find that, for Black men only, attitudes toward interracial dating are significantly related to achievement, and then only among males on Black campuses (B = .72, p < .001). It appears that males on Black campuses who do better academically are also more positively oriented toward intergroup contact; that is, they tend to approve of interracial dating. On the other hand, this factor is unrelated to male achievement on white campuses.

When personal attitudes are considered, we find that respondents' self-confidence is important in predicting achievement in both white and Black schools. However, this factor is more influential in the white university context (B = -.15 versus B = -.08). What this implies is that, in white universities, self-confidence is a much more valuable assistance to achievement than it is in Black universities, although self-confidence is an important factor in both contexts.

Similarly, for the secondary institutional dimension, high-school GPA is very important across environments. The effect is also slightly stronger in Black schools (B = .27, p < .05) than in white schools (B = .24, p < .001),

TABLE 7.2
Black Male College Grades: Traditionally Black (TBI) and White Institutions (TWI)

Variables	TBI Beta	TBI Standard Error	TWI Beta	TWI Standard Error
Age	.01	.01	−.02	.01
Fathers' Education	.01	.03	.01	.03
Mothers' Education	.00	.03	.03	.03
Fathers' Occupation	.00	.00	.01	.02
Mothers' Occupation	.00	.00	.02	.02
Parental Income	.01	.01	.00	.01
Black Party	.00	.04	−.03	.04
Mix Dating	.72**	.03	.00	.04
Class/Race	−.05	.03	−.03	.04
Physical Well-Being	.03	.04	.01	.06
Self-Confidence	−.08*	.05	−.15**	.06
Leadership Ability	.07	.05	.04	.06
Kind of Person	−.04	.05	.02	.06
Occupational Aspiration	.00	.00	.00	.02
High-School GPA	.27**	.06	.24**	.08
High-School Race	−.02	.02	−.01	.02
Intensity	−.01	.05	−.02	.06
Alienation	.06	.04	.08*	.05
Family/Financial	−.22	.18	−.12	.38
Self/Financial	−.16	−.09	−.09	.38
Institutional/Financial	−.12	.19	−.12	.38
Family/Social	.00	.09	−.28*	.17
Self/Social	−.07	.09	−.26	.19
Institutional/Social	−.10	.11	−.33*	.18
Advising/Academic	.08**	.03	−.05	.05
Tutor/Academic	−.05**	.02	.02	.05
Intercept	1.89		3.43	
R^2	.18		.21	

* $p < .05$.
**$p < .10$.

but also not overwhelmingly so. This automatically implies, however, that high-school GPAs have better payoffs in Black schools than in white schools.

Turning to the postsecondary institutional dimension, we find some rather interesting contrasts. The degree to which the respondent feels a part of campus like and relies on family and institutional support in coping with problems are all significantly related to academic performance in the predominantly white universities. However, these factors are insignificant predictors of academic achievement at traditionally Black institutions. As a further contrast, both academic support indicators were significant influences on achievement in the Black campus environment, while being non-significant in the white campus environment.

These results reveal profound differences in terms of how high academic performance is generated in the postsecondary context. The more that Black male students attending white schools feel themselves to be a part of campus life, the better they will perform (B = .08, p < .05). This particular variable is irrelevant on Black campuses. In addition, on white campuses, the more that males turn to their families for socioeconomic support, and the more that they turn to their institutions for help in solving their social problems, the less well they will do academically (B = −.28, p < .05 and B = −.33, not significant).

Again, these factors are irrelevant in Black universities. On the other hand, academic support systems are determinants of academic success in Black universities (B = .08, p < .001), while being irrelevant in white universities. The results indicate that the performance of students enrolled in white schools are more affected by social factors than are those of students enrolled in Black schools. In Black schools, males' academic performance, at least in terms of the postsecondary dimension, was more affected by academic support systems.

Thus, we found significant differences for males enrolled in Blacks universities as compared to males enrolled in white universities. The findings support our basic contention that certain factors are important for successful performance in one environment, while being unimportant in the other. Further, we find that males on white campuses were more affected by social-type factors, whereas males on Black campuses were more affected by academic factors. We also found similarities across the different-race campuses, primarily in terms of self-confidence and high-school GPA as positive correlates of high achievement.

Estimates of Female Performance

Turning our attention to females (Table 7.3), we find rather interesting contrasts by gender and by campus race. Here as before, the generation process differed depending on the particular institutional environment. Background factors were considerably more important for females attending white universities than for those enrolled in Black universities. These important differences centered around the respondents' mothers. Both mothers' education (B = .05, p < .001) and mothers' occupation (B = .04, p < .001) were significant determinants of performance in the white campus context, while being statistically unrelated on Black campuses. Although age was significant in both environments, its patterns of effect differed by campus race. The older the respondents were on Black campuses, the better they performed ($B = .01$, $p < .05$); while in the white schools, younger respondents performed better ($B = -.02$, $p < .001$).

When attitudes are considered, we found little or not complementarity between the two contexts. In the white campus context, one racial indicator was important—that being the degree to which the respondents thought relations were more a function of class than race ($B = -.06$, $p < .05$). It appears that the less racially-conscious the respondent, the less likely was she to perform well academically. This factor was unimportant in the Black campus context. What we *did* find for females in Black universities was that self-confidence was important for academic success, just as was the case for males. The less highly the respondent evaluated and believed in herself the less well she performed ($B = -.08$,). Interestingly, the factor was totally irrelevant in the white university environment.

When the secondary institutional dimension is considered, we find that high-school GPA is again important in both environments. Additionally, we find that it is considerably more significant in the Black campus context ($B = .34$, $p < .001$) than in the white campus context ($B = .20$, $p < .001$). African American women with high grades in high school were significantly more likely to have high grades in college.

We also find, with respect to this dimension, that racial composition of the high school attended was important for the white-university context ($B = .04$, $p < .05$), but insignificant for the Black schools. Apparently, Black females in white universities who come from racially integrated high schools tend to do better than female students who come from racially isolated environments. The same cannot be said for academic performance in the Black university context.

When the postsecondary dimension is considered, we find that only the academic support subdimension was significant in either context. In contrast to the male situation, this implies that female performance is more a function of background and past experiences than any present, postsecondary occurrences. Be that as it may, what we also find in the academic support component is that these factors are more dominant in Black than white universities. Both indicators were significant for students attending Black universities, while only one was significant for students attending white universities: as satisfaction with advising increased, so did performance. On the other hand, as satisfaction with tutorial services increased, performance decreased. Conceivably, these tutorial services do more to help socially adjust students, as indicated by their satisfaction, than to improve their performance as indicated by the effect of this factor. It should be noted that a similar situation existed for males enrolled in Black schools.

In contrast, tutorial services were also found to be significantly predictive in white universities. However, the effect was reversed. As the satisfac-

TABLE 7.3

Black Female College Grades: Traditionally Black (TBI) and White Institutions (TWI)

Variables	TBI		TWI	
	Beta	*Standard Error*	*Beta*	*Standard Error*
Age	.01*	.01	−.02**	.01
Fathers' Education	.02	.02	−.01	.03
Mothers' Education	−.03	.03	−.05**	.02
Fathers' Occupation	.00	.00	.01	.02
Mothers' Occupation	.00	.00	.04**	.02
Parental Income	.01	.01	.01	.01
Black Party	−.01	.04	.02	.04
Mix Dating	.04	.03	.01	.03
Class/Race	−.03	.03	−.06*	.03
Physical Well-Being	.04	.03	.04	.04
Self-Confidence	−.08**	.04	−.04	.04
Leadership	−.03	.04	−.04	.04
Kind of Person	.07	.04	−.03	.05
Occupational Aspirations	.00	.00	.00	.02
High-School GPA	.34**	.05	.20**	.07
High-School Race	−.02	.02	−.04*	.02
Intensity	−.03	.04	.03	.05
Alienation	.04	.03	.03	.04
Family/Financial	−.02	.17	−.06	.22
Self/Financial	.15	.18	−.02	.23
Institutional/Financial	.11	.17	−.14	.22
Family/Social	.01	.08	.14	.15
Self/Social	.01	.09	.21	.18
Institutional/Social	−.00	.09	.08	.16
Advising/Academic	.06**	.03	.01	.04
Tutor/Academic	−.06**	.02	.07**	.04
Intercept	1.41		2.86	
R^2	.23		.18	

* $p < .05$.

**$p < .01$.

tion with this service increased, so did performance ($B = .07$, $p < .001$). This implies that tutorial services on white campuses do, indeed, function to aid students academically.

All in all, what we find for females is that the means by which high academic performance is generated differs according to institutional environment. Background factors are significantly more important for females in white institutions than for females in Black institutions. In addition, we found that in two of the three situations where similar factors were significant in both environments, these factors affected performance differently. In other words, they had different and distinct patterns of influence or payoff.

CONCLUSION

We began by examining certain distributional differences that distinguished African American students enrolled in traditionally Black institutions from those enrolled in traditionally white institutions. We found several interesting contrasts between the two environments for both males and females. In both cases—the males and females—parental education and occupation tended to be higher on white campuses. Students enrolled in white universities also had higher high-school GPAs and tended to feel less a part of campus life. In addition, we found that African American students in white universities relied more on their families for financial support, while in Black universities, students relied more on institutional sources of support. And finally, we found that students on Black campuses had a tendency to solve their own problems to a much greater extent than did students on white campuses, who relied more on their families and institutional mechanisms. Even though these distributional differences are noteworthy in their own right, further examination revealed them to be insignificant for predicting academic performance. Our analysis revealed that certain factors tended to be considerably more important in one environment versus the other, thereby making some aspects of the distributional variation inconsequential.

When we examined predictive models for males, we found that the similarities across white and Black campuses were negligible. The only two factors that exerted similar influence across different race campuses were self-confidence (for higher payoffs in white universities) and high-school GPAs (with higher payoffs in Black universities). All other significant factors were restricted to a given environment. Social factors, such as feelings of alienation and sources of social support, were extremely critical on white campuses. On Black campuses, however, more academically oriented factors, such as advising and tutorial services, represented important predictors.

Among females, we found that background factors carried considerably more weight in the white-campus setting than in the Black-campus setting. In addition, we found that, in the majority of situations where factors were significant in both contexts, there were contrasting payoffs. Thus, not only does our analysis reveal differences between traditionally white and Black universities, but also between males and females within these two environments.

Policy makers will need to recognize these gender differences within campus-race contexts and campus-race differences across gender groups before effective policies can be implemented. For males in Black schools, more emphasis should be placed on the academic-support system, while for males in white schools, more emphasis should be placed on the social-support component. The situation for females enrolled in Black schools is similar to that of males in that more emphasis should be placed on the academic component; whereas for females in white schools, background factors need to be considered as more significant for predicting who is most likely to achieve academically.

ROBERT BOB DAVIS

Chapter Eight

Social Support Networks and Undergraduate Student Academic-Success-Related Outcomes: A Comparison of Black Students on Black and White Campuses

The concept of social support is the subject of considerable attention and research effort among social and behavioral scientists. Social bonds, social integration, and primary group relations have long been central concepts in sociological theory and analysis. These relationships "may be thought of as the basic building blocks of social structure; and their formation, mainte-nance, and severance are universal and fundamental social processes" (Hammer et al. 1978: 523).

The view that social bonds and supportive interactions are important to a person's health and well-being was represented in original form by Durkheim's theory of anomie. Durkheim argued that individuals lacking social support and integration were more prone to commit suicide. Without attempting a survey of the literature, it can be noted that Cobb (1976) and Dean and Lin (1977) have reviewed an array of studies suggesting that so-cial support may be an effective buffer or mediator of life stress. Other researchers report findings consistent with the view that social support mat-ters for psychological well-being independent of the level of adversity or stress (Andrews et al. 1978; Henderson 1980; Henderson et al. 1978; and

143

Miller and Ingram 1976). The general finding is that social support is positively related to health and well-being. The more social support an individual receives in the form of close relationships with family members, kin,
friends, acquaintances, co-workers, and the larger community, the better
his or her health and well-being.

A recent review of the "buffering hypothesis" by Thoits (1982) suggests a number of conceptual and methodological problems. These include
lack of a theoretically useful definition of social support; inadequate oper-
ational definitions of social support; and failure to distinguish among dimensions of social support such as number of supporters, perception of
support, alternate sources of support, and different kinds of support. Thoits
(1982:155) concludes that "although there exists some evidence that social
support can buffer the impact of life changes, it must be interpreted with
extreme caution."

To date, most research on social support has not focused on college
campuses. The importance of strong, supportive campus interpersonal relations, and social networking for cognitive, intellectual and career-related
functioning of Black students on Black campuses has been documented by
Fleming (1984). She concludes that, partly due to reasons of differences in
social support, Black African American students at predominantly white and
predominantly Black schools differ significantly in their intellectual and
psychosocial development. Fleming (1984) provides a comparative picture of
the intellectual development of Black students in Black and white colleges.

Fleming's results show that the patterns of intellectual development are
consistently more positive for students in Black schools. These students exhibit stronger personal attachments to faculty, enhanced involvement in the
career process, greater satisfaction with their academic lives, improvement
in measures of academic performance, more enterprising vocational interest
patterns, and maintenance of higher occupational aspirations. Black students in white schools, however, show quite the opposite. They report
increasing dissatisfaction with academic life, negative attitudes toward
teachers whom they feel grade unfairly, limited return for time and effort
invested in school work, and no net improvement in academic performance.
Among students in white schools, there were a few positive indications of
attachment to a role model and high educational aspirations. Nevertheless,
students in Black colleges seem to have a virtual corner on intellectual satisfaction and outcomes during the college years. In the subjective, psychosocial domain, African American students in Black schools experience
better social adjustment whereas Black students in white schools experience
a crisis in social adjustment.

In this broader light, there seems to be sufficient reason to warrant an
investigation of the relative contributions of Black students' campus social-

support networks in predominantly Black and white colleges. An important research question is: Do students on Black campuses experience different campus interpersonal relations and social networking compared to their peers on white campuses? If so, what are the negative and positive consequences for student outcomes?

Given that Black students are a minority on white campuses, they must rely, of necessity, on white students and professors in making their adjustments to campus life. Support systems and other coping mechanisms are structured and developed within a white environment, often with largely white participants. Black students on Black campuses, on the other hand, are not forced to cope with the unfamiliar, potentially stressful situation of being a minority on entering college. Consequently, they have opportunities to participate in social networks that are predominantly, if not exclusively, Black. Comparison of Black students' campus interpersonal relations, social networking, and outcomes—in particular, academic performance such as GPA—across different-race campuses should reveal useful evidence to assist our understanding of the importance of social support in the college experience.

It can be argued that Black students use support systems—specific sets of linkages among a defined set of persons and organizations—to help buffer and/or solve many of the social, psychological, and academic difficulties peculiar to campus life. In this sense, then, campus support systems may be seen as transactions among students, professors, and staff which are indicators of participation and integration into campus life. The specific roles that support systems are believed to play include:

1. The maintenance of individual self-esteem and life satisfaction;
2. Increasing social and academic competence and environmental mastery; and
3. The management of stress and coping.

CONCEPTUAL FRAMEWORK

This paper investigates the impact of campus interpersonal relations and social networking in Black and white college settings on student academic performance, satisfaction with academic life, and occupational aspirations. The model undergirding the proposed research suggests that African American students' college satisfaction, academic performances, and occupational aspirations are influenced directly and indirectly by preceding social-support variables in the model. It is assumed that academic-success-related outcomes of Black students suffer because of the difficulties experienced in adjus ting to the foreign environment of white colleges. Specifically, we hypothesize that:

Hypothesis 1: Students on Black college campuses will exhibit fewer adjustment-related academic problems than their peers on white college campuses due to their greater involvement in and use of social-support networks. We expect students on Black campuses to experience significantly more involvement and participation in student organizations and extracurricular activities than their peers on white college campuses.

Hypothesis 2: Students who use social-support networks are expected to have higher GPAs than those who do not regardless of racial identity of college attended.

Hypothesis 3: Black students in Black schools who use Black support networks will exhibit greater college satisfaction and higher occupational aspirations than their peers in white schools.

DATA AND METHODS

The proposed study will utilize as its primary data source the following computer data files from the National Study of Black College Students:

1. 1981 white college undergraduate data file (N = 695), and
2. 1983 Black college undergradute data file (N = 888).

A total sample of all Black undergraduate students attending both historically Black and predominantly white campuses in the NSBCS computer data files comprise our sampling design.

The computer files contain items about each student's experiences, evaluation of university condition, academic performance, future aspirations, problems, and needs. The Statistical Package for the Social Sciences (SPSS) is used to analyze the data. Comparative analyses of the data across key variables are undertaken to determine differential Black student outcomes. A combination of descriptive and summary, bivariate, and multivariate analyses is employed. As the situation dictates, cross-tabular, multiple regression, and correlational analysis are alternately used to unravel the complex relationships between access to and involvement in campus interpersonal relations, social networking, and differentials in Black students' academic-success-related outcomes on Black and white campuses.

MEASURING SOCIAL SUPPORT

Social support is defined as the degree to which a person's basic social needs are gratified through interaction with others. Basic social needs include affection, esteem or approval, belonging, identity, and security (Kaplan et al. 1977). These needs may be met by either socioemotional support (such as affection, sympathy and understanding, acceptance, and esteem from significant others) or the provision of instrumental support (such as advice, information, help with academic problems, and financial aid).

The social-support system will be defined as that subset in the student's total social network upon whom he or she relies for socioemotional support, instrumental support, or both. Thus, students, teachers, counselors, and chaplains may be members of a student's social-support system, in addition to his or her spouse, relatives, and friends.

The primary measures we employed to index social support include a variety of indicators that are directly tied to:

1. Campus interpersonal contacts, for example, relations with students, faculty, and staff persons;
2. Students' experiences at their particular universities, such as participation in campus extracurricular activities; and
3. Black support networks, including opinions of Black student unity and Black male/female relations on campus.

Relations with students, faculty, and staff persons at respective campuses is measured on a four-point scale with 1 = Excellent; 2 = Good; 3 = Poor; and 4 = Very Poor. Participation in extracurricular activities sponsored by student organizations is also measured on a four-point scale with 4 = Hardly Ever; 3 = Sometimes; 2 = Often; and 1 = Very Often. The final two social-support measures are assessed by asking students to indicate the strength of their agreement or disagreement concerning statements about Black student unity and Black male-female relations on campus. The measures are as follows: 1 = Strongly Agree; 2 = Agree; 3 = Disagree; and 4 = Strongly Disagree.

MEASURES OF STUDENT OUTCOMES

The indicators of college satisfaction are the extent to which students feel themselves to be a part of the general campus life insofar as student activities and government are concerned; and whether the student ever seriously considered leaving the university. The scale for the first query is 1 = Not at All; 2 = Very Little; 3 = Somewhat; 4 = Considerable. A dichotomous 1 = Yes or 2 = No response is utilized for the latter query.

Academic achievement is measured by college grade-point average; and occupational aspirations are empirically assessed by students' responses to the following query: "considering your abilities, personal contact, the job market, and so forth, what occupation do you actually expect to go into once your education is completed?" The occupational responses were coded along the Duncan SEI occupational prestige scale which ranges from a low of 1 to a high of 100.

RESULTS

Since participation and membership in group-oriented activities and organizations is believed to help bolster or maintain self-esteem and social identity, we compare Black students' experiences on predominantly white and historically Black college campuses. Three empirical indicators of social support are utilized here. The first measure asks: "To what extent do extracurricular activities on campus reflect your interests?" The second measure asks: "To what extent do you participate in extracurricular activities sponsored by student organizations?" The third measure compares membership and participation in clubs and organizations.

Black students in white colleges reported that campus extracurricular activities reflected their interests "very much" substantially less often than did their peers on predominantly Black college campuses (12.4 percent versus 28.3 percent). The proportion of students responding that extracurricular activities do not reflect their interest at all (9 percent versus 7 percent), or only somewhat (42.8 percent versus 42.7 percent) is nearly identical. Finally, more than a third of the Black students attending white colleges (36 percent) responded that their interests were reflected "very little." The corresponding percentage for Black colleges was 22.2 percent of students responding to the query.

In terms of actual participation in extracurricular activities sponsored by fraternities and sororities, professional organizations, clubs, and the like, there appears to be very little difference in the proportion of students responding "sometimes" or "often." However, a larger percentage of students on white campuses "hardly ever" participate (31.4 percent versus 23.4 percent). Slightly more of the students attending Black colleges (16 percent versus 13 percent) participate in extracurricular activities "very often."

Although the majority of Black students on both predominantly white and Black college campuses belong to and participate in clubs and organized activities, students attending Black colleges and universities do so more often. More than two-thirds of the students on Black campuses (69 percent) are members and participate. The corresponding percentage for Black students on white campuses is 61 percent. In summary, our compar-

TABLE 8.1

Descriptive Statistics of Student Outcomes and Social support for Black and White Colleges

		White Colleges		Black Colleges	
	Outcome Measures	*Mean*	*S.D.*	*Mean*	*S.D.*
	University GPA	2.43	0.77	2.60	0.76
A	Dropping Out	1.66	0.48	1.57	0.54
	Expected Occupation	29.00	9.04	66.50	20.69
B	Feeling Part of Campus Life	2.22	0.89	2.81	0.93
	Social Support				
C	Participation in Student Organizations	2.14	1.03	2.30	1.02
D	Relations with Faculty	2.02	0.63	1.65	0.69
D	Relations with Students	2.07	0.68	1.53	0.64
D	Relations with Staff	1.88	0.66	1.87	0.87
E	Black Student Unity	2.49	3.36	4.23	3.35
E	Black Male/Female Relations on Campus	4.63	3.10	2.28	0.89
		N=695		N=888	

Scale

A: 1=No 2=Yes
B: 1=Not at All 2=Very Little 3=Somewhat 4=Considerable
C: 1=Very Often 2=Often 3=Sometimes 4=Hardly Ever
D: 4=Very Poor 3=Poor 2=Good 1=Excellent
E: 1=Strongly Agree 2=Agree 3=Disagree 4=Strongly Disagree

ison of students' experiences suggests that students attending predominantly Black colleges tend to view campus extrcurricular activities as reflecting their interests more, and they participate in these activities more frequently than do their peers on predominantly white campuses.

Means and standard deviations of four student-outcome measures (dependent variables) and six social-support measures (independent variables) are presented in Table 8.1 for Black students attending both historically white (N = 695) and Black (N = 888) state-supported universities. The average GPA is higher at Black colleges (2.60 versus 2.43), with the spread around the mean being identical. Black students on white and Black campuses were equally likely to respond "no" when asked if they had ever seriously considered dropping out of their respective universities (1.66 versus 1.57). Black students attending white institutions expected to be employed in sales and health-related occupations after graduation (29.0). Their peers on Black campuses expected to be managers and administrators (66.5). In terms of "feeling a part of the general campus life," Black students on white campuses fared worse than students on Black campuses (2.22 versus 2.81).

Scanning the social-support variables, we see that students in both samples indicated that they participated in student organization activities "sometimes" (Table 8.1). Relations with faculty, students, and staff persons are generally good for both samples. However, the means are slightly higher for the white college sample (2.0 versus 1.7). The average response to queries concerning Black student unity differed markedly. The Black college sample strongly disagreed that there was unity among students on their campuses, whereas the white college sample strongly agreed (4.2 versus 2.5).

Finally, students in the white college sample strongly disagreed with the statement that Black men and women on their campuses don't get along well (4.6). Interestingly, students in the Black college sample tended to agree that Black male/female relations were poor (2.3).

A correlation matrix of all variables for the white college sample is presented in Table 8.2. Correlations above the diagonal are for Black students on Black campuses, while correlations below the diagonal are for Black students on white campuses. University grade-point average is most strongly correlated with positive relations with white faculty and staff on Black campuses ($r = .12$ and $r = -.15$), and with a student having "considered dropping out" on white campuses ($r = -.20$). Moving to the other student-outcome variables, we see that students who have never seriously considered dropping out have high occupational aspirations on white campuses ($r = .2$), and on Black campuses, they feel that Black male/female relations are positive.

Students who expected to be in managerial, professional, and technical occupations after graduation feel very much a part of both Black ($r = .51$) and white ($r = .29$) campuses (Table 8.2). In addition, on Black campuses, these students participate more often in student organizations ($r = -.19$) and maintain more positive relations with white students on their campuses ($r = .21$). On white campuses students with high occupational aspirations are active in extracurricular activities ($r = -.24$) and maintain positive relations with white faculty ($r = .22$) and with white students ($r = .18$). Black students who feel themselves to be a part of the general campus life participate in student organizations on Black campuses ($r = -.20$). No strong correlations of other predictor variables with "feeling a part of campus life" are revealed on white campuses.

Summarizing the analysis of the zero-order correlations for both samples, we conclude that students who have good relations with other students and faculty on their campuses tend to have higher GPAs and occupational expectations, feel themselves to be a part of campus life, and have never seriously considered dropping out of school. Interestingly, the Black support network measures are related in the same manner to all student-outcome variables for both samples. Three of the four measures are positively related to opinions about Black student unity on campus, and university GPA is negatively related to this measure of social support. The

TABLE 8.2
First-Order Correlation Coefficients between Student Outcome and Social Support
for Black Students on Black Campuses (above diagonal) and Black Students
on White Campuses (below diagonal)

Scale	Variables	1	2	3	4	5	6	7	8	9	10
	University GPA	—	.11	.11	.08	−.02	.12	.09	−.15	.11	−.03
A	Ever seriously considered dropping out?	−.20	—	.12	.05	−.07	.07	.11	−.04	−.06	−.19
	What occupation do you expect once completed?	.08	.20	—	.51	−.19	.16	.21	−.06	.09	−.10
B	How much do you feel a part of campus life?	.07	.13	.29	—	−.20	.15	.14	−.07	.10	−.05
C	To what extent do you participate in extracurriculars?	−.13	−.16	−.24	.11	—	−.38	−.37	−.03	−.03	.17
D	How do you characterize relations with white faculty?	.05	.14	.22	−.09	−.66	—	.59	.02	.01	−.10
D	How do you characterize relations with white students?	.04	.08	.18	−.07	−.48	−.45	—	.01	−.03	−.14
D	How do you characterize relations with white staff?	−.06	.04	.10	.10	−.07	−.09	−.10	—	−.08	−.10
E	Great deal of unity/sharing among Black students?	.05	−.01	.01	.05	.05	−.06	−.02	−.09	—	−.02
E	Black men/women students don't get along well.	.05	.02	.05	.05	−.02	.00	−.01	−.04	.16	—

second Black support network measure (Black male/female relations) is
positively related to each outcome measure for the white college sample.
Oddly enough, the observed correlations for the Black college sample on
this measure are all negative. Good relations among Black males and females on campus tend to be related to student outcomes in a manner contrary to expectations at the zero-order level.

To test the simultaneous effects of all social-support variables for each
of the four student outcome variables, four separate regressions are presented; one for each of the four student outcome variables with social-
support variables entered on a stepwise basis. The standardized regression
coefficients (Beta weights = "B") in Table 8.3 are for both the white college sample and the Black college sample.

TABLE 8.3

Stepwise Regression for Social-Support Measures as Predictors of Student Outcomes for Black and White Campuses

Student Support Predictor	Black Campuses				White Campuses			
	Univ GPA	Drop out	Occ.	Campus Life	Univ. GPA	Drop out	Occ.	Campus Life
Participation in student organizations	.06*	.03	.07*	.48*	.08*	.15*	.11*	.32*
Relations with faculty	.11*	.00	.03	−.01	.19*	.13*	.01	.17*
Relations with students	−.06*	.01	−.04	.05*	−.05	.07	.06	.10*
Relations with staff persons	.04	.08*	.01	.12*	−.02	−.01	.08*	.08*
Black student unity	.11*	−.06*	.08*	.04	.05	−.01	.08*	.00
Black male/female relations	−.02	−.18*	.10*	−.06*	.04	.01	.03	.03
R-Square	.03	.05	.02	.29	.03	.05	.03	.17

*Indicates $p < 0.05$

Of the social-support variables analyzed for the white college sample, only participation in student-organized extracurricular activities is related to the outcome variables in the expected direction. Each relationship is positive and significant at the .05 level. Furthermore, this variable is the strongest predictor for students feeling a part of campus life (B = .32), seriously considering dropping out (B = .15), and expected occupation (B = .11).

Relations with faculty are positively related to university GPA (B = .19), considering dropping out (B = .13), and feeling a part of campus life (B = .17). These relationships are also significant at the .05 level (Table 8.3). Interestingly, there is no relationship between relations with faculty, the strongest predictor of GPA, and expected occupation after graduation. Only one of the four outcome variables—feeling a part of campus life—is significantly related to relations with students. The relationship is positive (B = .10) and consistent with expectations. Relations with staff persons proved to be statistically significant and positively related to expected occupation and feeling a part of campus life. The magnitude of the coefficients is identical (B = .08) for both outcome variables.

The Black support network measures are uniformly weak predictors for each outcome variable. Significance is obtained for only the relationship between Black student unity and expected occupation (B = .08). None of the observed relationships between student-outcome variables and Black male/female relations are significant for the white college sample.

Overall, the social-support model best accounts for variation in "feeling a part of campus life" since approximately 17 percent of the variation is explained by our model (Table 8.3). Furthermore, four of the six Betas are significant at the .05 level. The multiple R and R^2 for the remaining three outcome variables are relatively modest. The model explains only

3 percent of the variance in GPA and expected occupation, and 5 percent of the variance in dropping out.

Scanning results for the Black college sample in Table 8.3, we see that three of the four student outcome variables—university GPA (B = .06), expected occupation (B = .07), and feeling a part of campus life (B = .48)—have significant positive relationships with participation in extracurricular activities sponsored by student organizations. This social-support variable is also the strongest predictor of feeling a part of campus life.

Of the professor/students/staff relation variables, relations with faculty is only significantly related to university GPA (Table 8.3). As expected, the relationship is positive (B = .11). The remaining regression coefficients for this variable are extremely low. Relations with students proved to have significant relationships with both university GPA (B = −.06) and feeling a part of campus life (B = .05). However, the relationship with GPA is negative and not in the expected direction. Relations with staff persons is positively related to all outcome variables, with significance attained for expected occupation (B = .08) and feeling a part of campus life (B = .12).

The Black support network variables have significant relationships with several of the outcome measures (Table 8.3). Specifically, Black student unity has significant positive relationships with university GPA (B = .11) and expected occupation (B = .08). Significance is also obtained for the relationship with dropping out (B = −.06). Our second measure of campus Black support networks—Black male/female relations—is significantly related to three of the four outcome variables. The regression coefficients are negative for dropping out (B = −.18) and feeling a part of campus life (B = −.06). Neither of these relationships is in the expected direction. The final outcome variable—expected occupation—is positively related to Black male/female relations (B = −.10).

Overall and as was the case for the white college sample, our social-support model best accounts for the campus-life variable as nearly 18 percent of the variable is explained (Table 8.3). A relatively high multiple regression coefficient is obtained, accounting for nearly 30 percent of the variance. For the remaining outcome variables, the model explains 3 percent of the variance in university GPA and expected occupation, and 5 percent of the variance in dropping out.

DISCUSSION

The aim of this analysis was to examine the relationship between social support and student outcomes within two distinct college settings. The strategy was to compare Black students on Black and white campuses to deter mine if variation in their use of social-support networks was related to four academic-success-related outcomes. It was hypothesized that Black students on Black campuses would experience more involvement and participation in extracurricular activities sponsored by student organizations than did their peers on white college campuses. The data provide modest support for this hypothesis. It was further hypothesized that students who use social-support networks will have higher GPAs than those who do not, regardless of racial identity of college attended. There is limited support for this hypothesis. Of the six social-support variables in our model, only participation in extracurricular activities of student organizations and relations with faculty are in the expected direction and significantly related to university GPA in both samples. Interestingly, the multiple regression analysis reversed the sign of the negative zero-order relationship between participation in student organizations and university GPA.

The stepwise multiple regression analysis further indicated that Black students on Black and white campuses who participate in student organizations often have higher occupational aspirations and exhibit greater satisfaction with their campus life. Clearly, participation in student organizations is the best predictor for the four outcome variables for both white and Black college samples. It is also responsible for the largest coefficients observed in both samples. We refer here to the relationship observed for satisfaction with campus life. In fact, the coefficients for the Black (.48) and white (.32) campus samples account for more than two-thirds of the multiple Rs recorded for the campus life variable by our social-support model.

Relations with faculty is only significantly related to university GPA for the Black college sample. However, Black students on white campuses who have good relations with faculty have never seriously considered dropping out of school and have greater satisfaction with their campus lives. Statistically significant positive relationships are observed for relations with staff persons and satisfaction with campus life for both samples. For Black students on Black campuses, good relations with staff persons is associated with never seriously considering dropping out of school. Blacks on white campuses, on the other hand, were found to have lower occupational expectations.

The conclusion is that professor/student/staff relations are strong predictors of satisfaction with campus life for Black students on white and Black campuses. For the remaining outcome variables, this particular block of social-support variables resulted in few significant relationships for either sample.

Finally, we come to the Black support network variables. This set of variables proved to be poor predictors of Black student outcomes on white campuses. The regression coefficients are uniformly weak, with significance observed only for one relationship. Black students who agree that there is unity and sharing among Blacks on their campus tend to have higher occupational aspirations. Contrary to the relationships observed for the white college sample, six of the eight regression coefficients proved to be significant for the Black sample. Having never seriously considered dropping out of school and higher occupational expectations were associated with favorable opinions concerning Black student unity and relations among Black males and females on campus. Black support networks are indeed important factors influencing college satisfaction and occupational aspirations of Black students attending Black state-supported universities. Therefore the final hypothesis is accepted that Black students on white campuses do not benefit from Black support networks to the same degree as do their peers on Black campuses.

The conceptual framework that undergirds this research—the buffering effect of social support systems—provides a useful perspective for interpreting and understanding the participation and membership in group-oriented activities and organizations, and it helps buffer and/or solve many of the social, psychological, and academic difficulties peculiar to campus life. Transactions among students, professors, and staff (campus support networks) are believed to help bolster or maintain self-esteem and social identity in addition to increasing social and academic competence and mastery of the institutional setting.

Black students' college outcomes in this study are indeed more favorable when there is involvement and participation in extracurricular activities sponsored by student organizations, such as clubs, fraternities and sororities, debating teams, and the like. Students attending traditionally Black colleges view campus extracurricular activities as reflecting their interests more, and participate in these activities more than their peers on predominantly white campuses. These findings suggest that satisfaction with campus life is greater for students on Black campuses.

Utilizing the logic of our conceptual model, it can be argued that, in the cases of Black campuses, Black students have more opportunities to become integrated into campus life. Support systems and other coping mechanisms are structured and developed within a Black institutional setting. Consequently, Black students on traditionally Black campuses have more slots to vie for without the issue of race becoming a factor in determining who becomes class president, editor of the campus newspaper, or captain of the debating team. Membership and participation in such student organizations enhance the self-esteem and life-satisfaction of Black students. Students on traditionally Black campuses are more likely to feel they are a part of campus life because of favorable interpersonal relations within predominantly, if not exclusively, Black settings.

The college experiences of Black students are also influenced by how other actors in the college setting interact and relate to them. Significant others in the university setting (such as students, faculty, and staff) on whom Black students rely for socioemotional support (for example, sympathy and understanding) or the provision of instrumental support (such as help with academic problems and financial aid) make up their social-support system. Thus, the way in which professors relate to Black students, the manner in which library or domitory personnel respond, or the character of interpersonal relationships with other students influence the college outcomes of Black students.

Overall, students on both Black and white campuses have cordial relations with faculty and staff. However, relations with faculty proved to be a better predictor of student outcomes for Black students on white campuses. One possible explanation is that, on historically white campuses, Black students have fewer significant others with whom to form meaningful interpersonal relationships. It should come as no surprise that these students who often "cry out for supportive conditions under which to pursue their educations" (Allen 1986) turn to their professors for social support. Basic social needs (such as esteem or approval) are gratified through interaction with faculty who identify themselves as caring and supportive.

Students on Black campuses, on the other hand, operate within an institutional setting that provides a broader range of choices for satisfying basic social needs. Hence, significant others are more likely to be other Black students and staff persons as well as friends and peers from surrounding Black communities.

Interpersonal relations with other Black students on campus is also important in determining student outcomes. The Black support network variables (Black student unity and Black male/female relationships) proved to be better predictors of Black student outcomes on Black campuses. Indeed, Black students on Black campuses are commonly assisted in feeling good about themselves and about their places in the university community through favorable interpersonal relationships with their fellow students. Campus support services are designed and operated specifically for the needs of Black students. There is no need for "minority support services" to ensure that there are activities (such as dances, homecoming festivities, or rallies) that allow Black students to mix and interact socially, politically, or culturally. Generally, the issue of on-campus interracial dating does not strain male/female relations on historically Black campuses as they sometimes do on white campuses. Unity and sharing among students on Black campuses may not be ideal, but the institutional setting and the likelihood of common geographical and socioeconomic characteristics enhance their probability of occurance.

We have seen substantial evidence documenting the fact that students on Black campuses experience differences in campus interpersonal relations and social networking in comparison to their peers on white campuses. It is clear that, on Black campuses, Black students are exposed to caring and supportive institutional settings that foster psychological well-being and the positive direction necessary for learning.

The challenge facing policy makers, educators, and administrators is to make Black colleges and universities more attractive to middle- and upper-class Black parents who are sending their children in increasing numbers to white colleges and universities. Although Black colleges regularly restore positive direction to transfers from white campuses with shattered confidence, Black parents continue to send their children into environmental settings where they are treated as aliens and viewed as not belonging.

Too often, our best and brightest students are denied an educational experience that provides the academic and social successes that build positive self-images for the best education possible. The day must come when the number of caring and concerned faculty persons on a campus become equally as important as an integrated educational experience to Black parents when selecting colleges or universities for their children. If we are to improve the situation of Black students in U.S. higher education—whether they attend Black colleges and universities or white ones—we must focus our attention on social-support systems that buffer and/or solve academic difficulties and increase satisfaction with campus life.

Part Three

The Graduate and Professional Years: Empirical Research Findings

The graduate and professional years are generally underresearched in the literature; these papers however, do shed some light on the experiences and outcomes for African American students who choose to pursue postgraduate education. Braddock and Trent's paper addresses several important questions, chief among these are the following: Do the correlates of success differ for graduate and professional students? Is postgraduate students academic performance more the function of university or individual characteristics?

Mickelson and Oliver focus more on student characteristics in their paper, attempting to test the assumption that student quality varies in concert with institutional prestige. They challenge the assumption that "quality rises to the top" (as in the premise that the better Black graduate students are consistently found at the more prestigious institutions). According to them many factors operate to impede Black students access to the more prestigious programs for reasons other than personal qualifications.

In their focus on graduate and professional students, Matthews and Jackson ask a slightly different set of questions. Of particular interest to them is the status of Black women in postgraduate programs. They attempt to identify important differences by gender in the mechanism of postgraduate academic success. They seek to understand how individual differences combine with differences in institutional responses to penalize Black women in postgraduate study, thus limiting their access and success rates.

The important topics addressed by papers in this section have received only limited prior attention. For example, more research on the context of success and failure of Black women in graduate and professional school would greatly enhance their representation in postgraduate education *and* in the professions. The papers in this section draw on data from the National Study of Black College Students to aid our understanding of key actors, processes and policies that influence African American involvement in postgraduate education.

JOMILLS HENRY BRADDOCK II
WILLIAM T. TRENT

Chapter Nine

Correlates of Academic Performance among Black Graduate and Professional Students*

In recent years, fundamental changes have occured in African American students' access to graduate and professional schools. Black representation among full-time graduate students increased throughout the 1960s and early 1970s to 5.5 percent in 1974, but has declined to about 5 percent since then. Similarly, Blacks, as a proportion of all first professional degree students, decreased from a high of 4.9 percent in 1974 to 4.6 percent in 1980 (National Center for Educational Statistics 1983). And by 1980, Blacks represented only about 4 percent of all professional and doctoral degree recipients (Berryman 1983; and Trent and Braddock 1987). Thus, although Blacks have made gains in enrollment access over the past two decades, there is still a long way to go before parity is attained.

Issues of access to graduate and professional school are important because African Americans continue to be underrepresented in advanced degree programs, especially the hard sciences and technical fields (Blackwell 1981; and Thomas 1985). Issues of success in graduate school and professional school—academic performance, retention, and graduation—are equally important, yet they have received little attention from researchers and policy makers (Blackwell 1981). Academic performance is especially important as it, in large part, determines other success outcomes, such as retention and graduation.

Research focusing on grade-point average (GPA) as a measure of academic performance of African Americans in graduate and professional schools is both limited and ambiguous. Anderson and Hrabowski (1977) report a strong correlation between undergraduate GPA and graduate GPA among Black students at the University of Illinois. They found no difference between Blacks who had attended traditionally Black undergraduate institutions and Blacks who had attended traditionally white undergraduate institutions.

It also did not matter which field of study was being considered. In a larger study, Hall and Allen (1982) found Black graduate/professional students grade performances to be positively related to age, attending schools outside the South, prior experience with large university environments, and having favorable relations with faculty. Surprisingly, they also report that undergraduate and graduate/professional grades were unrelated statistically. Scott and Shaw (1985) found a negative relationship between Graduate Record Examination (GRE) scores and graduate GPAs for Black students attending the University of Florida. Their findings suggest that the predictive validity of the GRE is similar for Blacks and whites, albeit in different directions.

This paper extends the Hall and Allen (1982) analysis by separately examining factors affecting African American students' success in graduate and professional schools. Specifically, the study analyzes data from the National Study of Black College Students to explore three related questions: (1) Are the influences of social and academic backgrounds on academic performance different for graduate and professional students? (2) Is the academic performance of graduate and professional students more dependent on the nature of the college itself, or on experiences within colleges? (3) Do different college characteristics and experiences have a differential impact on the academic performances of graduate and professional students?

METHODS

The research model of determinants of Black graduate and professional students grade performance is presented in Figure 9.1.

Social background, academic preparation and commitment, institutional and program selectivity, academic demands, and social integration are included as blocks of factors which affect, directly or indirectly, the academic success of Black students. The model in Figure 9.1 symbolizes a five-stage, longitudinal process through which student social background exerts an influence on academic preparation and commitment. At stage

FIGURE 9.1

A Model of Determinants of Black Graduates/Professional Student Grade Performance

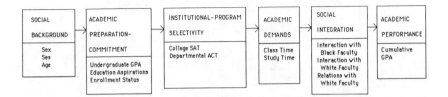

two, social background and academic preparation combine to determine the quality/selectivity of the students' college and program of study. Third, social and academic background, along with institutional and program selectivity, determine the academic demands which students face. Fourth, the academic demands, program-institutional selectivity, and social and academic backgound, in turn, affect the degree of students' integration into the social and academic subsystems of the university. Finally, all of these factors combine to influence academic performance.

Regression analysis following this model allows us to trace direct and indirect routes of influence on grade performances separately for Black graduate and professional student subpopulations. How the variable examined in this model are operationalized is shown in the Appendix. Table 9.1 presents means, standard deviations, and intercorrelations separately for graduate and professional students.

FINDINGS

To trace the effects of the predetermined background variables, Tables 9.2 and 9.3 examine the relations among social background, academic preparation and commitment, university-departmental selectivity, academic demands, and social integration for graduate and professional students.

ACADEMIC PREPARATION AND COMMITMENT

The first three columns of tables 9.2 and 9.3 present the effects of background variables on graduate and professional school commitment: educational aspirations (EDASP), enrollment status (STUSTAT) and academic preparation (UGPA). First, social background explains less than two percent of the variance in undergraduate GPAs for graduate students and less than three percent for professional students.

TABLE 9.1
Intercorrelations, Means, and Standard Deviations among All Variables*

Variables[1]	(1)	(2)	(3)	(4)	(5)	(6)	(7)	(8)	(9)	(10)	(11)	(12)	(13)	(14)	(15)	Mean	Standard Deviation
SEX		-.09	.03	.02	.00	.11	.15	.15	.16	.12	.10	.07	-.02	.05	-.15	.38	.49
SES	.12		.36	-.01	-.12	-.24	-.30	-.11	-.27	-.31	.00	.02	-.17	.02	.14	32.35	4.43
AGE	-.05	.27		-.02	-.07	-.35	-.33	-.32	-.29	-.35	.00	-.22	-.18	.09	.25	33.21	7.57
EDASP	.05	.05	-.03		.02	-.01	.06	.01	.04	.01	.04	.02	.03	.06	.02	3.94	1.56
UGPA	-.10	-.11	-.11	.07		.23	.23	.08	.20	.19	.04	.06	.00	.02	.08	3.03	.43
STUSTAT	.12	-.11	-.42	.18	.29		.59	.40	.56	.61	.08	.32	.31	-.02	-.01	.78	.41
SELECT	.11	-.12	-.17	.17	.36	.67		.46	.50	.42	.03	.20	.24	.03	-.16	1031.83	98.58
MAJOR	.25	-.05	-.17	-.02	-.07	.19	.03		.30	.33	.03	.17	.19	.08	-.29	19.31	1.52
STUTIME	.30	-.02	-.07	.25	.16	.43	.40	.38		.56	.00	.17	.25	-.08	-.20	4.49	1.45
CLSTIME	.05	-.11	-.29	.07	.15	.37	.23	.03	.26		-.08	.26	.25	-.09	-.24	3.96	1.35
RELWFAC	.06	-.15	.08	.10	-.06	.00	.07	.08	.09	.00		.15	-.03	.10	.13	3.84	.69
FINWFAC	.14	-.10	-.10	.03	.18	.29	.30	.10	.22	.37	.29		.08	.23	.02	3.15	1.43
BFACPRO	.19	-.11	-.12	.01	.00	.02	-.04	-.01	-.06	.05	-.01	-.06		.00	-.27	.65	.48
FINBFAC	-.07	-.10	-.05	.14	-.07	.05	-.03	.06	.06	.06	.10	.13	.12		.02	1.70	.86
GGPA	.10	-.12	.14	.35	.26	.02	.13	-.12	.10	-.03	.12	.02	.08	-.03		3.21	.46
MEAN	.50	323.60	32.53	3.71	3.12	.70	1014.63	19.85	4.08	3.23	3.85	3.39	.45	1.87	3.34		
Standard Deviation	.50	4.01	6.75	1.63	.44	.46	111.90	1.72	1.51	1.11	.77	1.25	.50	.92	.36		

*Professional students above diagonal, graduate students below.

[1]See Appendix for variable names and descriptions.

TABLE 9.2

Determinants of Black Graduate Students' Academic Preparation and Commitment, Institutional and Program Selectivity, Academic Demands, and Social Integration[1]

	UGPA	EDASP	STUSTAT	SELECT	MAJOR	CLSTIME	STUTIME	RELWFAC	FINWFAC	FINBFAC
SEX	-.09 (-.08)	.05 (.17)	.10 (.10)	.06 (13.13)	.23 (.79)*	.03 (.07)	.18 (.55)*	.05 (.07)	.11 (.28)	-.10 (-.19)
SES	-.70 (-.01)	-.05 (-.02)	-.01 (.00)	-.08 (-.22)	-.04 (-.02)	-.04 (-.01)	-.01 (-.00)	-.19 (-.04)*	-.06 (-.02)	-.09 (-.02)
AGE	-.10 (-.01)	-.01 (-.02)	-.41 (.00)	-.16 (-2.56)*	-.09 (-.02)	-.16 (-.01)	.13 (-.00)	.14 (.02)	.09 (.00)	-.00 (.00)
EDASP	-.01 (-.01)	.00 (.00)	-.03 (-.03)*	.04 (3.04)	-.05 (-.06)	.01 (.01)	.18 (.16)*	.09 (.04)	-.04 (-.03)	.14 (.08)
UGPA				.18 (44.93)*	-.11 (-.44)	.05 (.12)	.07 (.24)	-.09 (-.15)	.08 (.22)	-.10 (-.21)
STUSTAT				.66 (159.64)*	.16 (.59)	.32 (.76)*	.24 (.79)*	-.05 (-.09)	.06 (.15)	.08 (.15)
SELECT						-.04 (.00)	.18 (.00)	.10 (.00)	.16 (.00)	-.09 (.00)
MAJOR						-.06 (-.04)	.31 (.27)*	.08 (.04)	.07 (.05)	.04 (.02)
STUTIME							.02 (.01)	-.02 (-.01)	.05 (.03)	
CLSTIME							.01 (.01)	.32 (.36)*	.04 (.03)	
Multiple R2	.03	.01	.19	.5	.12	.17	.39	.07	.21	.07

* p < .05.

[1]See Appendix for variable names and descriptions.

TABLE 9.3

Determinants of Black Professional Students' Academic Preparation and Commitment, Institutional and Program Selectivity, Academic Demands and Social Integration[1]

	UGPA	EDASP	STUSTAT	SELECT	MAJOR	CLSTIME	STUTIME	RELWFAC	FINWFAC	FINBFAC
SEX	-.01 (-.01)	.02 (.06)	.11 (.10)	.08 (16.86)	.13 (.41)*	.04 (.11)	.08 (.23)*	.10 (.15)	.05 (.16)	.04 (.07)
SES	-.11 (-.01)	-.00 (.00)	-.11 (-.01)	-.13 (-2.87)*	.06 (.02)	-.14 (-.04)*	-.08 (-.03)	.00 (.00)	.17 (.05)*	-.03 (-.01)
AGE	-.03 (-.00)	-.02 (-.00)	-.31 (-.02)*	-.10 (-1.31)	-.23 (-.05)*	-.10 (-.02)	-.06 (-.01)	-.02 (-.00)	-.16 (-.03)*	.10 (.01)
EDASP				.07 (4.14)	.01 (.01)	.01 (.01)	.03 (.03)	.05 (.02)	.02 (.02)	.06 (.03)
UGPA				.09 (20.48)	-.00 (-.00)	.05 (.15)	.05 (.16)	.04 (.07)	-.01 (-.05)	.03 (.06)
STUSTAT				.50 (119.28)*	.31 (1.15)*	.49 (1.60)*	.37 (1.31)*	.19 (.33)*	.25 (.86)*	.03 (.07)*
SELECT				.01 (.00)	.20 (.00)*	-.03 (.00)	.03 (.00)	-.03 (.00)	.03 (.00)	.06 (.00)
MAJOR				.07 (.07)	.02 (.02)*	.02 (.01)	-.01 (-.01)	.02 (.01)	-.01 (.00)	.13 (.07)
STUTIME						.01 (.01)		-.01 (-.01)	-.07 (-.07)	-.10 (.06)
CLSTIME								-.21 (-.11)*	.13 (.14)*	-.11 (-.07)
Multiple R2	.02	.00	.15	.41	.21	.42	.37	.05	.15	.05

* p < .05.

[1]See Appendix for variable names and descriptions.

In neither case does sex, age, or socioeconomic status make a significant, unique contribution. These results are consistent with other research showing that, for Black undergraduate students, it is not social background but prior academic preparation (grades and tests) and other experiential variables which determine academic success in higher education (Braddock and Dawkins 1981; Nettles 1987; and Nettles, Thoeny, Gossman, and Dandridge 1985).

Examination of the educational commitment measures shows similar patterns for graduate and professional students (Tables 9.2 and 9.3). For both groups, social background explains less than one percent of the variance in educational aspirations. In contrast, social background factors, especially age, account for a significant portion of the explained variation in enrollment status. In both graduate and professional schools, older students are less likely to be full-time matriculants.

INSTITUTION AND PROGRAM SELECTIVITY

Now that we have explored how graduate and professional students' educational commitment and academic preparation are influenced by their social backgrounds, the analysis turns to how both sets of factors sort students into differentially selective colleges, departments, and programs (Tables 9.2 and 9.3).

First, among graduate students, those attending more selective universities are younger, full-time enrollees, and are better prepared academically. Among professional students, those attending more selective schools are found also to be full-time enrollees but, surprisingly, they are from less affluent backgrounds.

This may be partially understood in light of the fact that column one reveals a slightly negative but nonsignificant relationship between SES and undergraduate grades for both graduate and professional students. Thus, despite little variation in SES among this sample (see Table 9.1), it appears that students from less-affluent backgrounds have better undergraduate records which allows them access to more selective colleges. Similarly, it appears that younger students have (insignificantly) higher undergraduate grades which makes them more attractive to selective graduate schools.

Among selective graduate and professional schools there seems to be a preference to admit full-time rather than part-time students. Together, social background, academic preparation, and commitment account for more than 40 percent of the variance in college selectivity among both graduate and professional students.

With regard to major-field or program selectivity, we again find similarities and differences among graduate and professional students (Tables 9.2 and 9.3). For both groups, males enter the most selective or competitive fields. Put differently, major-fields distributions tend to be gendertyped, and males more typically enter engineering, mathematics, and the hard sciences—fields which attract students who score higher on standardized college entrance examinations.

Among professional school enrollees, younger students and full-time students enter the most selective of programs and major fields. These patterns may reflect the recent attempts by higher education to attract (and support) young and able minority students for advanced study in engineering and computer sciences, for example. Similar efforts have been made in law and medicine.

It might be argued that professional schools' recruitment efforts in engineering, law, and medicine have resulted in less gender-typed distributions since the unique effect of sex on major-field selectivity among professional school students (B = .412) is only 52 percent as strong as is this effect among graduate school students (B = .789). In any case, social background, academic preparation, and commitment account for nearly double the amount of variance in major-field selectivity among professional students (multiple R^2 = .213) than among graduate students (multiple R^2.115).

ACADEMIC DEMANDS

We turn next to a consideration of how social background, academic preparation, academic commitment, and university/departmental selectivity affect academic demands of class time and study time. For graduate and professional students, the most important determinant of amount of time spent in class is enrollment status (Tables 9.2 and 9.3). Clearly, full-time students spend more time in class than do part-time students. In fact, these measures would be proxies for one another except that graduate students can take a full-load of thesis, research, or independent-study credits and spend little, if any, time in class. In addition, for professional students, less-affluent students spend more time in class. This relationship is nonsignificant but in the same direction among graduate students.

Recalling the earlier observation that less-affluent students had better undergraduate records and were perhaps more academically prepared, it would not be surprising that these students might enroll for heavier course loads in professional school. Heavier course loads may also represent an attempt to shorten the duration of their programs as much as possible, perhaps with an eye toward minimizing any financial burdens on their families.

With regard to study time, again there are differences and similarities among graduate and professional students. First, among both groups, enrollment status is a major determinant of amount of time spent devoted to studying. As expected, full-time graduate and professional students spend more time studying than part-time students. Among graduate students, males and students in more selective disciplines also spend greater amounts of study time. It is not surprising that students in more selective or competitive fields would find the academic demands greater and thus requiring greater study time. It is surprising that after controlling for major field selectivity (where males are overrepresented in the more selective disciplines) we observe that males study more than females. This may in part be explained by males' lower undergraduate grade point averages (see Table 1). If males are less prepared academically and are disproportionate in highly competitive disciplines, it would be essential that they devote extra time to study. Professional students show little gender effect on either study time or undergraduate academic preparation. However, for professional students college selectivity is a significant determinant of study time. Students in more selective institutions spend greater amounts of time studying. In addition, graduate students with high educational aspirations devote greater amounts of time to studying.

SOCIAL AND ACADEMIC INTEGRATION

Our final set of predetermined variables in the model examine how graduate and professional students' social background, academic preparation, academic commitment, university-departmental selectivity, and academic demands. Among Black graduate students, relations with white faculty are better for less-affluent students. While no precise interpretation is possible with the present data, it does seem plausible that the behavioral style of less-affluent Black students may be more accommodating, deferent, and consistent with the expectations of white graduate faculty than the behavioral styles of their more affluent counterparts, thereby making possible more amiable relations. Black professional students who are enrolled full-time and who do not spend an inordinate amount of time in class have better relations with white faculty. This might suggest that Black students who are full-time participants in their programs or departments but who do not overload themselves with courses have more time to interact with white faculty. Consequently, they develop better relations with them.

Frequency of interaction with white faculty is determined primarily by enrollment status for professional students and by time spent in class for graduate students. That is, full-time students and students spending more hours in class show the highest rates of interaction with white faculty in professional and graduate schools, respectively. This is reasonable, since students who are enrolled full-time and who spend more hours in class will more often find it necessary and prudent to interact with their white instructors to discuss class assignments, clarify course content, and so on. In addition, younger and more affluent professional students also show higher rates of interaction with white faculty. Neither finding is unexpected. In addition, the younger, more affluent Blacks who are overrepresented among full-time students, are likely to be more experienced in dealing with interracial situations and, therefore, perhaps less reluctant to interact with white faculty. In contrast, our model does not adequately explain frequency of interaction with Black faculty for either graduate (multiple $R^2 = .055$) or professional (multiple $R^2 = .045$) students.

ACADEMIC PERFORMANCE

Finally, we turn to the question of how social background, academic preparation and commitment, college-departmental selectivity, academic demands, and social integration affect grade performance in graduate and professional school. Table 9.4 presents the multivariate regression results for the model of grade performance for both graduate and professional students.

Among graduate students, none of the social background effects are significant. Among professional students, however, both sex and age show unique effects on grade performance. Specifically, females and older professional students earn better grades. That Black females in professional schools earn better grades than their Black male counterparts is not surprising, given our earlier analyses which show that females are less likely to enter the highly competitive and male-dominated professional fields such as engineering, law, and medicine. Similar reasoning would apply with regard to age: older students earn better grades, in part, because they are also more likely to enter less competitive professional programs such as social work or education. By contrast, their younger counterparts are attracted to more selective and highly competitive fields such as engineering, law, and medicine. Parental social class has no impact on the grade performance of either graduate or professional students.

Academic preparation and commitment appear to be more important to graduate school success than to professional school success. Among graduate students, educational aspirations, undergraduate grades, and enrollment status combine for an R^2 increment of .181 while the corresponding R^2 increment for professional students is only .013—nearly a fourteen-fold

TABLE 9.4

Determinants of Grade Performance among Black Graduate and Professional Students[1]

	Graduate						Professional					
	(1)	(2)	(3)	(4)	(5)	(6)	(1)	(2)	(3)	(4)	(5)	(6)
SEX	-.08 (-.05)	-.07 (-.05)	-.06 (-.04)	-.07 (-.05)	-.07 (-.05)	-.06 (-.04)	-.16 (-.15)*	-.16 (-.15)*	-.12 (-.12)	-.11 (-.10)	-.13 (-.12)	.14 (.13)*
SES	-.16 (-.01)	-.12 (-.01)	-.12 (-.01)	-.11 (-.01)	-.11 (.01)	-.11 (.00)	.04 (.00)	.05 (.01)	.06 (.01)	.03 (.00)	.01 (.00)	-.02 (-.00)
AGE	.18 (.01)	.19 (.01)*	.17 (.01)	.16 (.01)	.15 (.01)	.16 (.01)	.24 (.02)*	.24 (.01)*	.18 (.01)*	.16 (.01)*	.19 (.01)*	.19 (.01)*
EDASP	.24 (.02)*	.34 (.08)*	.34 (.07)*	.33 (.07)*	.32 (.07)*	.33 (.07)*		.02 (.01)	.02 (.01)	.03 (.01)	.02 (.01)	.03 (.01)
UGPA		.25 (.20)*	.23 (.19)*	.23 (.19)*	.24 (.20)*	.24 (.19)*		.11 (.12)	.11 (.12)	.13 (.13)	.13 (.13)	.11 (.11)
STUSTAT		-.04 (-.03)	-.07 (-.06)	-.07 (-.06)	-.07 (-.05)	-.06 (-.05)		-.02 (-.02)	.06 (.07)	.18 (.20)	.13 (.14)	.17 (.19)
SELECT			.06 (.00)	.05 (.00)	.05 (.00)	.04 (.00)			-.02 (.00)	-.01 (.00)	-.01 (.00)	.00 (.00)
MAJOR			-.05 (-.01)	-.07 (-.02)	-.08 (-.02)	-.08 (-.02)			-.23 (-.07)*	-.22 (-.07)*	-.22 (-.07)*	-.20 (-.06)*
STUTIME				.06 (.02)	.06 (.01)	.07 (.02)				-.09 (-.03)	-.08 (-.02)	-.07 (-.02)
CLSTIME				-.05 (-.02)	-.04 (-.01)	-.05 (-.02)				-.18 (-.06)	-.17 (-.06)	-.17 (-.06)
RELWAC					.08 (.04)	.08 (.04)					.10 (.06)	.09 (.06)
FINWAC					-.03 (-.01)	-.01 (.00)					.15 (.05)*	.15 (.05)*
BFACPRO						.10 (.07)						-.21 (-.20)
FINBFAC						-.08 (-.03)						-.04 (-.02)
Multiple R^2	.051	.232	.236	.240	.245	.258	.091	.104	.148	.177	.208	.246

* $p < .05$.

[1] See Appendix for variable names and descriptions.

difference. For graduate students, educational aspirations and strong under-graduate grades both exhibit unique effects on academic success. That is, students with high educational aspirations and strong undergraduate grades earn better grades in graduate school. Comparing their total causal effect (column 2) with their direct effect (column 6) it appears that the impact of undergraduate grades and educational aspirations are primarily direct and unmediated. Enrollment status has no statistically significant impact for ei-ther group, although it approaches significance for professional students.

College and departmental selectivity are unrelated to grade perfor-mance for graduate students. For professional students, however, depart-mental or program selectivity is a significant determinant of academic success. Students who enter more selective or highly competitive fields earn lower grades. Comparing the effects of academic demands on grade performance, we see that neither amount of time spent attending class nor amount of time spent studying show unique effects for either graduate or professional students, although time attending class approaches statistical significance (negative) for professional students.

For graduate students, none of the social integration measures regard-ing contact with either white faculty or Black faculty has a unique effect on grade performance. Among professional students, however, we find that fre-quency of interaction with white faculty is significantly related to grade performance. Black professional students who have higher rates of interac-tion with white faculty earn better grades. Earlier analysis suggested that younger, more affluent students have higher rates of interaction with white faculty. These students are also more likely to be full-time but less likely to overload themselves with coursework, thereby permitting their interactions with faculty to be more productive. Finally, these younger students are better able to interact with faculty because they have fewer outside com-mitments (such as work or family responsibilities) competing for their scarce time.

Frequency of interaction with Black faculty shows no unique effect for either Black graduate or Black professional students. However, because many departments, in the graduate schools (55 percent) and professional schools (35 percent) studied, have no Black faculty members, we included in our analysis a measure of whether Blacks were represented on the faculty of the students' programs. Interestingly, while the presence of Black faculty had no significant effect on the grade performance of graduate students, it had a significant negative effect on the academic performance of profes-sional students. This is a very complex and confusing finding.

However, other patterns in the data lead us to believe that Black faculty in professional schools may perform nontraditional roles such as recruiters or support-services coordinators. This makes their impact on Black students' academic performances indirect or different from that of other professional school faculty, or that of Black graduate school faculty., For example, the Black professional students in this study report having significantly more Black faculty in their programs than Black graduate students, yet they also report having considerably less contact ($t = 1.85$, $p < .10$) with them than do Black students in graduate schools. In fact, for professional students the zero-order relationship between class time and contact with Black faculty is negative ($r = -.09$) while for Black graduate students this relationship is positive ($r = .06$). Thus, the often nontraditional role of Black faculty in professional schools seems a plausible explanation of the unexpected finding that the presence of Black faculty in professional programs does not directly enhance the academic (grade) performance of Black students. Other explanations for the negative relationship between gradepoint average and having Black faculty in the program might be suggested, but these data do not allow them to be tested.

DISCUSSION

Several things become obvious when the findings of this study are examined. First, it is clear that the determinants of grade performance differ for African American graduate and professional student. Although our model accounted for roughly one-quarter of the variance in Black students grade performance in both graduate and professional schools, different measures were significant for each group. For Black graduate students, grade performance is primarily explained by undergraduate grades and educational aspirations. For Black professional students, grade performance is explained by a more diverse set of factors including social background factors such as sex and age, major-field competitiveness, interaction with white faculty, and the presence and role of Black faculty in the students' programs. Thus, grade attainment in graduate and professional schools appears to reflect two distinct causal processes for Black students. While more extensive research on this topic is called for, the present findings suggest that admissions officials should become more sensitive to these subtle differences in the correlates of Black students' success in graduate and professional schools.

Second, college or university characteristics and experiences appear to be important factors affecting African American students' success in advanced degree programs, especially professional programs. Attention should be given to the racial makeup of the faculty or department *and* to the role assigned to Black faculty personnel. Simply having Blacks represented on the faculty, even as counselors or recruiters, is important to the issue of equity of access in advanced degree programs (Blackwell 1981), but as our data suggest it is vital to the academic success of African American students that Blacks be an integral part of the teaching faculty as well.

Finally, there are clearly factors other than those used in this study which account for Black graduate and professional students' grade performances. One obvious missing factor is performance on standardized admissions tests such as the Graduate Record Examination (GRE). Despite its well-known limitations as a predictive device for Blacks (Scott and Shaw 1985), use of the GRE in combination with other relevant information of a traditional nature (such as grades) and of a nontraditional nature (educational aspirations, for example) could well increase the explanatory power of our model of determinants of African American academic performance in graduate and professional schools.

APPENDIX

Operationalization of Variables

SEX—1 = male; 0 = female

SES—represents a linear weighted composite socioeconomic index composed of mother's education; father's education; mother's occupation; father's occupation; and combined parental income.

AGE—represents self-reported year of birth.

EDASP—represents student's current educational aspirations. Code: 1 = some graduate school; 2 = M.A. or M.S. degree; 3 = Professional M.A.; 4 = Professional Ph.D; 6 = Ph.D.

UGPA—represents self-reported undergraduate grade-point average scored on a four-point scale.

STUSTAT—represents student's enrollment status. Code: 1 = full-time; 0 = part-time.

SELECT—represents the selectivity of the student's college or university as measured by the average combined SAT score of entering freshmen.

MAJOR—represents the selectivity of the student's program or department as measured by the average combined ACT score of students planning to enter the field.

STUTIME—represents the self-reported number of hours spent studying weekly. Code: 1 = none; 2 = 1 to 5 hours; 3 = 6 to 10 hours; 4 = 11 to 15 hours; 5 = 16 to 20 hours; 6 = more than 20 hours.

CLSTIME—represents the self-reported number of hours spent attending class weekly. Code: 1 = none; 1 = 1 to 5 hours; 3 = 6 to 10 hours; 4 = 11 to 15 hours; 5 = 16 to 20 hours; 6 = more than 20 hours.

RELWFAC—represents self-reported relations with white faculty members. Code: 1 = no contact; 2 = very poor; 3 = poor; 4 = good; 5 = excellent.

FINWFAC—represents self-reported frequency of interaction with white faculty members. Code: 1 = no contact; 2 = less than once a week; 3 = at least once a week; 4 = several times a week; 5 = at least once a day; 6 = several times a day.

BFACPRO—represents the whether or not there are Black faculty members in the student's program or department. Code: 1 = yes; 0 = no.

FINBFAC—represents self-reported frequency of interaction with Black faculty members. Code: 1 = no contact; 2 = less than once a week; 3 = at least once a week; 4 = several times a week; 5 = at least once a day; 6 = several times a day.

GGPA—represents self-reported graduate/professional grade-point average scored on a four-point scale.

ROSLYN ARLIN MICKELSON
MELVIN L. OLIVER

Chapter Ten

The Demographic Fallacy of the Black Academic: Does Quality Rise to the Top?*

Since the mid 1960s we have seen a marked increase in the aggressiveness of major white colleges and universities in recruiting African Americans, women, and other minorities into the ranks of their academic faculties. This aggressiveness has been due, in large part, to challenges issued by Black student protests and the threatened cutoff of federal funding. Despite the almost twenty years of this strategy, minority scholars—and particularly African Americans—remain significantly underrepresented at practically all levels of faculty employment. This paper addresses one aspect of the traditional search process in academia which contributes to continued minority underrepresentation.

We argue that significant numbers of highly qualified African American candidates are overlooked or deemed unqualified, in part because of the untested assumption in academia that "quality rises to the top." According to this assumption, if Black candidates are not found in the graduate programs of the universities considered to be the best in a field, then it is often incorrectly concluded that no other qualified Black candidates are available.

We argue that this pattern leads to the faulty perception of a greater shortage of *quality* African American academics than is actually the case. In reality, the search process itself is to blame for not uncovering highly qualified Black candidates.[1] The assumption that the demographic

177

distribution of qualified Black scholars is coterminous with the top institutions in a particular discipline ignores the fact that Black academic talent is broadly dispersed throughout many types of institutions of higher education. It is a fallacy to assume that quality Black academics only rise to the top of the academic hierarchy.

Using data from the National Study of Black College Students (NSBCS), we show that there are few, if any, differences in the quality of African American graduate students from highly ranked and less highly ranked institutions of higher education. This challenges one major assumption of the academic search process—that high-caliber minority candidates are trained only in the most highly regarded graduate departments. Quality exists not only in top educational institutions, but also at the mid-level schools, where for various reasons, one finds good students capable of highly successful academic careers.

SOME HISTORICAL CONSIDERATIONS

The appearance of noticeable numbers of African American faculty in the major institutions of higher education in America is a fairly recent phenomenon. When W. E. B. DuBois, for example, finished his doctoral degree in history at Harvard in 1899, he was unable to obtain an academic appointment from an American university (DuBois 1940/1968). Instead, he became a research assistant at the University of Pennsylvania, and subsequently spent the remainder of his academic career at Atlanta University. Indeed, the Black college became the refuge for early American Black academics. Unable to obtain employment in the white colleges and universities with research traditions and funds, Black scholars were forced to spend tremendous amounts of time teaching and doing administrative work in Black college settings. What research they were able to accomplish was produced in spite of these serious impediments.

This early exclusion of Blacks from American colleges and universities reflected a whole array of racist beliefs and attitudes that were held by highly educated American scholars, as well as by society at large. Emblematic of this situation is the life and academic career of the most significant biologist Black America has yet to produce: Ernest Everett Just.[2]

A 1907 magna cum laude graduate of Dartmouth College with a degree in English and science, he was eagerly sought as an instructor by both Howard University and Morehouse College. Just chose Howard where, after first teaching English, he became an instructor in a newly formed zoology major, and subsequently became an important teacher and administrator in the Medical School. He fought many racist obstacles to gain advanced training at the Marine Biology Laboratory at Woods Hole, Maine. There he came to the attention of its director, Frank Lilly, who was also chair of the Department of Biology at the University of Chicago. Impressed with Just's intelligence and acumen in the laboratory, Lilly arranged to have Just's work at Woods Hole count toward earning a doctorate at the University of Chicago. After several years of working at Howard, attending summer institutes at Woods Hole, and studying at the University of Chicago, Just earned his Ph.D. in 1916. His dissertation was the basis of a series of articles on the structure of the cell which was published in the top biology journals. Just was also named the first recipient of the NAACP's Spingarn medal for "foremost service to his race" in recognition of his contributions to biology and the Medical School and medical education at Howard.

One of the few African Americans to have a Ph.D. in the biological sciences, Just grew tired and impatient at Howard where he was given neither the time nor the resources to do really scientific work. Feeling heavily weighted by onerous teaching and administrative duties, Just attempted to gain funds to free himself from this burden and to allow him time to do the work to which he was so deeply committed. He knew, however, that the only way to accomplish this would be to gain an appointment at a research university. But this was not to be.

Although he had a superb publication record and had made important scientific discoveries, Just was never seriously considered for a position at a major white university. Even those with whom he had worked and who knew him well wrote recommendations with comments like the following: " . . . very good for a Negro, but not for a white," "very well-qualified to be a teacher in a colored university," or they recommended that Just should go on to high-school teaching for such a move would be "a good thing for science and, in the long run, for Just himself." The only white university to really consider Just was Brown but, in the end, it concluded that he would have been "just ideal except for his race" (Manning 1983: 227).

Just's contributions to science have, of course, outlived many of those who offered these evaluations but, with such general attitudes, it is not surprising that Blacks were hardly ever found in the major white colleges and universities before the 1940s.

The 1940s have been characterized as a period of "experimentation" for white colleges and universities. While hiring African Americans as full-time faculty continued on a miniscule level, white higher education seemed more than willing to give visiting or temporary appointments to Blacks who regularly taught at traditionally Black schools. Only when foundations or external groups placed intense pressure on college administrators were Blacks hired in full-time positions. Allison Davis' appointment at the

University of Chicago, for example, was prompted by pressure brought by the Rosenwald Foundation, which even provided a stipend to partially cover his salary (Fleming et al. 1978: 27).

Such token appointments characterized the recruitment of Black scholars during this period. But Black scholars of outstanding talent were, for the most part, excluded from teaching and doing research in the nation's most prestigious institutions of higher learning (Winston 1971). Among that group were such eminent scholars as E. Franklin Frazier, Rayford W. Logan, Charles R. Drew, Ralph J. Bunche, Alain Locke, Charles H. Houston, and Arthur P. Davis, to name only a few.

The rather lackluster record of white colleges and universities in hiring Blacks for their faculties continued into the 1950s. Even though the 1950s marked the most energetic use of the courts by civil rights organizations in breaking down the legal basis of "separate but equal," institutions of higher education maintained resistance equal to and, in many instances, stronger than other sectors of the society. Caplow and McGee (1958: 226–27) categorically stated that " . . . discrimination on the basis of race appears to be nearly absolute. No major university in the United States has more than a token representation of Negroes on its faculty, and these tend to be rather specialized persons who are fitted in one way or another for such a role."

Even during the expansionary era of the 1960s, African American employment in the major centers of higher education reflected little interest on the part of administration and faculty to open its ranks to qualified Blacks. While college enrollment, and consequently faculty positions, increased rapidly during the 1960s, Black faculty employment actually decreased. In 1960, approximately three percent of all faculty in colleges and universities were Black, but the percentage declined in 1968–69 to only 2.2 percent. Even as recently as 1972–73 the percentage of Black faculty (2.9 percent) had yet to recover to 1960 levels (Fleming *et. al.* 1978: 36). (By 1983, the percentage of Black faculty in four-year institutions rose to approximately four percent [National Center for Educational Statistics 1988]).

Clearly the free market in academia up to that point had not opened its doors to previously excluded Black scholars. More importantly, however, this failure of the nation's universities and colleges came at precisely the time when, with the expansion of higher education, opportunities to diversify the pool of faculty were a real problem. Because of exclusionary patterns of hiring throughout higher education, an entire generation of white scholars were locked into available slots in universities. Their presence has made it much more difficult to increase faculty racial diversity in the current era of limited growth and retrenchment toward policies of affirmative action.

AFFIRMATIVE ACTION AND THE RISE OF THE
RHETORIC OF MERITOCRACY

The complacency of academia was severely shaken, however, by the protest and demands that African American students made in support of the general goals of the Civil Rights Movement and in regard to specific reforms in higher education. These campus protesters questioned why universities appeared to be bastions of white privilege in both the content of the subject matter they taught and the composition of the faculty. On white campuses in particular, demands were made for the introduction into the curriculum of "Black Studies" and for the aggressive recruitment of Black faculty (Edwards 1970; and Prager 1982).

In addition, the passage of the Civil Rights Act of 1964 set the legal basis for affirmative action in higher education. Combined with several executive orders issued by President Lyndon B. Johnson, and requirements for federal contracts issued by the Department of Labor and the Equal Employment Opportunity Commission, universities were no longer as free to do as they pleased in the hiring of faculty and the admission of students. Job openings now had to be widely advertised and written evidence of the good-faith efforts of the institution to increase the pool of minority applicants had to be provided. But more importantly, federal contracts and grants, which provided significant income to the medical and scientific enterprises of most research-oriented universities, were subject to compliance review which monitored the affirmative action efforts of the institution in general (Fleming *et.al.* 1978; and Smelser and Content 1980). It was primarily pressure from these two sources which fueled real efforts on the part of institutions of higher education for diversifying their faculties and students.

However, the responses of universities to this challenge varied. Some hired Black faculty who were not completely qualified and who subsequently could not meet the tenure requirements of the institution. Others raided some of the best faculty from Black colleges, providing them with better-than-average salaries and very high ranks (Rafkey 1971). However, for the most part, institutions complained that qualified Blacks were hard to find, and that, if they could find them, they would certainly hire them. This was, and continues to be, the common response of the major research and teaching schools.

Of course, it is true that there is a real shortage of African American Ph.D.s to fill positions in higher education. And it is, indeed, the case that supply is uneven if one examines fields of specialization. For example, during the 1970s, a little more than one-half of all Black doctorates were in education or an allied field. By the mid–1980s, the proportion had remained the same (Hirschorn 1989). Consequently, all other fields had to divide among themselves only four of every ten Black doctorates earned during that period (Blackwell 1981; National Center for Educational Statistics 1988). In some fields, Blacks are not even represented as earning doctorates.

These facts certainly point to the need for increasing the pool of eligible Blacks. However, we argue that the available pool is not the *only* factor that inhibits schools from identifying and making offers to qualified Blacks. The process by which candidates are identified, screened, and selected is guided by a set of meritocratic values and untested assumptions which work against the identification and selection of qualified minority candidates who are not graduates of the leading institutions.

That merit is the overriding norm guiding the selection of faculty by U.S. colleges and universities cannot be denied. What *can* be questioned is the ability of whatever bodies that evaluate and select candidates for faculty positions to make such judgments based on a set of meritocratic criteria that do not inherently bias the decision-making process, especially for minority candidates. Seen in its sociological context, the process of selection turns out to be less of an expression of positive choices and more the result of negative choices (Smelser and Content 1980) where inappropriate and supposedly less-qualified candidates are cast by the wayside as the more appropriate and most qualified candidates buoy to the top of the list. At almost every turn, minorities seem to be disproportionately excluded by criteria which, on their face, appear to be based on merit but, in actuality, serve to depress the probabilities of a minority candidate rising to the top of the search. And indeed, the irony of affirmative action is that, just at the time when the recruitment and promotion of minority faculty has assumed great public interest, the ideology of meritocracy has become all the more vigorously defended and promoted in the halls of academia. As Alvarez (1973: 124) notes, when universities face real shortages of financial and other resources, "the cognitive fictions by which social stratification is made legitimate or justifiable are likely to receive vigorous endorsement."

BIASES IN THE ACADEMIC SEARCH PROCESS: THE FAILURE IN IMPLEMENTING MERITOCRACY

The proponents of meritocracy argue that the present system which allows an autonomous faculty to choose its peers within the context of meritocratic values is the best protection that minorities have against biases in the selection process (Glazer 1975; and Sowell 1975). When selection is based on neutral, objective, universalistic, and achievement-based criteria, the argument states, Blacks and other disadvantaged minorities are protected against the intrusion of particularistic and biased criteria which have previously excluded them from participation in this realm. However, this view disregards an established literature (Gilford and Snyder 1977; Duster 1976; and Lewis 1975) which finds the search process to be plagued by precisely the opposite—"objective standards are often vague, inconsistent, and weighted toward subjective judgments" (Exum 1983: 393). The implementation of meritocratic principles is thwarted somewhere between rhetoric and reality.

To understand just where the disjuncture between rhetoric and implementation occurs, we look more closely at the search process itself. Two very good studies (Caplow and McGee 1958; and Smelser and Content 1980) offer considerable insight into this process. One describes the operation of academic searches before affirmative action and the other describes post-affirmative-action efforts. Affirmative action has made a marked difference in the process but, sadly speaking, not in the results. Because of affirmative action, academic positions are now more widely advertised than ever, advertisements contain language which encourages women and minorities to apply, and procedures are generated which allow the monitoring of the size of minorities in the pool of eligible candidates. However, both studies show that the results of searches continue to be the same. Those who rise to the top of the lists of qualified candidates are graduate students from the most elite universities, who are recommended by the most eminent people in their fields, and who were, in many cases, encouraged to apply by members of the hiring faculty.

How does this occur? The academic search process proceeds from a unique perspective. The search for academic talent is both " . . . a competition *for* individual services and a competition *between* universities trying to advance or solidify their own positions in the prestige hierarchy" (Smelser and Content 1980: 7). Thus, extremes of inequality have developed over time between institutions. Some institutions have maintained reputations of excellence which allow them to be more selective in who they hire, and more attractive to the better people in certain fields, Thus, the recruitment patterns of schools become relatively fixed by the prestige hierarchy that has developed. Elite schools will hire only from schools at their level, while those in the second-rank will hire only from their rank or higher. And the pattern continues on down the line. Therefore, the system of competition between schools sets the pattern for the competition for individual academic talent. From the outset, the search process becomes biased, not toward individual merit, as the ideology of meritocracy would have us believe, but toward institutional reputation.

The power of institutional reputation (and likewise departmental reputation) is made all the more important by the inability of faculty and selection committees to agree upon the factors that constitute "excellence in research and teaching." Academic discipline and specializations differ as to the degree that excellence can be recognized. The hard sciences are somewhat more likely to have consensus on what constitutes good work, while the soft sciences are fragmented by varying schools of thought and paradigms—so much so that consensus is difficult, if not impossible, to achieve. Thus, institutional prestige becomes a firm proxy that can take the place of—or at least supplement—a candidate's claim for excellence in the face of shifting and vague standards of scholarship.

Contributing to this imbalance of attention to institutional sources of merit is the tendency for faculties to rely heavily on the sources of recommendations that accompany an applicant's file. Given an inability to autonomously evaluate a candidate's record in the light of conflicting or unclear standards, what becomes important is the nature and source of an applicant's supporting letters. They testify to a candidate's abilities and potentials. But more importantly, to the degree that the recommender is from a highly placed institution or is an important member of a disciplinary concentration—or as in some cases, the recommender is personally well-known among faculty—the more influence the recommendation will have. Thus Caplow and McGee (1958: 120) argue that "personal influence among networks of colleagues" is the most important carrier of the prestige that really counts. In other words, the academic market is not an objective competitive system, but rather a system of sponsored mobility (Turner 1960) where patronage from established scholars at elite institutions is the important indicator of potential merit.

That such a system radically departs from the model of meritocracy seems evident. Smelser and Content (1980: 27) argue that, what in actuality occurs, is a "succession of exclusions" whereby, after the application of criteria of exclusion, " only one candidate for the position remains." What is of interest to us is that the built-in biases of the system tend to *exclude* more African American scholars than to *include* them. In part, this is a consequence of the sponsored character of the search. In a quasi-objective manner, each field can claim to have knowledge of the best universities in a particular field. However, when this is used as an exclusionary criterion along with the network of colleagues associated with that institution and through which the prestige of the institution flows, the end result is to unfairly exclude those Blacks who do not have access to such prestigious institutions and colleagues.

Moreover, to the degree that inequalities have grown in the educational system due to such competition for talented scholars, the results of searches, more often than not, appear to meet the standards of meritocratic ideology only if the criteria are not questioned. As practically all studies note, the best scholars who have graduated from the best schools get the best jobs. In the process, highly qualified Blacks who have not graduated from the elite universities are overlooked and bypassed. Equally qualified whites who come from elite universities may have more opportunities to develop careers of distinction in major universities than do highly qualified Blacks from less prestigious universities. As Exum (1983: 391) notes, "Everyone desires minority superstars, but they may be less willing to gamble on minorities than on whites."

What gives the academic search process its legitimacy as a meritocratic system is the comforting assumption, buttressed by a good deal of sociological insight, that "quality rises to the top." A system that rewards those who are already at the top and assumes that their training, motivation, and skill-level will lead to a rewarding future, will indeed generate a series of self-fulfilling prophecies. Bright undergraduates are recruited by the elite and prestigious graduate schools which, in turn, are able to place them in the leading institutions; privilege begets privilege in such a situation (Smelser and Content 1980).

African Americans in this context seem to suffer more acutely because they lack the sustenance generated by initial privilege. A prime example concerns the myth of "quality rising to the top." A central tenet of this argument is that quality will in the end, conquer all barriers and find its true place at the top of the academic hierarchy. However, Blacks have severe difficulties conquering the personal and institutional barriers which they face in their quest for academic success. In the demography of higher education, Blacks are more inclined to be at the less prestigious and less elite institutions of advanced training. A 1977 report of the National Academy of Sciences (Gilford and Snyder 1977) reports that Blacks are least likely to earn their Ph.D.s from the top-rated institutions (those universities most research oriented), and that the proportion earned from that tier is less than their proportion of the total degrees granted.

Clearly, if graduation from these top institutions is a prerequisite for employment in major colleges and universities, then Blacks will be systematically excluded on this basis. Evidence bears this out as Black Ph.D.s are "found mainly in the less-prestigious colleges and universities—those which are public, rather than private, and which do not grant doctorates. They are less likely to be found in elite private institutions, especially at the university level" (Exum 1983: 385).

Thus, the assumption that "quality rises to the top" may be fallacious for African Americans and other minorities. Is it fair to assume that Black students who graduate from less prestigious universities and colleges are not as qualified as those from elite research institutions? If this is the case, then the traditional academic search process excludes only those Blacks who should be excluded. But if this is not the case, then the process overlooks a significant source of Black scholarly resources.

DOES QUALITY RISE TO THE TOP?:
EVIDENCE FROM THE NATIONAL STUDY OF
BLACK COLLEGE STUDENTS

The unique data provided in the National Study of Black College Students (NSBCS) allow us to address, in a tentative way, the issue of quality differences among Black students in variously ranked graduate institutions. Such an empirical inquiry is not without significant problems. Foremost is the question of how "quality" is defined. As our discussion notes, academics are themselves unable to agree upon what criteria constitute evidence of "excellence."

We have taken a performance-based model as our lead. What skills are necessary for success in academia, and which factors are academic search committees likely to examine? Four factors come to mind.

First, we considered the student's academic performance as measured by grade-point average: outstanding grades indicate that a student has mastered successfully the necessary coursework, and subsequently obtained the skills needed to do good work in an area. Second, we looked at the receipt of fellowships, research assistantships, and grants: this is a precursor to the competitive process of securing grants and prized fellowships that make for a successful career. Third, we noted the presentation of scholarly papers at conferences and professional meetings. And finally, we considered the publication of scholarly articles or books. A combination of these four factors consititute our indicator of quality.

Since the NSBCS contains a sample of graduate students ranging from first year to those in the process of writing dissertations, it would be inappropriate to demand that first-year students meet the same standards in our ranking of quality as fourth-year or fifth-year students. Therefore, we have used a sliding scale which takes into account the natural history of the development and maturation of students in graduate school. So, for example, first-year students do little more than coursework. Therefore, we weight the criteria which they are most likely to meet—a high grade-point average and the receipt of a fellowship or grant—more heavily for them than we do for more advanced graduate students. But for third- and fourth-year students, all the criteria are applicable and, here, excellence is based on a fuller range of factors. Ideally, we would like to factor into this formula the *number* of paper presentations and publications, but the data do not permit this elaboration.

Respondents' quality index scores range from a low score of .5 to a high of 8.0. The formula for ascertaining each student's score on our quality index works as follows: a first-year student with a high grade-point average and a research grant would receive a quality index score of 4.5 (GPA $>$ 3.0 (2.0) + grant (2.5) = 4.5), while a third-year student would receive a score of 3.5 for the same accomplishments (GPA $>$ 3.0 (1.5) + grant (2.0) = 3.5), and a fourth-year student would score only 2.5 (GPA $>$ 3.0 (1.0) + grant (1.5) = 2.5). In this way, we weight the scale to the length of the graduate careers of our respondents.

However, we adapt this formula to the extremes of our scale as well. Extraordinary first-year graduate students who have high GPAs and who have grants, paper presentations, and publications, can exceed our 8-point scale (GPA $>$ 3.0 (2.0) + grant (2.5) + paper (2.5) + published (2.5) = 9.5). In these circumstances, we truncate their scores to 8. Certain respondents, primarily a few first-year graduate students, have no papers, grants, or publications, and have grade-point averages which are below 3.0. To prevent their quality index score from taking a value of zero, which would cause the student's case to be dropped from the data analysis, we assign the individuals the score of .5 in order to retain the case.

We have divided the eight graduate training institutions from the NS-BCS into three groups based on the national reputation of their graduate departments. The top group represents those institutions which, across-the-board, have consistently highly ranked departments whose size and influence have made them traditional suppliers of faculty for other elite institutions around the country (University of Michigan, University of Wisconsin, and University of North Carolina-Chapel Hill).

The middle group contains institutions which, in particular specializations, have departments that are nationally ranked but are not consistently strong across-the-board and are usually young universities relative to the first-ranked institutions (University of California-Los Angeles, Arizona State University, and State University of New York-Stony Brook).

The lowest ranked grouping represents those schools without national reputations and with relatively newly inaugurated graduate programs. These schools, located for the most part in urban areas, developed most rapidly during the 1960s when expansion in higher education was the norm (Memphis State University and Eastern Michigan University). While they have recruited high-quality faculty, they have yet to gain more than regional, and in some cases, local recognition as important institutions of graduate training.

The sample we use consists of all graduate and professional school students enrolled in the eight universities contributing to the NSBCS in both 1981 and 1982. We combined the 1981 and 1982 data sets primarily because of the small number of students in each year who attended schools in the lowest ranked category. Without combining the two data sets, we would risk having insufficient cases in the lowest rank of colleges to make meaningful comparisons. Our sample consists of 387 students from the top group of universities, 224 students from the middle group, and 122 students from the lower group, for a total of 733 respondents.

A potential problem arises when we combine data sets from two separate years. There is a possibility that respondents from each year have different histories. However, the subjects from both years are allocated throughout the three school ranks. This compensates for any bias which may occur due to history since our analyses are done *across* years, not *between* years.[3]

The questions we ask of our data are the following:

1. Are there quality differences among graduate students in variously ranked graduate institutions in our sample?
2. Do the backgrounds of these students differ so as to confirm the notion that students from better-quality institutions also come from more advantaged backgrounds?
3. Are students' aspirations about careers in their fields different for various graduate schools?

These questions directly test some of the assumptions that undergird present-day academic searches. To the degree that differences are not found in our data, we argue that the search process may unfairly impact Blacks by overlooking an important source of Black scholarly resources in the nonelite institutions of graduate training.

Quality Differences

We examined mean differences in students' quality index scores by conducting a series of analyses of variance (ANOVA). Our ANOVAS reveal no significant differences among quality index scores by rank of university (Table 10.1). The average score on the quality measure for students from the lowest ranked schools (3.35) was only slightly smaller than those from the middle (3.51) and the highest ranked schools (3.59).

The analyses reveal that institutional differences are less important than certain individual attributes in the prediction of whether students will be high or low on our measure of quality. Two significant attributes are gender

TABLE 10.1
ANOVA Summary Table of Dependent Variables by Rank
of University, Gender, or Marital Status

Dependent Variable	N	Mean	Standard Deviation	F
Student Quality Index				.492
High Rank	387	3.51	2.16	
Medium Rank	224	3.59	2.11	
Low Rank	122	3.35	2.23	
Gender				10.48***
Male	320	3.80	2.28	
Female	413	3.28	4.14	
Marital Status				4.28*
Single	427	3.37	4.53	
Married	219	3.74	5.01	
Father's Education (1 to 6 Scale)				4.13**
High Rank	375	2.93	1.48	
Medium Rank	219	2.59	2.12	
Low Rank	118	2.95	2.20	
Mother's Education (1 to 6 Scale)				9.79***
High Rank	386	3.10	1.31	
Medium Rank	221	2.67	1.32	
Low Rank	126	3.00	1.34	
Father's Occupation (Duncan SEI)				.82
High Rank	345	40.40	28.75	
Medium Rank	194	36.18	26.17	
Low Rank	106	42.30	28.75	
Mother's Occupation (Duncan SEI)				1.47
High Rank	338	40.51	24.94	
Medium Rank	179	36.64	24.04	
Low Rank	110	39.74	24.44	
Age at First Job				10.42***
High Rank	285	20.40	9.78	
Medium Rank	197	20.72	9.40	
Low Rank	92	18.91	14.02	
Occupational Prestige of First Job (Duncan SEI)				5.57*
High Rank	243	51.95	21.18	
Medium Rank	151	56.11	17.31	
Low Rank	106	42.34	28.75	
Motivation to Succeed ("Hunger")				1.159
High Rank	222	3.60	2.25	
Medium Rank	127	3.61	1.91	
Low Rank	76	3.88	1.51	

* $p = < .05$.
** $p = < .01$.
*** $p = < .001$.

and marital status. Black men and married graduate students have significantly higher mean scores on our index of quality than do women and single respondents (see Table 10.1). Married students can devote more time to their studies without spending inordinate energies directed toward their social lives. Also, in a marriage, a spouse can help share certain responsibilities (including financial support), thus freeing up more time for the pursuit of studies. But for Black women, marriage seems to have the opposite effect. Marriage ties Black women to domestic duties and this appears to detract from their academic pursuits.

From this examination of the data, it is clear that quality Black graduate students are found not only in the highest ranked institutions. Indeed, better predictors of student quality are gender and marital status!

Background Differences

Implicit in the academic search process is the assumption that the best and brightest students attend the best universities and become the best Black Ph.D.s. This assumes that the educational-attainment process for Blacks in academia is similar to that for whites. The evidence regarding white students reveals a strong relationship among family background, academic achievement, and the prestige of the university (Gottfredson 1981). Thus, the better white students are likely to come from more privileged backgrounds and attend better graduate schools. Can we find evidence of this educational-attainment process in our sample of Black graduate students? If the same social forces are at work, we should find the very best Black graduate scholars come from more affluent families and are trained at the elite universities. But this is not the case.

Among Black students, the educational and occupational backgrounds of parents can be quite diverse, and the analyses reveal that parental background is not related to the rank of the school students attend (see Table 10.1). For example, the mean educational level of mothers and fathers of Black graduate students from the highest and lowest ranked graduate departments are almost identical. As Table 10.1 indicates, those who attend the middle-level ranked schools appear to come from social backgrounds where parents are less educated and held lower status jobs than do students from both the lower and higher ranked schools.

Black graduate students from all social backgrounds appear to attend a variety of graduate schools. This may be because the paths to graduate school that Blacks take differ drastically from those traditionally associated with white males. Black students do not necessarily take the traditional route of four years of baccalaureate work and then directly enter graduate school. The work experiences of graduate students in our sample illustrate this pattern. Students from the lowest ranked schools both worked at significantly earlier ages and held significantly less prestigious first jobs than did students from either middle- or top-ranked schools (Table 10.1). But these facts do not seem to affect their quality rankings. What becomes increasingly clear is that differences among Black students in terms of our measure of faculty potential—the quality index score—are not linked to the institutions in which they received their graduate training.

Motivational Differences

Inherent in the "quality rises to the top" argument is the assumption that students at elite institutions see themselves as the best, are the most highly motivated and, therefore, aspire to higher accomplishments in their chosen fields. To see if this difference is found among graduate students in our sample we examine an item related to this theme. Students were asked the following question:

> After you are in the profession which will be your life's work, when do you think you will be able to consider yourself successful enough so that you can relax and stop trying so hard to get ahead?

Students could respond to one of five categories which ranged from "When you are . . . doing well enough to stay in the profession" (scored 1) to "When you are . . . recognized as one of the top persons in the profession" (scored 5).

We descriptively label this the "hunger for success" question: how motivated are these students to achieve at the highest levels possible? According to assumptions inherent in how graduate students are evaluated for jobs in the market today, the "hungriest" students are thought to be found among those at the most elite institutions.

The data demonstrate that, for our sample, those students from the most elite or prestigious graduate programs are no more likely to be "hungry" for success in their chosen fields than those from less prestigious universities. While the differences are not statistically significant, those students from the least highly ranked schools have higher mean "hunger" scores (3.88) than those at the most highly ranked (3.60). Once again, there is no evidence to support the notion that Black academic resources, in the form of highly motivated graduate students, are found exclusively in a narrow group of elite universities (see Table 10.1).

As a final examination of the "quality rises to the top" thesis we examine the quality differences among Black graduate students in our three ranks of universities in a more complex fashion. We explore the differences in quality index scores by university rank, while we control for social structural and individual factors that typically influence academic performance.

TABLE 10.2

Analysis of Covariance Models Predicting Mean Scores on the Student Quality Index
for the Three Ranks of Schools

Source of Variation	*Analysis of Variance (N=395)*			
	Degrees of Freedom	*Sum of Squares*	*Mean Square*	*F*
Between Means	2	19.79		
Covariates	5	100.44	20.08	4.32***
Error	388	1803.90	4.64	
Regression	5	103.97		
Equal Adjusted Means	2	16.27	8.13	1.74
Error	388	1803.90	4.65	
Overall Regression	5	103.97		
Equal Regressions	12	77.61	6.46	1.40
Equal Adj Means	2	16.27		
Equal Slopes	10	61.35	6.13	1.30
Error (Each Regr)	378	1742.60	4.61	
Total	395	1924.20		

Coefficients for Covariate				
Covariates	*Coefficient*			
Sex	−.579**			
Marital Status	.299			
Children	.172			
Hunger for Success	−.275***			
Year in Program	−.067			

**Significant at < .01.
***Significant at < .001.

Using an analysis of covariance models, we examine graduate student differences in quality index score controlling for gender, marital status, the presence of children in the home, the degree to which students express "hunger for achievement," and, finally, their year in the program.

As Table 10.2 indicates, once we control for these factors the difference among quality index means is still not significant. However, the covariates taken together explain some of the differences we observe. Thus, we note that gender and the motivational variable of "hunger" are significant covariates. We conclude, therefore, that any significant difference in the academic quality scores of individuals is associated with factors like their gender, marital status, and motivation, and not the graduate schools which they attend.

SUMMARY, CONCLUSIONS AND POLICY IMPLICATIONS

This study attempted to demonstrate that biases which are inherent in the traditional search process in academic hiring serve to exclude rather than include minorities, particularly African Americans. After reviewing the history of Blacks in higher education, we examined the rise of affirmative action and how it affected a previously openly racist and exclusionary process.

However, affirmative action in itself has limits, since greater numbers of minority faculty are not the direct goal. Rather, the opening up of the process by widely advertising positions and expressing the nondiscriminatory intention of employers became the "be-all" and "end-all" in evaluating the effectiveness of affirmative action. In addition, affirmative action cannot deal with the lack of a sufficiently large pool of qualified African American applicants. But even given these limitations, we argue that the way in which candidates are identified, screened, and selected biases against the probability that Blacks will find their way into the final categories of the process and ultimately be hired.

The emphasis on an ill-defined and ambiguous notion of merit tends to create a situation where faculty rely, by default, on so-called "proven categories of evaluation", namely candidate's graduation from a leading school and department, and recommendations from prestigious, influential, and well-known scholars. Yet these allegedly proven categories of evaluation are actually indirect evaluations of candidates. The individual candidate is not at issue; rather it is the schools and reputations of the referees used as proxies for the merit of the candidate. To the degree that minorities are found less often at top institutions, and to the degree that they are left out of prestigious patronage networks, then "the institution as proxy" process will tend to exclude perfectly qualified African American candidates. The cry often heard in faculty search committees that qualified minorities cannot be found is one that should be amended to "properly sponsored and credentialed" minority Ph.D.s cannot be found.

Implicit in such a model is what we term the demographic fallacy of the Black academic. By this we refer to the prevailing assumption that Black academic human resources are to be searched for and can only be found in a few elite institutions of higher education. Those not present in these types of schools are deemed not qualified. The assumption that "quality rises to the top" may reflect some truth in the case of nonminority male students, but for Blacks and other minorities who continue to confront barriers to obtaining the prerequisites for higher education—and higher education itself—such an assumption is fallacious. Thus, well qualified minorities—because of family obligations, financial need, hostile social and racial climates on elite campuses, inadequate social and psychological support systems at the leading schools, or limited knowledge about the prestige of various institutions—may enroll in a wide variety of schools rather than follow the traditional white male path to the elite universities.

Using the National Study of Black College Students data, we examined underlying assumptions of the demographic fallacy—that African American graduate students from elite schools would be advantaged over those in lesser ranked universities in terms of quality, social background, and motivation. Using a performance-based model of quality, our data show that there are minimal differences in the quality of students from elite and lesser ranked institutions in our sample.

While these findings are clear, there are certain limitations inherent in the NSBCS that make a definitive test of the "demographic fallacy of the Black academic" difficult. For example, we would like to be able to compare students across disciplines as we are well-aware that some disciplines can be more affected by the institutional resources that students have available to them than can others. Realistically, universities with well-funded labs or research projects can be expected to provide a level of training not available in less-funded and less-prestigious universities. Our data do not permit us to make these comparisons. However, even though these data are limited and our conclusions tentative, it is worthwhile to extrapolate some recruitment policy implications from our findings.

In all probability, departments will be slow to change their process of recruiting and hiring in the near future. This means that, when searches are conducted and exclusion begins, minority candidates will most likely not reach the final stages. Currently, the only time that minority candidates are in an advantageous position is when searches are structured specifically to obtain a minority candidate—as when subject matter itself is "Black " (as in Black Studies) or when universities are under pressure to hire minorities. Our analysis suggests, however, that one strategy universities can use to successfully reconcile commitments to equity and merit is to expand the pool of universities from which credible candidates are recruited. This may require keeping an outstanding minority candidate in the running longer than normal, although this candidate may have attended a nonelite school.

While this will not necessarily ensure that minority candidates will be hired, it will provide them the opportunity of a closer evaluation without being subjected to a perfunctory rejection on the basis of what school they attended. This policy will benefit graduate faculties as well. To the degree that a department gains a reputation as one that seriously examines the merit of minority applicants, even when they are not graduates of elite institutions, the more likely is it that such departments will generate more applications from minorities who see the position as a real possibility rather than a "wired" job.

Another strategy that can take advantage of the Black academic resources found in nonelite universities could be their more intensive use of postdoctoral training programs as a recruitment strategy. These programs should be designed to provide African American scholars with some of the resources to which they allegedly had little access in their less-prestigious graduate training. Minority Ph.D.s can then become stronger candidates for positions at the university where they have taken their postdoctoral training or in the job market in general. In this way, universities can assess for themselves whether a candidate from a lesser ranked school has the abilities, aptitude, and skills necessary to contribute to the discipline at the highest levels of scholarship.

It is our contention that African American academic talent is not demographically isolated, but rather broadly dispersed throughout institutions of higher education. The overriding issue at stake here is the continuation of institutional racism inherent in the faculty recruitment and search process. Since access to eminent scholars and elite universities whose reputations, in turn, attract the interest of search committees is not yet free from the fetters of discrimination, reliance on these criteria as the litmus test of merit for Black scholars is essentially a racist practice. So long as sponsored mobility and attendance at premiere institutions of higher education remain proxies for individual quality, the underutilization of minority talent will continue. The proper utilization of Black academic resources requires a recognition of this fact.

WESTINA MATTHEWS
KENNETH W. JACKSON

Chapter Eleven

Determinants of Success for Black Males and Females in Graduate and Professional Schools

INTRODUCTION

While blacks have increased their share of the college-age population (eighteen to twenty-four) they have gained no ground as a proportion of those enrolled in or graduating from colleges. The proportion of Black high-school graduates going on to college dropped by 11 percent between 1975 and 1981. Also, there has been registered a decreasing proportional share of enrollments at all postsecondary levels since 1976.

Examination of the data over the past decade will also reveal that Blacks have experienced losses in their proportional share of degrees earned (American Association of State Colleges and Universities 1985). This is especially true at the postgraduate level. Of the 31,190 doctoral degrees conferred in 1982–83 across all fields (not including professional degrees such as M.D., D.D.M.D., or D.D.S.) Blacks represented only one thousand.

There is a somewhat different picture presented for professional degrees. Between 1976 and 1982, Blacks registered a slight increase from 4.5 percent to 4.6 percent in professional degree recipients. Based on evidence presented by Blackwell (1981), one might speculate that this slight increase is a function of increased female enrollment and subsequent graduation from professional schools. Indeed, during 1982–83, female degree recipients

197

reached an all-time high in percentage of total Black degrees as well as in numbers awarded (34 percent and 10,845, respectively). Nevertheless, when compared to their proportion of the college-age population that would normally graduate, females are still largely underrepresented.

For those who do graduate, the situation appears to be somewhat traditional. Women continue to be concentrated in education and in the arts and humanities (National Research Council 1984), even though Blackwell (1981) has indicated that women are beginning to enroll and graduate from professional schools in much greater numbers. Thus, in a general sense, the educational situation has not altered over the past decade. However, in accordance with the findings of the American Council on Education (1984), evidence indicates that the increased enrollment and graduation of Black women is primarily responsible for the few areas of higher education where gains or steady growth have occurred for Blacks as a whole.

There has been very little research that directs its attention primarily to Black women in higher education, especially at the postgraduate level; and certainly, little has been published in the last few years. There is even less evidence directed toward identification of those critical factors that are responsible for success among this population. What *does* exist is primarily of the descriptive variety—such as enrollment trends, graduation rates, or group differences. The study by Blackwell (1981) is a definitive example of this type of research. Blackwell examines each of the above areas (enrollment trends, graduation rates, and the like) for both graduate and professional schools. And, although the information presented is quite informative with respect to changes in enrollment patterns and graduation rates, it is only speculative in terms of identifying those factors that contribute to outcomes such as increased female graduation or access to nontraditional fields. The work of Anderson (1984) on the production of Black Ph.D.s is another example of descriptive studies of Black women in higher education.

The studies by Fleming (1984), Miller and O'Connor (1969), and Hedegard and Brown (1969) go beyond the merely descriptive accounts. Although they, too, are quite informative—especially in terms of causal factors—these studies suffer from the limitation of an exclusive focus on undergraduate populations.

The Fleming (1984) study consists of a sample of 874 undergraduate students at seven major universities. Her efforts centered primarily around the effects of social-psychological factors on student success. One of the more significant findings was that similar educational environments tended to have different effects on males and females. That is, in both Black and white environments, measures of stress, satisfaction, motivation, and achievement orientation all tended to function somewhat differently for males and females. Hedegard and Brown (1969), examining Black students enrolled in a predominantly white environment, found similar results.

Miller and O'Connor (1969), focusing more on traditional educational indicators, found significant male/female differences in terms of important determinants of success. Specifically, they found that high-school percentile rank and SAT scores were quite insignificant with respect to grades and retention for males, while SAT scores were rather significant predictors of grades for females. Additionally, the researchers were unable to determine any significant determinants of retention for males, while finding that a scale of achiever personality predicted female retention quite well.

Considering both the descriptive as well as inferential assessments of Black postsecondary success, it may be concluded with a fairly high degree of confidence that the mechanism by which success is generated is different for males and females, at least at the undergraduate level. Data on this point relating to the graduate and professional school experience is a bit more speculative.

In fact, a cursory review of data taken from the National Study of Black College Students reveals only minor differences in the characteristics of males and females at the postgraduate levels of graduate and professional schools. All students, regardless of the type of postgraduate setting, tended to come from fairly stable homes. About 50 percent of their fathers and mothers had also earned at least a bachelor's degree.

For the graduate students, there were only minor differences in fathers' and mothers' higher education, with 16 percent of males' parents and 23 percent of females' parents holding B.A. degrees. However, at the professional level, the fathers of Black males (19 percent) were more likely to have earned a professional degree than were the fathers of Black females (10 percent). This difference narrowed for mothers with professional degrees (15 percent of the Black males' mothers, and 12 percent of Black females' mothers).

About 60 percent of the males and 75 percent of the females, in both graduate and professional schools, were single. About one-third of the black males' and one-fourth of the Black females' parents' income was below $8,000. In fact, over 70 percent of the students reported that their parents' income was less than $25,000, and only about 7 percent reported incomes of more than $50,000.

Thus, from these preliminary observations, one could assume that there are few gender-related differences in factors that influence the academic performance and retention of Black graduate and professional students. Nevertheless, based on research at the undergraduate level, as well as cursory evidence of student outcomes at the postgraduate level provided in the works of Blackwell (1981) and Anderson (1984), we can speculate that there are important differences by gender in the mechanism of generating success. It is to an examination of these expected differences that this study is directed.

METHODOLOGY

Information for this analysis is taken from the National Study of Black College Students. It includes data on Black males and Black females enrolled in seven predominantly white graduate and professional school programs. The sample is composed of 152 males (63 graduate and 89 professional) and 229 females (80 graduate and 149 professional).

As we have conceived the process, success is primarily a function of background factors, institutional/structural factors, and social-psychological factors. We have further subdivided background factors along two subdimensions and institutional/structural factors along three subdimensions.

For *background* we have two sets of variables: personal characteristics and family characteristics. The *personal characteristics* are represented by two indicators: respondents' age in terms of years (AGE), and whether respondent is married or not (MARRY). The MARRY variable is coded O if the respondent is single, separated, divorced, or widowed, and coded 1 if the respondent is married. The *family background* group has five indicators. They are father's education and mother's education, measured as a seven-category variable ranging from a low of one-to-eight years to a high of PH.D., J.D., or M.D.: Father's occupation and mother's occupation are measured in terms of Duncan SEI occupational prestige scores, ranging from lowest (1) to highest (2). Parental income is measured as a sixteen-category variable, ranging from a low of less than $8,000 to a high of more than $150,000 in annual earnings.

The *institutional/structural* component has three sets of variables. For the first, *institutional characteristics,* we have two indicators: respondents' undergraduate grade-point average measured along the standard four-point scale, and the percentage of Black enrollment at their undergraduate institutions. This latter variable is measured as a six-category variable, ranging from a low "of less than 10 percent" to a high "of greater than 81 percent." *Scholarly activity* is the second subdimension, and is represented by four indicators. They are: the number of times a paper has been presented at a conference, and the number of times a paper has been published; the number of times a paper has been coauthored; and the number of times a project has been funded. Each of these indicators are measured in terms of the actual number of occurrences. *Financial aid* represents the final subdimension and has a total of six indicators. They are: the amount of funds received via each of the following sources: grant, loan, fellowship, teacher assistantship, research assistantship and work-study.

Each of these factors are measured as an eight-category variable ranging from a low of "no funds" to a high of "$6,000 and above."

For the *social-psychological* dimension, we employ one indicator—a measure of self esteem. It is a four-category ordinal type variable that asks "If you were compared to most other students at this university, how would you be rated on the following points by an unbiased observer?" The categories ranged from 1 (high) to 4 (below average).

As *success outcomes*, we employ two indicators. The rationale here is to be as inclusive as possible in terms of understanding the generation of success. Separate equations are estimated for each dependent variable with comparisons being made across these equations in an effort to determine consistency. The first dependent measure is the respondent's graduate grade-point average (GGPA), measured along the standard four-point scale. The second is a measure of retention which asks whether the respondent plans to return to his present institution (RETURN). This particular measure is a six-category variable ranging from a high of "definitely will" to a low of "definitely will not return." Additionally, the analysis is stratified by whether the postgraduate program is a graduate and professional school. It is our basic belief that the criteria for success may be quite different in these two academic environments. As a result, we propose to estimate each separately.

RESULTS

Professional Schools

In Table 11.1, the means and standard deviations for males and females enrolled in professional schools are presented. An examination of this table is consistent with the preliminary observations cited earlier. We find that the characteristics of males and females enrolled in these postgraduate programs are quite similar. From among those postulated as being important to the postgraduate experience only four factors were found to have significant differences:

1. Whether or not the respondent was married;
2. The respondents' GPAs;
3. The number of times the respondent has presented a conference paper; and,
4. Whether the respondent planned to return to the program.

TABLE 11.1
Means by Gender and Program Status

Variables	Professional School		Graduate School	
	Males	Females	Males	Females
Age	30.57	30.04	29.19	29.81
Marital Status	.36	.20**	.37	.27
(1=Married)				
Father's Education	3.43	2.99	3.05	3.23
Mother's Education	3.45	3.48	3.50	3.46
Mother's Occupation	31.67	35.57	32.52	32.68
Father's Occupation	37.10	31.10	38.59	37.81
Parents' Income	5.79	5.81	5.62	6.46
Undergraduate GPA	3.03	3.03	3.07	3.16
Graduate GPA	3.12	3.26*	3.30	3.37
Percentage of Blacks at UG Instn.	2.54	2.67	2.97	3.44
Conference Papers	1.74	.73*	1.66	1.24
Publications	.26	.08	.09	.12
Coauthorship of Papers	.09	.05	.11	.07
Funded Projects	.06	.07	.15	.11
Grant	.76	1.04	.75	.78
Loan	1.85	2.08	.89	.93
Fellowship	1.73	1.27	2.20	1.95
Teacher Assistantship	.13	.14	.31	.12
Work-Study	.13	.16	.45	.06*
Self-Esteem	1.91	1.93	.26	.11
Return	4.49	4.14*	2.00	1.91

*Indicates two-tailed difference in means test where $p < .05$.
**Indicates difference in means test where $p < .01$.

We found that males were more likely to indicate that they would return to the program. Females, on the other hand, tended to have higher graduate GPAs.

Of these four factors, two were what we have identified as outcome measures, the respondents' graduate GPAs, and whether the respondent will return to the program. In an empirical sense, this merely adds credence to the conclusion that the characteristics of males and females enrolled in professional schools are not fundamentally different. On the other hand, it also implies that males and females tend to have different experiences within these contexts and as the dynamics of the educational process are played out. That is, it appears as if the mechanism by which outcomes are generated is different for males and females. Table 11.2 presents evidence relating directly to this issue. Here, regression estimates were obtained for the two outcome measures: graduate GPA (GGPA), and whether the respondent would return to the program or not (RETURN). Table 11.2 presents these estimates for females and males.

TABLE 11.2
Linear Probability Model (students in professional school) Dependent Variables:
GGPA and RETURN

	Females				Males			
	GGPA		Return		GGPA		Return	
Variables	beta	se	beta	se	beta	se	beta	se
Age	.01	.02	.00	.02	.02	.01	.00	.02
Marital Status	.21*	.10	.17	.33	.07	.13	.19	.33
Father's Education	.06	.04	−.15	.13	−.05	.06	−.04	.14
Mother's Education	−.02	.04	−.12	.14	.02	.06	.13	.14
Mother's Occupation	.00	.00	.00	.00	.00	.00	.00	.00
Father's Occupation	.00	.00	.00	.00	.01**	.00	.00	.00
Parents' Income	−.01	.01	.11	.05	−.03	.02	.03	.05
Undergraduate GPA	.09	.10	−.28	.31	.11	.15	.50	.37
Graduate GPA			.35	.32			−.02	.35
Percentage Blacks	−.01	.02	−.14*	.07	.03	.03	−.11	.08
Conference Papers	.01	.02	.15*	.08	.01	.01	.02	.04
Publications	.19	.11	.38	.35	.03	.08	−.06	.20
Coauthorship	.16	.17	−.01	.54	−.28	.15	.31	.38
Funded Projects	.07	.12	.08	.36	.14	.28	−.22	.70
Grant	.00	.02	.00	.06	−.05	.03	.02	.08
Loan	−.03*	.02	.17**	.05	−.02	.02	.00	.06
Fellowship	.01	.02	.05	.05	.00	.02	−.02	.05
Teaching Assistantship	.02	.07	−.58**	.21	.07	.07	.16	.17
Research Assistantship	.05	.05	−.16	.14	.14*	.07	.05	.18
Work-Study	.09	.55	.07	.18	.15	.10	.00	.26
Self-Esteem	.00	.55	−.11	.18	−.07	.09	−.02	.23
R^2	.26		.41		.37		.23	

*Indicates two-tailed difference in means test where $p < .05$.
**Indicates difference in means test where $p < .01$.

An examination of Table 11.2 reveals that, for females, our model is capable of accounting for approximately 25 percent of the variance in academic performance and 37 percent for continuation in the program. For academic performance, we find that age, marital status, and the amount of financial aid received via loans were significant determinants. Two of these determinants were personal background factors (such as age and marital status), thereby implying that the more-successful female, at least in terms of grades, is the more-mature and married individual.

Findings for the other significant factor—amount of financial aid received from loans—are rather puzzling. Results indicate that, as loan aid increases, females tend to have lower GPAs. It may be that those females who rely on loans are not of the same academic quality as are those who are successfully able to compete for grants, fellowships, assistantships, and the like—assuming that females have equal access to meritorious support.

As a result, the indicator itself would be a proxy for past academic achievements rather than an indicator of how financial considerations impact success.

On the other hand, the results for the amount of financial aid received via loans could simply be a methodological artifact of a poorly specified model. Note that we were able to account for only 26 percent of the variance in this estimation with only three variables proving to be significant. Additionally, of the three that were significant, none had a significance level beyond the .05 level. Obviously, there are other more important factors that influence females' GGPAs in professional schools which are not specified here. Thus, conclusions regarding this outcome are tenuous.

For retention (RETURN), we do a much better job of understanding the generating mechanism (Table 11.2). There were a total of five significant determinants:

1. Parental income,
2. Percent of blacks in undergraduate institutions,
3. Number of times that respondent presented a conference paper,
4. The amount of aid received via loans, and
5. The amount of aid received via teacher assistantships.

Of the five, three were related in some way to financial resources through parental income, the amount of aid from loans, the amount of aid from teacher assistantships and the like. Both amount of aid from loans and from teacher assistantships were significant at the .01 level. These findings imply that female retention in professional schools is more a function of financial exigencies than of any other factor or group of factors postulated here. Additionally, given the much better fit of the model, we can also conclude that finances are among the more critical determinants of retention, even assuming that some as yet unidentified dimension exists (as was evident from the estimation of GGPA).

Thus, in an overall sense, we find that the traditional criteria used to estimate attainments do a rather poor job of estimating female grade-point averages in professional schools. We do have tentative evidence which indicates that personal background factors are among the more critical determinants of this outcome. These factors were not relevant in terms of retention. Here, we found that factors relating to financial resources proved to be quite dominant. We had much more confidence in this estimation using traditional criteria than we had for grades. As a result, we are quite confident that retention and academic performance are generated differently. We cannot say exactly how, but we can conclude that academic performance is not a function of financial resources while retention is.

TABLE 11.3
Linear Probability Model (students in graduate school) Dependent Variables:
GGPA and RETURN

					Dependent			
		GGPA				Return		
	Females		Males		Females		Males	
Variables	beta	se	beta	se	beta	se	beta	se
Age	.01	.01	−.02	.03	.03**	.10	.07	.04
Marital Status	−.25	.12	.58	.49	.11	.14	−.18	.55
Father's Ed	.02	.04	−.25	.17	.03	.05	.06	.18
Mother's Ed	.05	.05	.30	.22	.06	.06	−.04	.22
Mother's Occ	.00	.00	.00	.00	.00	.00	.00	.00
Father's Occ	.00	.00	.00	.00	.00	.00	.00	.00
Parents' Income	−.02	.02	−.06	.07	−.01	.02	.07	.08
Undergraduate GPA	.15	.12	−.07	.51	.51**	.14	−.36	.65
Graduate GPA	—	—	.35	.00	—	—	−.78	.70
Percentage of Blacks	.00	.02	.04	.10	−.08	.03	.00	.13
Conference Papers	.10	.10	−.02	.04	.01	.02	−.08	.07
Publications	.04	.12	.30	.48	.05	.16	1.04	.99
Coauthorship	.08	.13	−.97	.55	.13	.16	−.39	.60
Funded Projects	.07	.10	.27	.43	.21	.11	−.15	.46
Grant	.02	.03	.02	.11	.02	.03	−.10	.10
Loan	−.02	.03	.04	.10	.02	.03	.16	.11
Fellowship	−.00	.02	−.05	.07	.03	.02	−.05	.09
Teaching Assistantship	.17	.09	.42	.35	−.05	.05	−.06	.20
Research Assistantship	.00	.00	−.50	.38	.02	.04	.04	.14
Work-Study	.02	.07	.16	.28	.01	.06	.08	.22
Self-Esteem	−.07	.08	−.07	.31	.00	.10	−.31	.38
R-Square	.28		.51		.30		.38	

* $p < .05$.
** $p < .01$.

If we compare these results we find that our model is even less effective in modeling the process for males than it was for female grades (Table 11.2). For male grades, even though we obtained an R^2 of 41 percent, only two factors emerged as significant determinants of this outcome (father's occupation, and financial aid or research assistantship). This implies rather serious specification problems for this particular outcome. The situation is not improved when we consider explanations of male retention (RETURN). In fact, in a relative sense, we do better for male academic performance than we do for male retention, which was just the opposite of what we found for females.

This indicates that the model proposed here works moderately well in terms of explaining retention for females, but is quite inappropriate for males, either in terms of GGPA or retention. What we can discern from this is that male processes are quite different from female processes, especially with respect to retention in professional schools. It is not possible to definitively state whether a similar situation exists in terms of GGPA. However, given the moderately poor fit for females as compared to the extremely poor fit for males, we might speculate that the mechanism that generates the GGPA academic performance is different as well.

Graduate School

Turning attention to the graduate school context, (Table 11.3), we find that the characteristics of males and females are more similar than in professional school context. As a matter of fact, there was only one factor that emerged as statistically different for the two groups—the amount of aid received from research assistantships. It was found that males had tended to receive more funds from research assistantships than did females, thereby implying that males were more likely to do research in a structured setting with some sense of institutional guidance than were females. This aside, all other differences, including outcome differences, were not statistically different.

When regression estimates were computed for the outcome measure we found that the model specification worked only fairly well for male academic performance (see Table 11.3). For females, the situation was quite similar to that of males in professional school. These traditional criteria were incapable of accounting for any significant portions of the variation in either outcome measure. We can conclude then that academic performance and retention for females in graduate school is contingent on nontraditional criteria or, more appropriately, factors that are not normally found in attainment models of the sort employed here.

For males (Table 11.3), we have a situation similar to that for females in professional school. The traditional specification has a tendency to work fairly well for one outcome measure while functioning less adequately for the other. In this case, however, the best fit was for grades rather than retention, as it was for females in professional schools. Specifically, we found that three factors emerged as significant predictors of males' GGPAs, with two of those factors (age and undergraduate GPA) being significant at the .01 level. Two of the three factors (undergraduate GPA and percentage of Black enrollment at undergraduate institutions) were institutional type factors—implying the dominance of this subdimension. As undergraduate GPA went up, graduate GPA also had a tendency to rise. Similarly, the smaller the proportion of Blacks at the undergraduate institution, the higher the graduate GPA.

Such findings shed very little light on the graduate school experiences of females, other than it differs substantially from males in terms of academic performance. We can further speculate that the difference is in terms of the generating mechanism as opposed to differences in the characteristics of males and females. Such speculative conclusions can not be made about retention in that the model did not fit well for either males or females.

CONCLUSION

Our findings indicate that, in both graduate and professional schools, males and females are quite similar in their characteristics. That is, there does not appear to be any substantial differences between the types of males and the types of females enrolled in these two postgraduate settings. We did find, however, that, in the professional schools, males and females exhibit significant differences in the outcome measures employed in this analysis. This finding added considerable credence to our contention that outcomes are generated differently for males and females. Such findings were not evident in the graduate schools. Here, males and females exhibited similar characteristics, even in terms of outcomes.

The results of our descriptive analysis also implied a significant difference across educational contexts. Such a conclusion was supported in part by the results of our attempts to model postgraduate academic performance and retention. We found that the traditional attainment models used to estimate outcomes had varying degrees of success depending on which group was considered and in what context.

We were able to explain substantial portions of the variance in retention for females in professional school. Similarly, we were able to account for a modest proportion of the variance in GGPA for males in graduate school. That is, traditional criteria carry considerably more weight in the professional context for females than it does for females in the graduate context, but only with respect to retention. Specifically, we found that financial resources were the most dominant predictors of female retention in professional school. A similar pattern holds for males in the graduate context, as opposed to males in the professional context, but only with respect to grades. Here, we found that institutional characteristics were, by far, the stronger of the determinants of academic performance in graduate school.

We suspect that our inability to model the female graduate school experience, as well as the male professional school experience, may have a lot to do with some missing dimension which is not traditionally included in such models of educational outcomes. The missing dimension could very well be of a more social nature having to do with feelings of alienation, perceptions of progress, and the existence of mentors. Such factors have proved to be quite successful in helping explain outcome variation for

Blacks at the undergraduate level. It may be that such factors are quite crucial at the postgraduate level as well.

In an overall sense, then, we must conclude that females have different experiences from males in both graduate and professional school—different experiences in the sense that factors tend to influence outcomes in different ways for the two groups. We must go on to say that these conclusions are tentative at best, owing to a better specification of the educational outcome model for males in professional schools and females in graduate schools. Suffice it to say here, that educational outcomes for males in professional schools and females in graduate schools are more significantly affected by nontraditional criteria than are their counterparts in the same settings.

Part Four

Practical Issues in the Higher Education of Black Americans

The practical issues arising from the experiences, status, and outcomes of Black students in U.S. higher education are considered in this section. The earlier papers in this book identified important factors which contribute to the welfare of Black college students. At this juncture it is appropriate to consider solutions to these problems, and to ask what are effective strategies for improving African American access and success in U.S. higher education.

Hare opens this discussion with an insightful examination of the educational philosophy underlying the use of school desegregation as a tactic to achieve educational equity for African Americans. He offers an analysis of and prescription for the creation of effective schools in general, and for the creation of effective desegregated schools in particular. Hare's paper reminds us that racial diversity and high academic achievement are not necessarily antithetical. Instead, racial inequities in academic achievement result from inequities in educational opportunities.

Frierson recognizes the serious hurdle that standardized tests often present for African American students and outlines effective strategies for intervention. Although standardized tests are integral to the U.S. educational system, as a rule, Black students do not perform well on these tests. Frierson's paper reports on an effective intervention program which equips Black students to meet the challenge posed by standardized examinations.

Kleinsmith and Johnston address another set of barriers commonly encountered by Black students who attend college—the natural science program distribution requirement. Many a career has floundered on the shores of introductory biology or physical chemistry. Thus, the search for effective ways to equip students to successfully meet these challenges becomes critical. This paper overviews one such successful program in the form of a computer-based study center designed to overcome "fear of science" and to enhance student achievement in biology.

Nesha Haniff's Epilogue overviews the book, highlighting important findings and recurring themes. She also critiques the book, identifying topics such as gender that are not adequately considered. Haniff's commentary locates the book in a larger tradition of inquiry and challenges the field to move beyond time-worn, culturally inappropriate paradigms. She speaks of the struggle, the love, the hope, promise and frustration that shapes the African American experience. In the process she provides a larger sociohistorical and cultural context for our consideration of Black college students.

This section ends by addressing a practical matter of a different sort—the need for up-to-date source materials on the literature that considers Black students in U.S. higher education. Hall, Gooley, and Presley provide a selected annotated bibliography of important studies and sources in the area. This bibliography provides a useful survey of the literature and a starting point for students, administrators, and researchers seeking information about African American students in college.

Chapter Twelve

Toward Effective Desegregated Schools

DESEGREGATION AND EFFECTIVE EDUCATION: PROMISES AND OBSTACLES

There remains for consideration the manner in which relief is to be accorded. [Earl A. Warren, Chief Justice of the United States in delivering the opinion of the Court *Brown v. Board of Education.* 349 U.S. 294 (1954).]

As we approach 1990 and the thirty-sixth anniversary of the Brown decision, there is an understandable increase in the amount of attention being focused on the real consequences of the prolonged drive for educational equity through school desegregation. There has simultaneously been, as a consequence of concern regarding declines in national test scores and the perceived need to increase our ability to compete internationally in the emerging computer age, a recent rise in concern regarding school academic effectiveness. In fact, as we hope to illustrate, the two terms have frequently been interchanged although rarely fusioned, leading to some significant confusion about both the requirements of desegregated education and effective education.

It is the intent of this monograph to provide some clarity regarding the relationships between these two educational concerns by (a) separating and defining them, (b) indicating under what conditions they may either or both be present or absent, and (c) suggesting issues that must be addressed if either or both are to be attained. Specifically, we will concentrate on the question of desegregation as it has been assumed to—as well as it actually

211

appears to—relate to questions of school academic effectiveness; it should be emphasized that there exists more than one road to take to that end as well as positive steps that may be taken in route to effective desegregated schools.

In order to accomplish this task, we must, first, of course, define both what we mean by and what we see as the objectives of desegregation and effective education. Although a more detailed explanation of the terms will be provided later, for now, we may loosely define desegregated education as the significant mixing in schools of children and other school-system personnel of various racial, ethnic, and/or social class background. The objective of such mutual exposure, along with appropriate adjustments in the curriculum and organization of the school, might be said to be the development of what Edgar G. Epps (1974) would call "cultural pluralism," or what others (Glazer and Moynihan 1963) may have wishfully deemed a "melting pot." As will be illustrated, many people (including judges, lawyers, and researchers) further presumed that some increase in educational effectiveness would automatically occur for minorities as a consequence of desegregation.

The school effectiveness literature, on the other hand, can be said to primarily concern itself with increased academic outcomes and a decrease in the traditional attainment gaps across groups. The important point is that, in our opinion, as we will attempt to illustrate, these two events, desegregation and effective education, may or may not occur at the same time. The intent here is to engage in what we consider to be a kind of intellectual surgery that will allow us to see both of these objectives more clearly, as well as to recognize the pitfalls of failing to be able to distinguish between them as we pursue their concurrent presence.

DESEGREGATION FOR EFFECTIVE EDUCATION

The 1954 United States Supreme Court decision declaring "separate-but-equal" schooling to be inherently unequal marked a significant turning point in public education. It is important to note that the Court not only ordered desegregation with "all deliberate speed," but also concluded, for the first time, that, even if the physical facilities and other tangible factors were equalized, the segregated minorities would still be deprived of their equal education opportunities. Notably, the plaintiffs from Delaware in the Brown case had already been granted relief and ordered admitted to the white schools by the Supreme Court of Delaware on the grounds that the white schools were physically superior. That decision simply indicated that the authorities failed to make the separate systems physically equal, and left unchallenged the theoretical possibility of separate-but-equal facilities. In fact, some school systems rushed to equalize and even duplicate their segregated educational facilities in the hope of forestalling a desegregation order.

The important point here is that the 1954 Supreme Court decision was not based simply on the assumption of the existence of unequal facilities, but rather on the belief that the consequences of segregated education were detrimental, even if the facilities were equal. This is what killed the separate-but-equal doctrine established by *Plessy v. Ferguson* in 1896. One might conclude then, that academically effective education, not cultural pluralism (which is not even mentioned in the Court's opinion) was the objective of the Court's decision.

In writing the Court's opinion, Chief Justice Warren referred to the "intangibles," such as the ability to engage in exchanges and exposure, as well as to the potential psychological danger of transmitting messages of inferiority to the segregated minorities. Subsequent works on desegregation perpetuation, networking, and the advantages of early interracial exposure substantiates the concern of the court with the relationships between desegregation, effective education, and educational attainment.

Nevertheless, as we will attempt to show, the tying of desegregation to effective education and segregation to inferior education for so-called "minorities" may have created an unnecessary tolerance of mediocrity in minority-segregated school systems. In cities like New York and Chicago, for example, and in the name of waiting for desegregation, serious declines in attainment and excuses for not educating are being accepted. Conversely, prior to the rise of concern with effectiveness and knowledge of how to enhance it, we may have overestimated the degree to which desegregation can be assumed to automatically deliver effective academic education, especially when questions of school organization, curriculum, power, control, and social class characteristics are not addressed. Just as 1954 allowed the Supreme Court to see the limitations of its decision of 1896, so 1984 may have allowed us to fine tune our thinking of the events of 1954.

DESEGREGATION FOR PLURALISM

Aside from the underlying and perhaps racist assumption that desegregation would automatically upgrade the quality of the educational experience for minorities and hopefully not depreciate the educational experience of the majority, desegregation is expected to provide multicultural exposure. While the older literature optimistically suggested that such exposure would lead to an American "melting pot," time and experience have indicated that later southern European immigrants and people of color were no more likely to abandon their cultural baggage than were the proponents of the melting-pot philosophy. Perhaps that was because these groups sensed as Epps (1974) indicated, the implicit racism in a melting pot philosophy which assumes Anglo-European culture to be superior. The thrust of such an educational goal is unidirectional and assumes that, if the "heathens" can be acculturated (civilized) to the Anglo-European way, then all would be well.

It is important to note that, for such a process to take place, the majority curriculum had to be taught and, of course, it helped if such children were available to provide role models. Implicitly, if not explicitly, as noted by Epps, the typical school with a melting-pot orientation required the minority children to regard their own culture as inferior and to abandon it. The degree to which this "civilizing" function had been ingrained among some members of minority groups themselves was expressed in the willingness of Booker T. Washington, as indicated in *Up from Slavery* (1970: 67), to civilize American Indians.

Having theoretically experienced the process at Hampton Institute, Washington indicates that he and General Armstrong, his mentor, went out west to bring back one hundred of the most "perfectly ignorant" Indians they could find, so that the Black students at Hampton could civilize them similarly. Ultimately, as indicated by Glazer and Moynihan (1963: 290), although the idea of the melting pot is as old as the republic, "the point about the melting pot is that it did not happen." As Kopan (1974) suggests, the schools did acculturate and Americanize but not melt.

Desegregation for pluralism, on the other hand, advocates a pluralistic concept of equality and stresses respect for diversity in cultural patterns and learning styles in America. As defined by Epps (1974: 178), "cultural pluralism involves the mutual exchange of cultural content and respect for different views of reality and conceptions of man." It is worth noting that, although the courts cannot and will not mandate desegregation for pluralism, desegregation nevertheless creates circumstances in which questions of pluralism and melting-pot philosophy must be addressed. The consequence of failing to take such questions into account will produce a significant liability within the asset of desegregation. As Epps (1974: 178) warns, " . . . if the integrated school does not accept the basic premise of the pluralistic position and provide opportunities for cultural exchange and the development of respect for cultural and racial diversity, the educational benefits may be achieved at considerable psychic cost to individual students."

EFFECTIVE EDUCATION FOR ACADEMIC ACHIEVEMENT

There has, of late, been a renewed outcry regarding the quality of the education black American children are experiencing. Just as the technological advances that allowed the Soviet Union to place Sputnik in space in the 1950s produced a great uproar and review of our educational policies, so the emerging computer age and fears of America being left behind have reemerged in the 1980s.

Furthermore, facilitated by slight national declines in standardized achievement test scores, there has been a significant increase in debate and research regarding what constitutes an effective education and what practices and structural characteristics are common to effective schools. Just as scholars have begun to systematically study what makes schools work better—aside from questions of desegregation—so commensurately some "minority" educators, tiring of the wait for school desegregation, have begun to ask how the schools in which minority and poor youngsters currently exist can be made more academically effective—questions of desegregation aside. The consequence, on both sides then, is a growth in the literature which looks explicitly at the ways in which schools can be organized to generally raise standards of performance on the one hand, and decrease the size of historically produced performance gaps between groups on the other hand.

More detailed attention will be paid to the promising specifics of recent research findings in this area, including through the works of Michael Cohen (in press), Robert Slavin (1983), Elizabeth Cohen (1980), Willis Hawley (1982), Ron Edmonds (1979), and Stewart Purkey and Marshall Smith (forthcoming), among others.

This work is promising on two important planes. First, it raises new questions about organization of schools and classrooms, and their implications for attainment. Second, it suggests that there are possible "universal" strategies that can be applied to *any* school to elevate the level of attainment, whether such schools are desegregated or not. In fact, it is this new literature which most clearly suggests the need to clarify the relationship between desegregation and effective education.

Hawley (1982: 1) for example, suggests that, since homogeneous populations are easier to treat, "desegregation renders effective education more difficult" in some instances. It is also worth noting that it was—and still is—assumed that segregated majority schools can deliver an academically effective education, while it has also been assumed that segregated minority schools cannot.

The promise of this new knowledge is in demonstrating that neither premise is necessarily true, and that there do exist pragmatic steps that can be taken in *any* school to increase academic effectiveness, even en route to the ideal goal of academically effective pluralistic education.

EFFECTIVE SCHOOLS FOR DESEGREGATION

The idea that the goal of desegregation might be more easily realized if the schools were made more academically effective and therefore attractive was one of the more romantic notions to emerge in the 1960s. While it is true that specialized schools—such as a High School for Music and Art, or a Bronx High School of Science—would remain attractive to white students despite a sprinkling of small numbers of Blacks who could pass the test and gain admission, it is unlikely that such schools would remain attractive, or for that matter esteemed, were large numbers of Black students to attend. Although attaining academically effective schools remains a worthwhile goals in its own right, the possibility that effectiveness will deliver a population of whites to Black school districts, for example, is probably unlikely. There have, nevertheless, been attempts to do just that.

At one point in the 1960s, for example, there was a plan to make Intermediate School 201 in Central Harlem into a magnet school. The idea was to put the latest equipment and newest programs into I.S. 201 in the hope that the quality of the school would override its location and that white parents would send their children uptown, across town, and across the Triborough Bridge to the new effective magnet school in Harlem. It did not take the planners long to realize that most white parents—and many middle-class Black parents—did not care, as some stated, "if Jesus himself were in that building." They were not sending their children to school in Harlem.

In other cities, such as Boston, for example, there has been limited success with creating effective magnet-type schools, so long as they were not located in the minority communities. The notion that making an effective school could facilitate desegregation assumes that parents hold attainment preponderant over fears of racial contamination. This notion appears true of minority parents who do and have sent their children off to predominately white schools in the hope that they be better taught. But such behavior is questionable of, and probably seems unnecessary to, most white parents.

Fear of racial contamination, for example, led some white South Bostonians to open their own schools, just as Lester Maddox closed down his restaurant rather than serve Blacks. The important point is that, while we hold that the pursuit of academic excellence is a worthwhile goal in its own right, and we recognize that no parent with good sense would send his or her child off to a school that was known to be academically ineffective, it seems unlikely that making a school effective for purposes of desegregation would work at this time, unless it is very strategically located and the "racial balance" is carefully controlled.

SEPARATING THE OBJECTIVES; DESEGREGATION AND EFFECTIVE EDUCATION

It is clear by now that effective education and desegregation are not synonymous and cannot be expected to deliver each other. It should also be clear that we have been very imprecise about these two issues and have sometimes acted as if they *would* automatically deliver each other, at least to selected groups and under selected conditions.

For example, consistent with the importance of the 1954 Court decision, we have assumed that desegregation would deliver quality education for minority youngsters who could then go from their presumed ineffective segregated schools to the presumed majority segregated effective schools. This kind of thinking precluded recognizing, for example, that, prior to desegregation, there also existed effective segregated all-Black schools as well as ineffective segregated all-white schools. We were furthermore incapable of recognizing that there could exist, heaven forbid, academically ineffective desegregated schools.

Hare et al. (1983), for example, indicated that, even in public higher education, access to predominantly white universities and success in them cannot be assumed to be synonymous for minorities. It is again worth reemphasizing that we agree wholeheartedly with a support both for the drive for desegregation and its promise of pluralism, and for the drive for academically effective schools and its promise of attainment.

Moreover, we believe in the "intangible" advantages to be offered to *all* youngsters in a multicultural effective educational setting. We merely suggest that such goals are not simultaneously accomplishable unless they are separately understood. Such an understanding not only provides clarity, but, as the following model shows, will sometimes allow necessary optional roads to the ideal type of attainment/pluralistic school, as well as an awareness of unseen pitfalls along the road.

AN ATTAINMENT/PLURALISM MODEL

If our argument is correct and the two educational concerns for academic effectiveness and desegregation can be theoretically separated, then

FIGURE 12.1
An Attainment/Pluralism Model

		Effectiveness	Ineffectiveness
Pluralism Axis	Desegregation	4	2
	Segregation	3	1

Attainment Axis

the following two-by-two model offers four possible paired school characteristics for consideration. It is our opinion that prototypes of all four boxes
have existed as illustrated in the following discussion.

The horizontal "pluralism axis" separates racially and/or ethnically
segregated from desegregated schools. The vertical "attainment axis" separates academically effective and ineffective schools.

The model offers four potential educational experiences which will be
discussed in turn: One, ineffective segregated schools, which we label "lost
and alone."; second, ineffective desegregated schools, which we call "losing together"; third, effective segregated schools, which we label "making
academic progress"; and fourth, effective desegregated schools, which we
call "hitting the mark."

Box 1. Lost and Alone: Ineffective Segregated Schools

This is the box no one wants to be in. It is characterized by an absence
of educational academic effectiveness and is simultaneously segregated. It
is distasteful to the segregationist who wants to be *taught* in a "pure" environment and to the integrationist who wants pluralism *and* effective education. It is probably the box about which the U.S. Supreme Court was
most concerned when it made its 1954 decision in favor of minority youngsters. It is important to note, however, that many majority youngsters, especially of lower class and/or rural status, also attend schools of this
characteristic.

The solution to this problem has been much more actively sought
for minority than for majority populations, who have somehow frequently

been assumed to attend effective schools simply on the basis of the color of the student population. These schools have existed in such places as Boston, where Black-segregated Roxbury and white-segregated South Boston both sent less than 10 percent of their students on to college, even prior to desegregation. They have existed in the inner cities of America where eighth-grade graduates have had reading scores as low as fourth-grade, sixth-month. Desegregation plans which have included school improvement components in such places as New Castle in Delaware, San Diego, and Boston have implicitly recognized that these schools exist.

Box 2. "Losing Together": Ineffective Desegregated Schools

While we applaud the value of intercultural and interracial exposure, we recognize, as we have continually stressed, that desegregation does not, by definition, deliver quality education. Box 2 represents the existence of desegregated schools which are educationally ineffective. For example, Judge Garrity's decision to include a "university component" as part of his desegregation plan recognized the potential for newly desegregated Roxbury and South Boston to simply move from Box 1 to Box 2 together.

There also exist many other desegregated lower- and lower-middle class school districts which, while clearly desegregated, can hardly be argued to be effective. The emerging effectiveness literature has begun to awaken scholars to the idea that schools can be desegregated and still fail to be structurally and programmatically organized to deliver effective education. The hope for these schools resides in activating school effectiveness programs.

While desegregated mutual under-attainment is egalitarian, we know of no parents, Black or white, who would trade the adequate training of their children for racial proximity. As Derrick Bell (1983: 574) points out, " . . . Black parents have sought not integrated schools but schools in which their children could receive a good education." If forced to choose then, between ineffective desegregated schools and effective segregated schools, most parents would agree with W. E. B. DuBois' position (1935) that what the children *most* need is a good education.

Box 3. Making Academic Progress: Effective Segregated Schools

Either by default, inability to obtain desegregation, or by design, these schools do exist. It has been assumed, as indicated, that all majority schools can be, and frequently are, effective although segregated, but that all minority schools are ineffective by definition. The drive for desegregation which labeled separate facilities for minorities as "inherently unequal" (even if the physical facilities were equal) implicitly led us to assume that effective education for minorities was impossible without desegregation. The result of this assumption has, furthermore, been additional tolerance of academic ineffectiveness in minority and lower-class segregated school systems, such as in New York and Chicago.

Here again, the rise in concern with school effectiveness has begun to deliver hope and rethinking of this assumption. Works by Levine and Eubanks (1983), Edmonds (1979), Hawley (1983), Chessler (1981), and Sizemore, Brossard, and Harrigan (1983), among others, have documented the conditions under which even minority segregated schools have and can attain academic effectiveness. The point here, of course, is that, while effective desegregated schools remain the ideal type, we cannot afford to, nor do we have to, wait for desegregation before we demand academic effectiveness in schools servicing minorities.

If we are capable of assuming that majority youngsters can be effectively taught in a segregated setting, we should assume that minority youngsters are capable of the same thing. Given variations in local conditions, it may be necessary to programmatically pass through Box 3 from Box 1 en route to Box 4. Such understanding of the conditions conducive to effective education, needless to say, should be applied to improving education in general and even in the segregated majority schools, since the new literature also suggests that schools can no longer be assumed automatically effective even if they are majority and/or middle-class schools.

Box 4. Hitting the Mark: Effective Desegregated Schools

This elusive and yet increasingly present setting is one in which attention to the requirements of desegregation and attainment are found. Such schools are frequently characterized by such practices as heterogeneous grouping at both the school- and classroom-levels, equal status conditions, emphasis on academic effectiveness, and a flattening of the performance differentials.

Suffice it to say that, in addition to the avoidance of school building or classroom resegregation, such schools make explicit and directed decisions regarding such issues as leadership style, teacher training, discipline, parent involvement, individualized instruction, and curriculum development, and they are attuned to issues of cultural diversity and learning-style differences.

This type of school thus provides the kind of environment that can both maximize academic attainment while simultaneously providing the kind of desegregated schooling experience that will prepare the children for a pluralistic society. We believe that this remains the ideal type of education for American children and constitutes "hitting the mark."

Moving around the Model: Promises and Pitfalls En Route to Box 4

Without going into too much detail, we would like to illustrate some possible problems and pitfalls which school systems may encounter in search of effective desegregated education. If one were to start from Box 1, ideally one might go directly to Box 4, but we believe that, in poorer school districts, examples exist of movement from Box 1 to Box 2 in such cities as Boston, although Judge Garrity hoped that his university component would eventually deliver Box 4. Thus, desegregated systems with effectiveness programs can be said to be moving from Box 2 to Box 4.

In most cases, educational achievement falls short because insufficient attention is paid to questions of effectiveness or, as previously suggested, erroneous assumptions are made about the ability of desegregation to automatically deliver effectiveness. Interestingly, community control and school improvement movements in such cities as New York, San Diego, and Atlanta could be viewed as attempts to move from Box 1 to Box 3 in the absence of faith that Box 4 was attainable in the foreseeable future.

While many majority schools were presumed to move from Box 3 to Box 4 with desegregation, some argue that many Black schools—particularly in the South where many Black teachers and administrators lost their jobs—are thought to have backslid from Box 3 to Box 2. One might argue that, in transitional communities, schools may be found to move from Box 2 to Box 3 if the class character of the neighborhood is rising, or from Box 4 to Box 3, Box 2, or even Box 1 under varying circumstances.

Finally, the negative assumption that minorities could not have effective education without desegregation has allowed many of the schools to slip from Box 3 to Box 1. While this discussion is merely suggestive, it is intended to make the reader aware of the academic ineffective pitfalls of Boxes 1 and 2 and aware of the possible necessity to move through Box 3 en route to Box 4 among minorities and schools which are currently trapped in Box 1. Again, it is worth stressing that all strategies should be directed toward the ultimate attainment of and maintenance within Box 4.

Before closing, it seems appropriate to raise concerns regarding the limitations of these concepts, given the overriding needs of the social system and the conditions under which effective education and desegregation are being sought. These issues are simply *raised*, and others are invited to treat them in greater detail in other papers.

THE LIMITATIONS OF DESEGREGATION: IT'S NOT THE BUS——IT'S US

As indicated by the works of Diana Pierce (1980; 1983) and Gary Orfield (1975), among others, a significant issue in school desegregation is housing segregation—and the major issue in housing segregation is class segregation. So long as resource allocations for schools are inequitably distributed and the courts are not allowed a "front-door approach" to class desegregation through housing desegregation, a significant amount of inequality and segregation in education is inevitable.

THE LIMITATIONS OF EFFECTIVE EDUCATION: WHO WILL CLEAN THE BATHROOMS?

Aside from important questions regarding the roles of teachers' unions and public bureaucracies in inhibiting the attainment of demands for effective education, there exists in the social system a wide structural requirement that someone "lose" in school in order that they accept and occupy low-status jobs in the social system. While we are conventionally led to believe that everyone in America begins the great quest for status wearing the same track shoes, there is sufficient evidence to suggest that such egalitarian notions are myths and distortions of fact. While people speak of high-school dropout rates, for example, few are aware that there are "eviction" rates as well (Hare 1982).

It should be noted that the school plays a unique role in allocating people to different positions in the division of labor through routing and grading practices. Relative success in school is, in fact, the major avenue through which discrimination in the job market is justified.

Given racism, sexism, and classism, in a stratified America, it can be argued that the disproportional allocation of Blacks, other people of color, women, and people of lower-class origin to the lowest labor slots is functional. Their relative academic failure is essential to getting the job done. For example, such procedures as allocating girls to home economics and sewing courses, lower-class youngsters to vocational and commercial academic tracks, and minority youngsters to slower tracks are common school practices with long-term educational and occupational implications. Thus, structured educational failure legitimizes job discrimination, while eliminating legal recourse. One cannot successfully sue an employer for failing to give him or her a desired job if one arrives at the point of application relatively unqualified.

It should be noted that such discriminatory processes do not require a conscious conspiracy to operate; rather we posit that Newton's law of inertia regarding material objects, is also applicable to notions. Setting aside the issue of origins, continuing discriminatory practices merely requires that school personnel, like any other people, act on socialized unconscious beliefs in established stereotypes, which then have the capacity to become self-fulfilling prophecies. Such a process requires intervention to stop, not to continue—particularly if it occurs consistently within the stratification needs of the social system.

Thus, educational "effectiveness" may have different meanings for different categories of people, and, at some levels, may mean effectively limiting as well as effectively enhancing. The rising concern among some conservative writers with the "over-education" of some sectors of the American population—particularly women and minorities—speaks to the premise that too much education for too many people may result in a crisis in aspiration management and the filling of all slots in the division of labor.

HENRY T. FRIERSON

Chapter Thirteen

Intervention Can Make a Difference: The Impact on Standardized Tests and Classroom Performance

For numerous reasons, the educational outcomes of postsecondary students vary widely. These differences may be related to factors involving students' aptitude, intelligence, motivation, and the quality of instruction experienced. For African American and other minority students, factors related to societal inequities may depress achievement even if aptitude, intelligence, and motivation are present. Because the effects of such factors have been continuous and cumulative, there is a compelling need for ongoing development of effective intervention methods. The intent of intervention would be to effectively address the potentially depressing effects of inequity on Black students' academic outcome.

As it is, major areas of concern for many college students are their academic achievement, as measured by grade-point averages (GPAs), and their performances on a variety of standardized tests (used as entrance examinations to graduate or professional programs or for licensure or certification purposes). For African American students in particular, these concerns are pressing, especially the issue of standardized-test performance. Because of the heavy reliance on test scores in various educational scenarios, a Black student's standardized-test performance will often take on greater importance than the evidence provided by his or her years of classroom achievement.

Indeed, many individuals who, in effect, serve as "gate keepers" for the various educationally related systems of this society appear to have the impression that, for Black students, standardized-test performances have greater validity than years of classroom achievement. Although such ideas are fallacious, in many admissions decisions that involve Black students this is, nonetheless, the guiding premise.

STANDARDIZED-TEST PERFORMANCE

In the United States, standardized tests have acquired a status of critical importance and prevail at essentially every level of formal education (Frierson 1986). Such tests are used as the instruments of gate keepers, and are thus used to allow only a certain number of individuals into various selective educational programs and/or occupations. The Medical College Admissions Test and the Legal Bar Examination, are two examples of the former and latter categories.

Most commonly employed standardized tests are norm-referenced, therefore scoring is based on how examinees perform in comparison to others taking the same test. But because of the inequities experienced by many Black and other minority students, a system based on norm-referenced standardized testing often proves to be detrimental.

We are supposedly operating in a meritocratic, but just, society where equal opportunity is touted as the norm and individuals can advance on their own merits. Thus, one would logically assume that equity would prevail in a system where standardized tests play such an important role in determining individuals' educational and career options. But, in reality, equity does not exist for a substantial portion of this country's minority population. The effects of inequities are often seen in results related to academic outcomes. Relative to performances on achievement, entrance, and licensure standardized tests, it is clear that Black scores lag substantially behind those of whites.

For example, the average total Scholastic Aptitude Test score of Blacks as compared to whites from 1976 to 1985 is approximately 725 to 940 (Ramist and Arbeiter 1985); the average total 1983–84 Graduate Record Examination scores of Black and white aspiring scientists and engineers are 730 and 1104 respectively (Vetter and Babco 1986); and the 1985–1986 average Medical College Admissions Test subtest score of Black medical school applicants was approximately 6.0 compared to 8.5 for all applicants (Association of American Medical Colleges 1987). Finally, Rolph, Williams, and Lanier (1978) reported that, on the National Board of Medical Examiners examination, Part I (an examination used for medical licensure purposes), the average score of a sample of Black medical students was 76 points below that of white students. The reasons for such discrepancies are myriad, but a major reason could be attributed to the absence of equity relative to the education of Blacks.

Clearly, competitive performances on standardized examinations are critical for attaining access to educational and occupational advancement. But given this country's history, Black students, when compared with white students, are seldom on equal footing in competitive testing situations. For example, the generations of oppression which Black students experienced are further compounded by gross educational disadvantages with far-reaching negative consequences. One upshot is that many Black students develop negative attitudes or apprehensions concerning standardized tests. Often, they are quite intimidated by the tests. Moreover, many Black students appear to internalize the lowered achievement expectation maintained by others regarding their performances on such tests, and, in effect, have lowered expectations of themselves.

ACADEMIC PERFORMANCE RELATED TO CLASSROOM OUTCOMES

Classroom performance reflects a student's mastery of the content, and, in some situations, it is a reflection of his or her preparedness to perform in real-life settings. Further, classroom performance is regularly used as a criterion for admittance to advanced educational programs, and, in some situations, job selection. Generally, it is reported that the classroom performances of Black students are not at the level observed in the general student population.

For example, the 1985–1986 GPA of Black medical school applicants was approximately 2.8 as compared to 3.3 for all medical school applicants (Association of American Medical Colleges 1987). Again, the presence of inequities may be attributed as a factor in the creation and perpetuation of such discrepancies. In addition, as briefly cited earlier, the lowered expectation phenomenon may also be a crucial factor relative to Black students' classroom performances.

MODELS OF INTERVENTION

A likely conclusion is that in many situations, the historic and continuing inequities of racism create the need for academic intervention. It is apparent that racial inequities in education are not going to be significantly mitigated in the near future. Thus, in trying to reduce the negative direct and indirect effects, alternative promotion and effective intervention approaches must be utilized. The application of such intervention would be to ensure that more Black students gain experiences that allow them to offset some of the residual effects of inequality. They would, in effect, be made more competitive academically.

Are there, however, intervention methods that are effective for Black and other minority students? The answer is yes.

One intervention model, a combination of test-taking skills instruction and participation in learning teams, was shown to be effective and will be described in this paper. The interventive approach was applied to two different composite groups of minority students.

One group was a class of senior nursing students from a predominantly Black college (Frierson 1986 and 1987). For this group, two criteria variables were examined: standardized test scores on the State Board Examination (SBE) for nurses, and performance in nursing curriculum courses. For the latter, the GPA was the empirical measure.

The other group consisted of minority medical students from a predominantly white medical school west of the Mississippi River (Frierson 1984). Those students' performance on the National Board of Medical Examiners (NBME) and the associated effect of the applied intervention were examined.

PURPOSE OF INTERVENTION

The intent of the applied intervention was two-fold: first, to expose the students to test-taking approaches that, if incorporated, would assist them in becoming more effective test-takers; and second, to encourage students to work cooperatively in learning teams while taking courses or while preparing for major examinations (whether related to courses or standardized formats).

Thus, an additional system would be formed that could address both learning and socioemotional support. Support for learning would be manifested through the sharing of information, peer-tutorial teaching—both as recipients and instructors—and ruminating over and discussing information that had been learned. Socioemotional support is promoted through the camaraderie that normally develops within the learning teams. This camaraderie is usually reflected in the concern and attachment that participants develop for one another.

The use of learning teams in which members work cooperatively to assist one another in learning information related to a course or an impending examination has proven to be effective (Frierson 1984). The learning-team activities enhance learning, facilitate content review, reinforce acquired test-taking skills, and expedite preparation for examinations. A combination of test-taking instruction and learning team participation has been shown to be quite effective for enhancing both standardized test performance and classroom achievement among post-secondary minority students.

Concerning test-taking instruction, after working with students over the years at both the undergraduate and graduate-professional level, it has become apparent to the author that many minority students are not adequately exposed to effective techniques that can be applied on tests, particularly those that are standardized and contain multiple-choice formats. Consequently, minority students may experience anxiety and intimidation about taking such tests. (Other students, however, are certainly not immune to such phenomena, but the problem may be more widespread among Black and other disadvantaged minority students).

As a result, because of emotional and cognitive interfering factors and a relative lack of test-taking sophistication, those students' scores may not be accurate reflections of their levels of acquired knowledge. Test-taking acumen is, of course, very rarely taken into account when test scores are employed for decision-making purposes. The acquisition of effective test-taking skills can reduce errors related to test-taking that affect the performances of many minority students.

COMPONENTS OF THE INTERVENTION PROCEDURE

The major components of the applied intervention presented to students were:

1. Instruction related to a general and systematic approach to effective test-taking;
2. The opportunity to practice the suggested approaches on trial tests;
3. The use of trial tests that contained items which were relevant to the materials which students were studying;
4. Promoting the use of trial tests as self-assessment measures; and
5. Regular (at least once a week) and cooperative participation in learning teams to either review course materials or to prepare for future examinations.

From an instructional standpoint, the intervention procedure is time-efficient. Related instructions can be accomplished in twelve contact hours.

The contact hours involve test-taking-skills instruction and the establishment of learning teams. It is expected that the students will be self-initiating and carry out the activities basically on their own. Follow-up activities, however, can be employed to ensure that students are building on the skills acquired during the didactic instructional phase. The learning teams will usually be the major impetus behind individual students following through on the steps presented during the instructional phase.

RESULTS RELATED TO THE INTERVENTION PROCEDURES

Nursing Students and State Board Examination Performance

Although nurses may have graduated from an accredited nursing education program and have successfully demonstrated knowledge and skills in the classroom and hospital wards, to become licensed members of their profession, they must pass the State Board Examination for Registered Nurse Licensure (now known as the National Council Licensure Examinations or NCLEX). For many graduating nursing students, the State Board Examination (SBE) can be a formidable barrier. For example, in one state over a two-year period, more than 25 percent of the recent nursing school graduates failed the examination on their first attempt (Overstreet 1983). As Black students generally score below the national mean on standardized test such as the State Board Examination, such a situation would take on added ominous significance for graduating minority nurses.

At the time of the study, a mean score of 350 was required for passing. The examination consisted of five subtests that covered the five major areas of nursing: medicine, obstetrics, pediatrics, psychiatry, and surgery. The national mean standard score for the total test and for each subtest was 500. The reliability coefficient (KR–20) of the examination was reported to be around 0.80 (McQuaid and Kane 1981).

Intervention Procedure: Nursing Students. To determine the associated effects of the intervention on State Board Examination performance, 139 senior nursing students, consisting of four classes over a four-year period, were involved in this study (129 Black and 10 white students). The students attended a predominantly Black, southern state-supported college. The sample comprised four graduating classes, one class for each of four consecutive years. Based on year of graduation and the type of intervention received, three groups were formed. One group received test-taking instruction and participated in learning teams. The second group received only test-taking instruction. The third group, serving as a historical control or comparison group, received neither intervention method.

The comparison group consisted of seventy-five students (seventy-one Black and four white students) who graduated during the first two years of the four-year period. The group that received test-taking instructions and participated in learning teams (the Test Skills/Learning Teams group), contained thirty-four students (thirty-two Black and two white students) who graduated in the third year of the four-year period. The group that received test-taking instructions only (the Test-Taking Skills group), consisted of thirty students (twenty-seven Black and three white students) who graduated in the final year of the period. All participants took the State Board Examination for the first time in the month of July following their graduation.

For the two groups receiving intervention, the procedures began in the first half of the spring semester. The intervention methods for the Test Skills/Learning Instruction group covered six weeks in six two-hour sessions. The first two sessions consisted entirely of instructions and exercises related to test-taking skills. After the students were voluntarily placed in academically heterogeneous groups, the third session consisted of team building exercises centering on the use of practice tests. For example, students were instructed to answer practice test items by using consensus methods. The remaining three sessions consisted of continued reinforcement of effective test-taking approaches and learning team methods.

With an added purpose to determine how well the teams were functioning, team scores and team members' individual scores were recorded separately. Thus, any team producing a team score substantially higher than its highest individual score demonstrated effective teamwork in pooling knowledge to benefit its members. Hence, teams with the greatest positive difference between the team score and that of its highest scoring individual were recognized as those functioning most effectively.

The students were encouraged to work regularly (at least once a week) with their learning teams outside the scheduled intervention sessions. They were further encouraged to continue meeting at least until the end of the semester and, if possible, until the State Board Examination administration in July. Additionally, they were encouraged to continue reinforcing their test-taking skills by regularly (also at least once a week) using practice tests until the State Board Examination administration.

The Test-Taking Skills group received all the instruction related to test-taking; however, the members did not participate in the structured group activities as described for the Test-Skills/Learning Team group. The Test-Taking Skills group received eight hours of intervention over a five-week period that occurred in four two-hour sessions. The Test-Taking Skills students were encouraged to regularly use practice tests for reinforcing effective test-taking skills and for self-assessment purposes. They were strongly urged to follow this routine up to the time of the State Board administration.

TABLE 13.1
Covariate Means and Standard Deviations (In Parentheses)

Group	N	SAT-V	SAT-V	Junior Year GPA
Comparison	75	351.53 (62.86)	369.91 (56.93)	2.58 (0.39)
Test Taking Skills Instruction/ Learning Teams	34	346.53 (78.77)	370.21 (73.44)	2.47 (0.60)
Test-Taking Skills Instruction	30	346.25 (77.84)	385.27 (73.22)	2.35 (0.44)

TABLE 13.2
Observed and Adjusted SBE Means

Group	Observed		Adjusted Mean
	Mean	Standard Deviation	
Comparison	355.90	80.90	350.03
Test-Taking Skills Instruction/ Learning Teams	451.07	108.86	454.70
Test-Taking Skills Instruction	401.21	85.87	411.75

Results. Analysis of covariance (ANCOVA) was used to analyze the State Board Examination scores and to provide statistical control relative to prior academic performances. Three covariates were used to control for prior standardized-test performance differences, and the GPA from the junior year was used to control for academic performance differences that may affect scores. All three covariates were found to be significantly related to the examination scores. The means and standard deviations of the covariates are shown in Table B.1.

From the ANCOVA results, the three groups' State Board Examination mean scores differed quite significantly (F $= 26.81$, $p < .0001$). The groups' observed and adjusted mean scores are shown in Table 13.2, comparison of the adjusted means shows substantial differences among all three groups. The Test-Taking Skills group's adjusted mean score was 62 points greater ($p < .03$) than that of the comparison group. But the Test Skills/ Learning Teams group's adjusted mean score was 105 points ($p < .001$) and 43 points ($p < .025$) greater than those of the comparison and the Test-Taking Skills groups, respectively.

When effect sizes (the difference between the mean scores of the treatment and control groups, divided by the control group's standard deviation) were examined, the values were moderate for Test-Taking Skills methods

(ES = 0.56) and large for the Test Skills/Learning Teams method (1.18). Thus, 69 percent of the Test-Taking Skills group had scores greater than the comparison group's mean, whereas 86 percent of the Test Skills/Learning Teams group had scores greater than the mean score for the comparison group.

Further, when the predicted and actual mean scores of the two intervention groups are compared, the intervention groups' actual scores were significantly greater than those predicted (Table 13.3). The Test-Taking Skills group's observed mean score was 42 points higher than predicted (359 points predicted versus 401 points observed). But in keeping with the established pattern, the Test Skills/Learning Teams group displayed the greatest difference between observed and predicted scores. That group's mean score was 97 points higher than predicted (354 points predicted versus 451 points observed)—a difference of staggering magnitude.

Nursing Students and Classroom Performance

In examining the impact of the intervention methods on nursing students' classroom performances, essentially the same group of students participating in the study involving State Board Examination performance were also involved in the study of classroom performance. From the earlier study, it was demonstrated that both intervention methods—and the Test Skills/Learning Teams method in particular—were significantly associated with increased performance on the State Board Examination.

For this phase, the question was, did the procedures have similar effects on students' course performances? Course performance was represented by course grades during the period of the intervention administration. Some students in this study did not take the State Board Examination in the July following the graduation of their respective classes. Therefore, the same size for the classroom performance study was slightly larger than for the State Board Examination study.

Results. As in the initial study, Analysis of Covariance was used for analysis purposes. In this instance, Analysis of Covariance provided some statistical control for variability related to previous performance in nursing courses. Because the intervention occurred during the spring semester, the students' fall-semester GPAs from nursing curriculum courses were used as covariates to adjust for possible differences in the criterion variable, that is, the spring-semester GPA relative to the nursing curriculum.

The results from the statistical analysis showed a significant difference between the three groups' spring-semester mean GPAs (F = 28.66, $p <$ .001). As shown in Table 13.4, the adjusted spring-semester GPA means for

TABLE 13.3
T-Tests Comparing Intervention Groups' Predicted to Observed SBE

| Group | Predicted | | Observed | |
	Mean	Standard Deviation	Mean	Standard Deviation
Comparison	353.60	59.38	451.07	108.86**
Test/Taking Skills Instruction	358.95	53.13	401.21	85.87*

* $p < .05$.
** $p < .001$.

TABLE 13.4
Mean Fall GPA and Mean Adjusted Spring GPA

| Group | N | Fall | | Spring | | |
		Mean	Standard Deviation	Mean	Standard Deviation	Adjusted Mean
Comparison	79	2.24	0.49	2.39	0.51	2.40
Test-Taking Skills Instruction/ Learning Teams	36	2.21	0.48	3.09	0.49	3.11
Test-Taking Skills Instruction	37	2.40	0.50	2.64	0.51	2.59

the Test Skills/Learning Teams, Test-Taking Skills, and comparison groups were: 3.1, 2.6, and 2.4 respectively. Group contrasts showed that the adjusted GPA mean for the Test Skills/Learning Teams group was significantly greater than that of both the comparison group ($p < .0001$) and Test-Taking Skills group ($p < .0001$). Further, the adjusted mean of the Test-Taking Skills group was significantly greater than for the comparison group ($p < .0001$).

The effect size values for the Test Skills/Learning Teams and Test-Taking Skills groups were 1.37 and 0.50, respectively. Hence, 89 percent of the Test Skills/Learning Teams group had higher GPAs than the mean of the comparison group, whereas 67 percent of the Test-Taking Skills group had GPAs higher than the comparison group's mean.

Medical Students' Performance on Part I of the National Board of Medical Examiners Examination

The National Board of Medical Examiners standardized test is a three-part licensure examination used by graduating medical students as one of two routes to acquire certification. The Federal Licensing Examination, taken after graduation and under the auspices of individual state boards of medicine, is the other route.

To become certified as a National Board diplomat, an individual must graduate from an accredited medical school and pass all three parts of the National Board examination. Although the passing score levels are different for the three parts—380 for Part I and 290 for Parts II and III—the mean scores are the same: 500.

Performance on the National Board Examination (Parts I and II) is used at many of this country's medical schools as a major criterion for academic promotion and graduation requirements. In addition, it is frequently used to rate students against national norms (Association of American Medical Colleges 1982). Consequently, for a number of medical students, the National Board Examinations—particularly Part I which is normally taken after the second year of medical school—represents a major hurdle.

Like the State Board Examination for nursing students, the National Board of Medical Examiners test can be an especially formidable barrier for minority students. The anticipated failure rate for all students taking the National Board's Part I for licensure is approximately 13 percent (Hubbard 1978). But the failure rate for minorities taking the examination for the first time is probably several times that percentage.

As previously mentioned, the Rolph et al. (1978) study reported minority students' scores averaging 76 points below those of nonminority students. Further, those investigators found that, even when minority and nonminority students have equivalent preadmission characteristics, the predicted scores of minority students were at least 22 points lower on Part I and 36 points lower on Part II. (As an aside, Part II is normally taken after the third year of medical school, while Part III must be taken after graduation and at least six months of postgraduate clinical experience. Both Parts II and III have anticipated failure rates of no more than three percent, substantially less than is anticipated for Part I.)

The problems which minority medical students face regarding the National Medical Board Examination, Part I, have concerned officials at many medical schools. Unfortunately, however, there are relatively few documented attempts to widely address the problem. But there is evidence that intervention can have a significant impact on the performance of minority medical students. This section describes an intervention method for minority medical students using basically the same approach employed for nursing students.

The purpose of this study (Frierson 1984) was to evaluate the intervention method's effectiveness. Thus, three questions regarding the method were addressed:

1. Could the effects associated with intervention reduce disparities between minority and nonminority participants' National Medical Board Examination, Part I, performances?

2. Could the effects associated with intervention reduce disparities between minority and nonminority students' passing rates on the National Medical Board Examination, Part I?
3. Could the effects associated with intervention produce a higher passing rate for minority students when compared with the performance of minority students from the previous year?

The answer to all three questions was "yes."

Methods. To address the three questions, three comparisons were made using National Medical Board Examination, Part I, performances:

1. Comparison of the participants' mean scores with a random sample of second-year, nontarget or nonminority group students;
2. Comparison of participants' success (passing versus failing) rate with that of a random sample of nonminority students; and
3. Comparison of the participants' success rates with minority students' performances from the previous year.

As mentioned, the intervention methods were quite similar to those described for the nursing students. The target group consisted of twenty-one minority second-year medical students who were scheduled to take the National examination Part I for the first time. Of the target group, nineteen students chose to participate in the intervention program. The nineteen participating students' examination performances were compared with that of a randomly selected sample of nineteen nonminority second year students who did not participate in the program. Additionally, National Medical Board examination data from the twenty-five minority students who were in the previous second year class were collected.

Results. First, the 39-point difference between the mean examination scores of minority student intervention participants (mean = 451.84) and the nonminority student sample were statistically insignificant. Second, the passing rates of the participating and nonminority groups were 79 percent and 89 percent, respectively. Results from a test for significance of difference between two proportions revealed that the passing rates of the two groups were statistically similar ($z = 0.84$, $p < .20$). Third, the passing rates of the participating student group was 27 percentage points higher than the rate for the minority students in the previous second year class (79 percent versus 52 percent). This difference in pass rates between minority students in the two years was statistically significant ($z = 1.86$, $p < .04$).

CONCLUSION

The results of the studies presented here confirm the notion that intervention works and quite effectively for African American and other minority students. Indeed, intervention can have a substantial impact on those students' academic performances. For example, despite the relatively low SAT scores (a verbal mean of 346.5) for the nursing students in the Test Skills/Learning Team groups, those students achieved a State Board Examination mean of 451. The group's score approached the national mean of 500 and was well above what would be expected from students who recorded a mean SAT verbal score in the mid–300 range.

Further, the medical students who participated in the described intervention program recorded a mean National Board of Medical Examiners examination score of 452, which also approached the national mean of 500. The 79 percent passing rate of participating students was considerably above that from the previous year. The approximately 50 percent passing rate of the previous year rejected what has been generally observed for minorities students at that particular medical school.

In addition to having significant positive effects associated with standardized test performance, the intervention methods were associated with substantial positive effects on academic classroom performance. As shown in the study involving nursing students, not only were State Board Examination scores of the Test Skills/Learning Teams students enhanced, but their mean GPA was over 3.0 during the semester when intervention occurred. The GPA associated with intervention represented substantial improvement over the mean of 2.2 from the previous semester.

The implications of the results are many, in relation to university officials, faculty, and students. First, university officials need to recognize that intervention methods work for many students, and thus should provide sufficient support for related programs. Institutional support, both in spirit and financial form, should be made available for existing programs and for the development of other programs that may be more effective. The programs should emphasize high quality and continuity, rather than "quick-fix" or band-aid measures.

Given the legacy of racial inequality in the United States and the reality of persistent inequities, Black and minority student access, participation, and success in professional education continues to be negatively affected. Unless systematically and effectively addressed, these inequities will continue to limit the numbers of Black and minority students who qualify to enter the medical professions. University support and commitment is critical to the success of such efforts.

Second, faculty should be sensitive to the academic needs of many minority students who have not had the qualitative educational experiences common to most students in the general population. Further, when appropriate, faculty should encourage students to use interventive support services that may enhance academic performances. Moreover, faculty should seek to become directly involved in various aspects of intervention efforts for students. One benefit would likely be an improvement in overall teaching effectiveness; another might be heightened sensitivity to minority students' needs and an appreciation for what many of them have accomplished by attending a college or university. Indeed, for some faculty, such involvement may create additional research or funding possibilities, related to student learning and performance, or result in the identification of excellent minority candidates for research assistantships.

Third, Black and other minority students need to be more vigilant in ensuring that, when needed, appropriate assistance is sought and received. Our students should have faith in the effectiveness of intervention programs and not let pride stand in the way of academic survival. Students should be aware that they have academically related challenges which may be addressed by their own personal resources, such as perseverance and determination, but that their efforts can often be effectively enhanced by intervention measures.

The level of intervention described in this paper was effective but time-efficient and thus does not require an inordinate commitment of personnel time or institutional resources. Many of the activities, such as the group participation, were student-driven. The methods are clearly portable and can be presented to a range of students, from entering freshmen to graduate/professional students. Assuming that students participating in such an intervention are sufficiently interested in being students—that is, committed to striving and learning—the expectation is that performance results would be similar to those described here. Finally, effective support programs for minority and other students should be a major priority in institutions that purport to offer quality education.

LEWIS J. KLEINSMITH
JEROME JOHNSTON

Chapter Fourteen

Tackling the Fear of Science: The Impact of a Computer-Based Study Center on Minority Student Achievement in Biology

THE PROBLEM: UNDERACHIEVEMENT AND FEAR OF SCIENCE

Anyone who has taught an introductory science class at a major university for more than a few years eventually becomes aware of the fear and anxiety that such large courses can trigger in the minds of students. This problem is especially acute for individuals whose high-school science backgrounds leave them inadequately prepared; and the problem is further exacerbated by the unspoken, but unfortunately widespread, view among faculty that the purpose of introductory courses is to weed out individuals who are unqualified for careers in the sciences.

Hence, students interested in careers in the biomedical sciences—such as medicine and dentistry—have reason to fear college courses such as introductory biology and chemistry; if their background experiences in the sciences are even partially deficient, they are not likely to fare well against the intense student competition. And if they don't do well in the introductory science courses, their careers in the biomedical sciences are over before they have even had a chance to get started.

Although the preceding predicament applies to students whose inadequate preparation stems from a variety of sources, the problem has been exceptionally severe for minority students. In the early 1970s, the University of Michigan at Ann Arbor initiated an effort to increase its enrollment of underrepresented minorities, which led to a significant increase in minority student enrollment during the following decade. Unfortunately, analysis of retention rates and academic performances for this group of newly recruited students revealed some disturbing signs. One especially noticeable feature was the below-average representation and academic performance of minorities in the sciences. In introductory biology, for example, which is a prerequisite for all students interested in pursuing a career in the medical areas, minority students' performance in the early 1980s was almost two full grades below the class as a whole. Hence, careers in one of society's most prestigious and lucrative set of professions were effectively closed off for this population of students.

Having taught the introductory biology course for almost twenty years, I (Kleinsmith) was already well aware of the difficulties faced by inadequately prepared students. In fact, the basic problem encountered in this class is not really specific to introductory biology; it is encountered in most large introductory lecture courses where faculty must lecture to audiences of several hundred students of widely differing backgrounds and abilities. I have found that, if my lecture material is designed to challenge the better students in the class, the more poorly prepared students quickly get lost. If, however, lectures are instead focused on the needs of the bottom half of the class, the slower pace makes it difficult to cover all the necessary material, and the better students soon become bored. Faculty who teach such large introductory courses quickly experience the frustration of trying to walk this tightrope between the needs of differing student constituencies.

The underlying problem, of course, is that we are simply expecting too much from the lecture format. Lectures are an important tool for providing an overview of the subject matter, but they cannot ensure that all students will come away with an equivalent level of knowledge. If the goal of an introductory course is to provide all students with a roughly equivalent understanding of basic principles, then the great variability in student understanding that is virtually unavoidable following a lecture to several hundred individuals must somehow be made up outside of class. This is especially important in introductory courses, since the concepts involved provide the foundation for the following classes in the discipline.

But what can be done outside of class to help all students achieve a roughly equivalent understanding of basic concepts? Over the years, we at the University of Michigan have experimented with several approaches. The most obvious one—which is to recommend that students study the appropriate sections of the textbook—suffers from two serious limitations.

First, reading is a largely passive experience deficient in both feedback and interaction; this deficiency is largely insurmountable because a book has no way of knowing whether the student is understanding what he or she is reading. The second limitation is that printed words and diagrams are static, while biological principles tend to involve dynamic interactions occurring in time and place. Many important biological principles are, therefore, difficult to convey in textbooks.

In addition to textbook assignments, we also experimented with two other approaches for helping students outside of class. One involves weekly open-ended review sessions in which I responded to students' questions and difficulties by elaborating upon the concepts that were confusing them. The second approach I have tried is passing out old exams so that students can practice applying the principles which I have been teaching to the kinds of problems they are expected to understand.

To my surprise, neither of these approaches has led to a detectable improvement in overall class performance on exams! The lack of improvement in student performance after being given access to old exams has been especially surprising, since the types of problems used on exams are quite similar from year to year. In talking with students about how they go about studying from old exams, it has become apparent that they spent more time memorizing the old answers than trying to figure out the reasoning that allows one to discriminate between correct and incorrect responses. Hence, they were unable to generalize what they have learned and apply it to new situations.

THE INTERVENTION: MICRO-COMPUTER SOFTWARE

This is where the problem stood in the summer of 1982, when serendipity suddenly provided me with a novel insight. My twelve-year-old daughter, who had just taken a two-week course in computer programming, developed a simple riddle program in which the computer asks a series of questions and provides funny replies in response to answers chosen by the user. And it suddenly became apparent that this simple kind of interaction could form the basis of an educational program in which the computer's responses were designed to educate, rather than amuse, the user. If the program were well-designed, it might, in fact, mimic the kind of socratic feedback that I would provide to individual students sitting in my office as I was trying to help them understand a basic concept.

Armed with this idea, I solicited and soon obtained university funding for an experiment to see if microcomputer software could be developed to help students having difficulty in introductory biology. After examining the types of software that were commercially available at the time, it quickly became apparent that existing materials did not meet our needs, and that we would therefore need to develop our own programs. During the next year, I began to learn about computer programming—first from my daughter and, later, from two computer-literate students who happened to be working in my laboratory on other projects. As I developed some rudimentary programming skills and began to think in detail about the educational objectives of the project, it soon became apparent that two distinct types of software were required.

The first category of software to be developed consisted of programs designed to provide students with experience in applying the concepts and principles developed in lectures, which is exactly what they are required to do on our examinations. Although the large size of the class dictates the need for multiple-choice tests, the questions we use tend not to be of the rote memorization type that students typically encounter in high school. Instead, our questions generally require students to analyze, synthesize, and/or extrapolate from the information provided in order to draw the appropriate conclusions. Needless to say, it is difficult to acquire such skills by simply going to a lecture or reading a textbook.

I, therefore, decided to create a series of interactive "problem-set" programs in which students are presented with a broad spectrum of multiple-choice questions typical of those found on our exams. In fact, most of them *were* taken from old tests.

Moreover, the sequence of questions and the order of the multiple-choice answers are randomized; hence students cannot simply memorize patterns like "the answer to question 9 is choice 'a'," as they often do when studying from old exams. In this way, a virtually endless array of problem-solving exercises can be made available. The most important difference between these programs and simply looking at old exams, however, is that when students choose an incorrect answer, they are provided with feedback specifically designed to point out the error in their reasoning and/or to provide clues as to the appropriate approach (Kleinsmith 1987).

In the original version of the problem-set software, students were automatically advanced to the next question after they had picked the correct answer. However, they were first given an explanation as to why the answer was correct, in case they had chosen it for the wrong reasons. Students quickly complained that, even though they had chosen the correct answers, they wanted to be able to return to the question again to find out exactly *why* other responses were incorrect.

Now that our problem-set software functions in this way, I have repeatedly heard from students that they learn more from choosing wrong answers than they do from picking the correct ones! This unexpected insight into the question of how students learn suggests that the use of our software develops critical thinking and reasoning skills in a way that cannot be done by simply looking at old exams and seeing what the correct answers are.

The problem-solving programs, which represent the first category of software we developed, were designed to give students experience in applying principles and concepts with which they already had a basic familiarity. The second type of software we have produced is targeted at a slightly different problem—the teaching of complicated concepts involving dynamic interactions of various biological components in time and space.

At best, textbook diagrams can illustrate a few static pictures of such processes; and lecture presentations, using a blackboard or overhead projector, tend to be equally limited and even more cumbersome. Although good film-loops can overcome this problem and illustrate dynamic concepts and interactions quite well, films are non-interactive presentations over which students have little control.

We have, therefore, begun to develop a series of "animated tutorials" that utilize the animated-graphic and interactive capabilities of the microcomputer to create programs in which students can not only watch dynamic computer-generated animations of complex biological processes, but they can stop and start the action at any point, jump forward or backward, adjust the speed, observe the animations with or without explanations, and, finally, test their understanding of the processes involved by having the programs ask them questions along the way.

Although preliminary versions of our programs were tested on a limited number of students as development proceeded, it took almost two years before a sufficient number of "problem sets" and "animated tutorials" were refined to a degree that justified testing them on all 500 students in the class.

In order to facilitate student use of the software, a special room designated the "Biology Study Center" was outfitted with 15 microcomputer work stations, and the software was made available through a user-friendly network that requires absolutely no prior knowledge of computers. When a students sits down at a computer he or simply is confronted with the message "Press any key . . . ," and from there on everything is explained and runs automatically from a series of menus.

Although a graduate-student teaching assistant is always present to answer questions, student queries almost always concern the biological subject matter rather than how to run the computers or programs. Use of the Biology Student Center software is not required of students, nor is their attendance monitored in any way. Students are simply told that this study facility is a resource available for anybody to use outside of class as they desire, just as one might go to a library to study.

COMPUTERIZED TUTORIAL AND
MINORITY STUDENTS: RESULTS

Shortly after the Biology Study Center first opened in the fall of 1984, beneficial effects began to become apparent. To help us design ways in which this impact might be measured objectively, I enlisted the aid of Jerome Johnston, a social scientist who works in the area of evaluating educational interventions. Together we have designed, administered, and evaluated an anonymous questionnaire aimed at investigating some of the more obvious effects of the Biology Study Center on student behavior, attitudes, and performance. Although analysis of this data is still in progress, some interesting information that is especially relevant to this volume has begun to emerge about the behavior and attitudes of minority students.

One particularly interesting item concerns minority student attitudes toward the use of computers. When the biology software project was first proposed several years ago as a possible approach to dealing with the problems being faced by minority students in introductory biology, the question was raised as to whether minority students would feel comfortable going to computers for help. Some of our colleagues suggested that computers are impersonal and dehumanizing, and that a lack of prior experience with computers might cause minority students to shy away from trying to use them. That data that we have now collected, however, indicate that such fears were unwarranted.

When asked on our anonymous questionnaire how many hours they had spent using the Biology Study Center software, the average for minority students was, in fact, found to be greater than the average for the class as a whole (Table 14.1).

When asked how valuable they found the software to be in helping them study, minority student responses were again found to be extremely positive (Table 14.2).

TABLE 14.1

Student Estimates of the Amount of Time Spent Using the Biology Study Center Software Prior to the First Exam. (Data obtained from an anonymous questionnaire.)

Amount of Time Spent Using Software	Percent Responses	
	Minority Students (N=14)	Other Students (N=455)
None	0	3
Under three hours	0	8
Three to ten hours	21	44
Ten to twenty hours	64	39
Over twenty hours	14	7

TABLE 14.2

Student Estimates of the Value of the Biology Student Center
Software in Helping Them to Prepare for the First Exam.
(Data obtained from an anonymous questionnaire administered after the exam.)*

	Percent Responses	
Estimate of the Value	*Minority Students*	*Other Students*
of the Software	*(N=14)*	*(N=422)*
Very valuable	100	85
Valuable	0	13
Somewhat valuable	0	2
Not at all valuable	0	0

*Students not using the software are excluded.

TABLE 14.3

Class Performance on the First Examination in Introductory Biology before and after
Introduction of the Biology Study Center Software in 1984*

	Mean Score	
Time Period	*Minority Students*	*Overall Class*
1979–1983	48.0 (3.7)	65.6 (3.4)
1984–1985	65.5 (0.7)	75.0 (0.7)
1986–1987	81.1 (1.1)	81.9 (1.0)

*Cell entries are averages of the annual mean exam scores for each time period. (The numbers
in parentheses are standard deviations showing the variability in class means for each period.)

The written comments of minority students about their experiences
with the software were equally striking. One such student wrote that the
programs "were very helpful and . . . fun to do. They also helped me to
study for things I wouldn't have normally studied for. Thanks for the computers, hope my exam shows how much they helped." In a similar vein,
another student said, "It's the best way to study for the course and provides
very thorough understanding of the material." Such comments and the associated questionnaire data clearly reveal the absence of any significant barrier to the use of computer software among the minority student population.

The most exciting finding to have emerged regarding minority student
behavior, however, is a dramatic improvement in exam performance. Table
14.3 summarizes the mean score on the first examination in introductory
biology before and after the initial version of this software was introduced
in 1984.

Note that the mean for the class as a whole improved about 10 percent
during the first two years of software use, and improved even further during
the third year (1986) when the software was made more widely available by
placing it at various public work stations around campus in addition to the
Biology Study Center.

But what is even more striking about these data is the improvement in minority student performance! Note that prior to the introduction of this software in 1984, their performance was almost 20 percent below the class mean (roughly two full grades). By 1986, when minority students were strongly encouraged to use the software, this difference had virtually disappeared. Although it might be argued that the academic qualifications of our incoming minority student population are simply getting better, the incoming-grades and SAT scores of the minority student population in our biology course have not, in fact, changed significantly.

It should be emphasized that the improvement in exam performance observed during the past three years cannot be explained by any obvious change in the difficulty of the exam or in the effectiveness of the lecture presentations. Since the exams consist largely of problems designed to test the abilities of students to apply the basic concepts and principles discussed in lectures, the kinds of questions used on the exam can be made quite similar year to year (just as the kinds of problems used on a math test can be similar from year to year). Moreover, the number of questions and their distribution over the various subject areas stays basically the same.

In terms of the effectiveness of the lecture presentation, I have been teaching in the introductory biology course for twenty years and, after experimenting with content and style during the first ten years, the subject matter and my lecture notes have remained basically the same during the past ten years.

In addition, the standardized student evaluation forms administered every year have revealed no significant change in the perceived effectiveness of my lectures during the past three years. It, therefore, seems reasonable to conclude that the dramatic improvement in minority student performance observed in the past few years is related largely to the effectiveness of the tutorial activities in the Biology Student Center.

One of the most appealing features of the experiment described in this article has been that the Study Center is not a minority student facility per se, but is rather a heterogeneous environment utilized by the vast majority of the class as a learning resource center. Hence, minority students are not subjected to the indignity of being sent to a special facility for remedial help. They are simply taking advantage of a general facility whose overall goal is to provide all students, regardless of differences in background and experience, with the opportunity for achieving a roughly equivalent understanding of the basic principles of introductory biology.

One can only hope that the success of this approach will serve as a model for other disciplines where students of varying backgrounds and abilities must be handled within the context of large introductory courses.

Chapter Fifteen

Epilogue

THE INSTITUTION AND RACISM

This book of readings is a collective of perspectives and analyses of data from the National Study of Black College students. It provides at the most basic level information which has been desperately needed and is long overdue. This book is therefore, first of all, a service not only to the African American students struggling in the universities, but also those aspiring to become university students. It is hoped that these readings will inform the policy makers who direct the fates of the institutions of higher learning to make the universities a more conducive place for African American students.

There are many shades of information in these readings, but perhaps the most consistent is that African American students experience more adjustment difficulties on white campuses than on Black campuses. Although these difficulties seem predictable . . . obviously Black students would feel more at ease and adjust quicker on Black campuses. This is not now merely a truism confirmed by data, but a truth with profound implications for those students who attend predominantly white universities and who happen to be the best and brightest of African American students.

Compared to the students who attend Black universities, those who are admitted to predominantly white universities have higher grade-point averages, and come from families with more income and more education. Clearly it is the best and brightest who experience alienation and adjustment difficulties at these universities which, in the end, translates into high attrition rates among these Black students.

It is a question here not only of opportunity to attend the best universities or any university of one's choice, but making that opportunity *real* rather than *symbolic*. Perhaps the tottering Black universities with their fine traditions of learning and excellence can be bolstered both by financial and infrastructural support. The point is that Black students should have a chance.

If they attend Black universities, then they must be entitled to programs and choices as equally endowed as those at predominantly white schools. If the students choose to attend predominantly white campuses, then there must be mechanisms in place to support these students and alleviate their sense of alienation so that they can be successful students. Many universities studied here have attempted to set up such structures but with little effect on the students' sense of alienation.

These structures are, to some extent, artificial and reinforce the students' awareness of their separateness. By definition, therefore, these structures are contradictory. One finding discussed in this book is the importance of faculty and staff contact for Black students on white campuses. These relationships were important for both the students' sense of belonging and their performances in class.

What this means is that the contacts, which are spontaneous or emanate from faculty who do genuinely care, *do* make a difference, and it is this contact and caring which combats racism. This caring and these relationships cannot be legislated or programmed. It is precisely *because* such relationships cannot be legislated that programs to facilitate Black students on white campuses must exist, limited though they are. The point here is that such programs—which are easy to recommend—are only partial, temporary answers. In the end, these programs are run by persons who may or may not form meaningful relationships with students. The burden is on the institution to combat racism, and the institution's responsibility is not only to design programs but to use and inculcate persons who genuinely care for all students.

The further contradiction is that the institution is highly individualistic, competitive, and solitary, whereas the Afro-American culture is extended, affiliative, and interactive. In order to succeed—and many do—the African American student must learn to assimilate culturally. It is the price of this education that Carter G. Woodson addressed so many years ago.

> When a Negro has finished his education in our schools, then, he has been equipped to begin the life of an Americanized or Europeanized white man. (Woodson 1933/1969: 5)

There are of course unanswered questions here. If the best and the brightest Black students *did* succeed at these universities, would the Black community have gained?

To a large extent the problems that African Americans experience in these universities are the problems of assimilation. It is education which is the major vehicle for assimilation. The cultural difference between white America and Black America may appear minimal for those at the university level when, in fact, that is not the case. The differences are really quite large. It is not that the values of individuality and contest have not been internalized (Thomas, Chapter 3) but rather that the meaning of individuality and contest differs in the Black community, how it is expressed, its style, and its nuance. It is these small unarticulated expressions which make up a culture and, in the end, demarcate the lines of separateness. Further I am suggesting that there is an intact African American culture that is as legitimate as any other, but unrecognized as authentic and separate in its own right in the educational system because of the particular historical circumstances of the African American presence in this country.

This book does not address the content of education as in Illich (1971), Freire (1970), Woodson (1933), or Carnoy (1974). Instead, it addresses the issues of success and opportunity. Yet the content is an issue not so much because of what it *is* that the student has to learn but *how* that content is presented. It is, in effect, style.

In his paper, Nettles (Chapter 4) found that the most important contribution to the rapid progress of Black students was a nontraditional teaching style. If, in the predominantly white universities' teaching style, contact with faculty and social support are important, then the institution must become something radically different from what it is.

The university will not change because African American students have difficulties. It cannot be affiliative and supportive. To ask this is to ask the university to change intrinsically. The issue here is cause and symptom. The root of the problem is racism. Neither the university nor the society will change in a radical way. They cannot eradicate racism in the near future. At this point, the only solutions are symptomatic—programs to deal with African American students' difficulties on campus.

COLOR, DIFFERENCE, AND CULTURE

The argument has been made repeatedly that the problem may not be that the institutions are racist since other people of color succeed at these universities. Deskins' data (Chapter 1) show unequivocally that the greatest gains are being made by foreign-born students and Asian-Americans. These gains have their own contexts quite different from those of African American students. Those who make this comparison do so with little discernment. The act of moving from one country to another to improve one's life condition is predictably successful for such persons. The body of work on immigrants attests to this (Takaki 1987). A cursory look at very successful Americans will reveal that many of them are foreign-born or children of immigrants. This success is correlated to the dynamics of immigration, or a new opportunity in a new country, not with race (Ogbu 1978). This comparison is never made for the white population where foreign-born students and immigrants do extremely well in comparison to their white American counterparts.

On this issue of Asian-American students and their success in universities, this again is used to question the completely debilitating nature of racism towards African Americans in this country. Asians do well in school so, therefore, others can do well—meaning African Americans. But Asian-Americans have not only done well in school but have done well in business and in the professions regardless of whether they are schooled or not.

Although Asians and Jews in this country have had histories of trauma and incarceration, and continue to be discriminated against, it does not compare to the continued and relentless racial and cultural oppression of African Americans. One can see wave after wave of such oppression. It is not the invidiousness of slavery alone but the trauma before that, the wrench from home, the middle passage, slavery itself, the sharecropping system, de-facto segregation, lynching laws against Black men in particular, and an ongoing litany of oppressive and repressive norms that exist today. Credible arguments have even been made for the planned extinction of the African American male (Madhubuti 1990; Konjufu 1985). Despite this the achievements of African Americans have been outstanding both in school and out. How much more might they have accomplished had African Americans been allowed to hold on to their names, as in Chin or Goldberg or Kowalski—such a simple thing, a name.

This does not mean that the culture of African Americans has been decimated. It simply reiterates the nature of the onslaught and its effect on certain important aspects of culture. The argument that Jews and Asians, for example, had a culture that helped them survive and succeed is also true for African Americans. How that success is measured is the key here. That it does not translate into the areas of education in the manner that is expected is the problem. There have been many explanations for the educational problems of African Americans, racism, slavery, cultural disruption, persistent poverty and so on. I argue here that African Americans enter the school system with a sense of difference based on color not on culture or nationality. The Asian-American for example enters into the system with a consciousness of difference based on color, culture and nationality. It gives that student a concrete sense that this is a system very different from his life and therefore orients his stance toward learning.

This is not necessarily the case for the African American student. The system presumes that there is a shared culture between itself and African Americans. There is a mythological presumption of equality. Therefore there is no need for special programs concerning language, orality, writing, cultural difference, or adjustment difficulties. To base the explanation on race alone is insufficient, to base it on cultural strength or weakness is also insufficient. The first step is to recognize the difference, that African Americans are not only racially different but culturally different as well. Both the system and African Americans themselves must recognize this. The process of assimilating African Americans is profoundly different from any other group.

The crux of the matter is integration, the integration of African Americans into a dominant Eurocentric educational system (Ong 1982). Asians and other groups who enter the system understand this and become bicultural, they accept the new culture while keeping and valuing their own. African Americans accept integration with a sense that their separateness, their difference is inferior and must be eschewed. Many African Americans do know that they have a different existence from that of the dominant society, but they accept that existence as marginal and are ambivalent about that difference as a legitimate culture. The dominant forces in the society see the difference between themselves and African Americans as a manifestation of African Americans' maladjustment, not as a legitimate cultural difference.

GENDER

The other major point that this set of readings makes concerns gender. Men do better than women across race and campuses. This is surprising given the general notion that Black women do better than Black men because of the distinct impression that there is a feminization of education in the African American population. The data in the National Study of Black College Students show that, on white campuses, the enrollment of Black females is twice that of Black males, who do not do as well academically as Black females. The data, however, show that Black males are more ambitious, do better in the professional schools, and choose more competitive hard-science fields than do women. On Black campuses, men do much better and, on white campuses, women do better but only at the under-graduate level.

Black women have made gains but not in relation to the numbers who enter at the undergraduate level at both Black and white universities. This whole issue of gender in the Black Community is riddled with contradictions. In Farley and Allen's book *The Color Line and the Quality of Life in Black America* (1987), Black women in terms of income are either at the same level of white women or slightly ahead. The women, however, work more hours than white women for the almost comparable wages they receive. This highlights the additional burdens of Black women. Their income demands longer hours, is spent on children and family, and is almost always the only source of income. Black men lag far behind white men. There is no question that the African American male in this society is in crisis, this has always been so. The small cadre of Black men who do well are not in the categories of the unemployed or underemployed. The statistics concerning the income levels for Black women demonstrate clearly that they are the victims of both racism and sexism. Comparing the income levels of both Black men and women with the same education, reveal that Black women make $4,000 less than Black men annually (Farley and Allen 1987).

This is the context in which education achievements for Black men and women exist. But why are Black men doing better in graduate schools than Black women? Is it because Black women limit themselves? Or is it that universities and graduate schools in particular are sexist? The most plausible explanation is a combination of the two.

Black women who are already burdened with a socialization to achieve and with expectations of marriage and family are faced with a dilemma. The male-to-female ratio in the Black community makes life for a Black woman—particularly an educated Black woman—lonely, to say the least. The Black woman graduate student does better if she is married and more mature (see Matthews and Jackson, Chapter 11). This is a clear indication that social support and relationships are, again, central for the younger Black female graduate student.

The lack of such relationships in addition to the lack of other support, combined with the inherent sexism of graduate schools—like medicine and the sciences—make the pursuit of higher degrees in these fields formidable. This makes for a high attrition rate for Black women in such programs and their concerns about relationships and other female socialization agendas mitigate against pursuing degrees in these areas.

The data set of the National Study of Black College students is excellent in documenting the gender difference for Black men and women. However, it is lacking in the highly sensitive data needed to understand the complexities of Black women's lives at these universities. Although race has been pursued as an important variable, gender has been pursued mainly as a describer. This has often been the case in such large studies, and is one of the main reasons for gender-specific studies. More sophisticated information is needed on the peculiar status of Black women in graduate schools. Such a study would be an addition to both feminist and Black studies.

THE SOCIAL SCIENCE PARADIGM OF NSBCS

The National Study of Black College students, apart from supplying information, attempted also, in the tradition of classic sociology, to examine variables which can predict the success or failure of Black students on white campuses. Variables such as alienation, social and economic status, gender, mother's education, father's education, and social support on campus are scored according to the responses received on these items and then computed to determine their significance. Marriage, for example, is significant. Married students did better than unmarried students. It is this significance that leads to predictability.

This quest for predictability is an important tenet in the sciences and social science, and it has been met by this study. Together, these many variables add up to human behavior which in reality is a constellation of infinite variables. Social science is limited and can select only a finite number in predicting something as subtle and powerful as racism and its relationship to success and failure in education. In the end, one can only predict a few things, and even that is limited by time and context. A major feature of sociology in the last twenty years has been the increasing use of methods and technology to improve the accuracy in the measurement of variables—to discern more precisely the nature and predictability of its social phenomena. This effort at accuracy and sensitive measurement was, in effect, an attempt at making sociology more of a science, the feeling being that science was accurate.

In his book, *Chaos: Making a New Science* (1988), James Gleick examines the work of scientists who have made major breakthroughs in the last thirty years. These scientists have been grappling with a new phenomenon called "chaos" which essentially argues that there is order in chaos and that the physical reality of the world can only be predicted approximately. To put it another way, the "movement of a butterfly in China may be related to the wind flow in New York." This cannot be predicted.

There are in the lexicon of human behavior and the universe unending combinations of events that can lead to a certain result. It is how these combine, and the dynamics and the complexities of such combinations that we must seek out to fully understand.

> To some physicists Chaos is a science of process rather than state, of be-
> coming rather than being. (Gleick 1988: 5)

This sounds very much like the small band of qualitative social scientists who constantly argue for more than just measurement and quantity.
Even the physical sciences now are trying to find ways and methods of
capturing a more complex form of reality—in other words, a science that is
closer to reality, rather than a reality closer to science.

Will these events in the physical sciences force the behavioral sciences
to radically change? Chaos is the scientist's attempt to deal with the complexities of reality in a nonlinear way, and it is time that social scientists
take a second look at measurement and linear behavior.

> Lorenz put the weather aside and looked for even simpler ways to produce
> this complex behavior. He found one in a system of just three equations.
> They were nonlinear, meaning that they expressed relationships that were
> not strictly proportional. Linear relationships can be captured with a
> straight line on a graph. Linear relationships are easy to think about: the
> more the merrier. Linear equations are solvable, which makes them suit-
> able for textbooks . . . the pieces add up. (Gleick 1988: 23)

There are no nonlinear equations in this book, every variable is documented and correlated. It is either correlated or not. It is either significant
or not. In short, everything is measured in a linear way. When it does not
add up, then one explains *why*. One does not dismiss this lack of correlation. One simply looks at the method of going about this measurement and,
if the method is sound and within normal science, then that is good
enough. In effect, the science is more important than the reality. It is all
right to find no correlations. Perhaps they didn't exist in the first place.

What the physical scientists are doing is questioning themselves. If
things do not add up, what does it mean? What are we missing? What is it
within these systems that could teach us about cloud formation, about the
impact of butterflies or about the angle of the light? Things do add up in
the universe, but we have yet to discover how and what, after it has added
up, it is supposed to be.

Now, if these scientists are asking such questions, why shouldn't social
scientists? This research effort stays within the scientific paradigm evi-
denced by the many numbers and tables. All of these numbers attempt to
quantify the veracity of one issue—racism. Is being a Black student in
white universities in the United States truly "equal opportunity?" Does
equality exist for Black university students?

Racism is so complex and volatile that it could be measured ad infinitum. There are no nonlinear equations in this study. But still, the numbers are important, and more so are the voices and feelings of the students, of the bureaucrats, and, most of all, of the men and women who have written on these pages.

What a strange thing not to hear the voices and the feelings of the researcher and the researched! Is it perhaps these missing voices that are also the missing nonlinear equations? It may, after all, be quite simple for social scientists to devise their versions of nonlinear equations. Simply let us hear what people are thinking and feeling. Give us their own words, perhaps after a regression analysis or maybe before.

Despite this, the National Study of Black College Students represents an important break through for Black scholars and scholarship. African American researchers working on issues in the Black community are victimized. They must, themselves, constantly prove that they are entrenched in and know the paradigm. They must prove that they can do ordinary research. If they risk going outside the paradigm, then they are immediately suspect.

> Professional men of any specialty, university graduates or not, are men who have been "determined from above" by a culture of domination which has constituted them as dual beings. (If they had come from the lower classes this mis-education would be the same, if not worse.) (Freire 1970: 156)

The Black scholar, then, is caught in a tentacled web. To research issues in the Black community which have not been the purvey of Black researchers is, therefore, struggle. To rectify how traditional research has portrayed Blacks and Black lives by using the same research method is an act of courage.

These readings come from data which were generated because of a belief that education is a right for African Americans, and that right must become a reality. All of these things—struggle, courage, belief, and caring—cannot be quantified because they constitute love in the most profound ideological sense.

Words—like love—never appear in books of this ilk. It is not rigorous. It is not objective. And it is not knowledge. But love is rigorous.

The National Study of Black College Students has been an attempt to advocate for the rights of aspiring young African American university students to ensure that their chance to make better lives for themselves is real. This research has been, for these researchers, an act of love for one's race, one's self, and one's community.

- As an act of bravery, love cannot be sentimental; as an act of freedom it must not serve as a pretext for manipulation. It must generate other acts of freedom; otherwise, it is not love. Only by abolishing the situation of oppression is it possible to restore the love which that situation made impossible (Freire 1970: 78)

The National Study of Black College Students has played its part in removing a small piece of oppression.

Part Five

Appendices

JO ANNE HALL
CHERYL PRESLEY
RUBY GOOLEY

Appendix A

Black College Students in U.S. Higher Education: A Selected Bibliography

This selected bibliography is a list of published works compiled to focus specifically on issues related to the Black college student in the United States. The selected titles are drawn from a larger compilation currently being prepared for publication that reviews the literature on Blacks in U.S. higher education from a broader perspective.

Only published works, readily available in libraries, bookstores, or directly from publishers are listed. The bibliography covers the time period 1970–1987, although the emphasis is on the literature from 1980–1987. Items selected include bibliographies, general reference works, research studies, journal articles, and selected texts. The titles are arranged by broad topics and by type of publication. This bibliography, while selective, is an attempt to expose the reader to the works of both recognized and young scholars involved in creative research.

BIBLIOGRAPHIES

Chambers, Frederick. 1978. *Black Higher Education in the United States: A Selected Bibliography on Negro Higher Education and Historically Black Colleges and Universities*. Westport, Conn.: Greenwood Press.

Davis, Nathaniel, ed. 1985. *Afro-American Reference: An Annotated Bibliography of Selected Resources*. Westport, Conn.: Greenwood Press.

Jones, Leon. 1979. *From Brown to Boston: Desegregation in Education, 1954–1974.* 2 vol. Metuchen, N.Y.: Scarecrow Press.

MacDonald, A. P., and M. L. Rawlings. 1981. "Internal-External Locus of Control: A Selected Bibliography for Those Concerned with the Counseling and Education of High Risk Students." *Catalog of Selected Documents in Psychology* 11(59):59.

Newby, James Edward. 1980. *Black Authors and Education: An Annotated Bibliography of Books.* Washington, D.C.: University Press of America.

Swanson, Kathryn. 1981. *Affirmative Action and Preferential Admissions in Higher Education: An Annotated Bibliography.* Metuchen, N.Y.: Scarecrow Press.

United Negro College Fund Archives: A Guide and Index to the Microfiche. 1985. Ann Arbor, Mich.: University Microfilms.

Weinberg, Meyer. 1970. *The Education of the Minority Child: A Comprehensive Bibliography of 10,000 Selected Entries.* Chicago: Integrated Education Associates.

———. 1981. *The Education of Poor and Minority Children: A World Bibliography.* 2 vol. Westport, Conn.: Greenwood Press.

BLACKS IN U.S. HIGHER EDUCATION

Books

Abramowitz, Elizabeth A. 1976. *Equal Educational Opportunity for Blacks in U.S. Higher Education: An Assessment.* Washington, D.C.: Howard University Press.

Astin, Alexander W. 1982. *Minorities in American Higher Education: Recent Trends, Current Prospectives, and Recommendations.* San Francisco: Jossey-Bass.

Baca, Carlota M., and Ronald H. Stein. 1983. *Ethical Principles, Practices, and Problems in Higher Education.* Springfield, Ill.: C. C. Thomas.

Ballard, Allen. 1974. *The Education of Black Folk: The Afro-American Struggle for Knowledge in White America.* New York: Harper Colophon.

Blackwell, James E. 1981. *Mainstreaming Outsiders: The Production of Black Professionals.* Bayside, N.Y.: General Hall, Inc.

College Entrance Examination Board. *Equality and Excellence: The Educational Status of Black Americans.* 1985. New York: College Board.

Epps, Edgar G. 1972. *Black Students in White Schools.* Worthington, Ohio: Charles A. Jones Publishers.

Fleming, Jacqueline. 1984. *Blacks in College: A Comparative Study of Students' Success in Black and in White Institutions.* San Francisco: Jossey-Bass.

Green, Kenneth C. 1982. *Government Support for Minority Participation in Higher Education.* Washington, D.C.: American Association for Higher Education.

Gurin, Patricia, and Edgar G. Epps. 1975. *Black Consciousness, Identity, and Achievement: A Study of Students in Historically Black Colleges.* New York: Wiley Press.

Jones, Leon. 1979. *From Brown to Boston: Desegregation in Education, 1954–74.* Metuchen, N.J.: Scarecrow Press.

Lehner, J. Christopher. 1980. *A Losing Battle: The Decline in Black Participation in Graduate and Professional Education.* Washington, D.C.: National Advisory Committee on Black Higher Education and Black Colleges and Universities.

Morris, Lorenzo. 1979. *Elusive Equality: The Status of Black Americans in Higher Education.* Washington, D.C.: Howard University, Institute for the Study of Education Policy.

Myers, Michael M. 1982. *Fact Book on Higher Education in the South, 1981 and 1982.* Atlanta: Southern Regional Education Board.

Newman, Dorothy Krall, et al. 1978. *Protest, Politics and Prosperity: Black Americans and White Institutions, 1940–1975.* New York: Pantheon Books.

Ogbu, John U. 1978. *Minority Education and Caste: The American System in Cross-Cultural Perspective.* New York: Academic Press.

Peterson, Marvin, et al. 1978. *Black Students on White Campuses: The Impacts of Increased Black Enrollments.* Ann Arbor: The University of Michigan, Institute for Social Research.

Pifer, A. 1973. *The Higher Education of Blacks in the United States.* New York: Carnegie Corporation of New York.

Preer, Jean L. 1981. *Minority Access to Higher Education.* Washington, D.C.: American Association for Higher Education.

Simmons, Ron. 1982. *Affirmative Action: Conflict and Change in Higher Education After Bakke.* Cambridge, Mass.: Schenkman Publishing Co., Inc.

Sowell, Thomas. 1972. *Black Education: Myths and Tragedies.* New York: David McKay Company.

Stikes, C. Sully. 1984. *Black Students in Higher Education.* Carbondale, Ill.: Southern Illinois University Press.

Thomas, Gail E. 1981. *Black College Students in Higher Education: Conditions and Experiences in the 1970s.* Westport, Conn.: Greenwood Press.

Willie, Charles Vert. 1981. *The Ivory and Ebony Towers.* Lexington, Mass.: Lexington Books,; D. C. Heath and Co.

Willie, Charles Vert, and Arline Sakuma McCord. 1972. *Black Students at White Colleges.* New York: Praeger.

Wilson, Reginald. 1982. *Race Equity in Higher Education: Proceedings and Papers of the Ace-Aspen Institute Seminar on Desegregation in Higher Education.* Washington, D.C.: American Council in Education.

Articles

Harleston, Bernard W. 1983. "Higher Education for Minorities: The Challenge for the 1980s." *Journal of Negro Education* 52(2):94–101.

Harvey, William B., and Diane Scott-Jones. 1985. "We Can't Find Any: The Elusiveness of Black Faculty Members in American Higher Education." *Issues in Education* 3(1):68–76.

Jewell, K. Sue. 1985. "Will the Real Black, Afro-American, Mixed, Colored, Negro Please Stand Up?: Impact of the Black Social Movement, Twenty Years Later." *Journal of Black Studies* 16(1):57–75.

McClain, Benjamin R. 1982. "Racism in Higher Education: A Societal Reflection." *Negro Educational Review* 33(1):34–45.

Miller, Carroll. 1981. "Higher Education for Black Americans: Problems and Issues." *Journal of Negro Education* 50(3):208–223.

"Minorities in Higher Education." 1984. Special Issue. *Integrated Education* 22.

Moody, Ferman. 1980. "The History of Blacks in Vocational Education." *VocEd* 55(1):30–34.

Price-Curtis, William. 1981. "Black Progress Toward Educational Equity." *Educational Leadership* 38(4):277–80.

Reed, Rodney J. 1983. "Affirmative Action in Higher Education: Is It Necessary?" *Journal of Negro Education* 52(3):332–349.

Rossner, J. M. 1972. "Higher Education and Black Americans: An Overview." *Journal of Afro-American Issues* 1(2):189–203.

Spearman, Leonard H. O. 1981. "Federal Roles and Responsibilities Relative to Higher Education of Blacks since 1967." *Journal of Negro Education* 50(3):285–98.

Watson, Bernard C. 1979. "Through the Academic Gateway." *Change* 11(7): 24–28.

RECRUITMENT, ENROLLMENT, ATTRITION, AND RETENTION

Bennett, C., and J. Bean. 1984. "A Conceptual Model of Black Student Attrition at a Predominantly White University." *Journal of Educational Equity and Leadership* 4:173–188.

Davis, DeWitt, Jr. 1980. "Locational Preferences of Black University Students." *Phylon* 41(3):247–56.

Deskins, Donald R. 1983. *Minority Recruitment Data: An Analysis of Baccalaureate Degree Production in the U.S.* Totawa, N.J.: Rowman and Allaheld.

Nettles, Michael T., et al. 1985. *The Causes and Consequences of College Students' Performance: A Focus on Black and White Students' Attrition Rates, Progression Rates and Grade Point Averages.* Nashville, Tenn.: Tennessee Higher Education Commission.

Oliver, John, and Roland Etcheverry. 1987. "Factors Influencing the Decisions of Academically Talented Black Students to Attend College." *Journal of Negro Education* 56(2):152–161.

Pearson, Willie, Jr., and LaRue C. Pearson. 1985. "Baccalaureate Origins of Black American Scientists: A Cohort Analysis." *Journal of Negro Education* 54(1):24–34.

Pruitt, Anne S., and Paul D. Isaac. 1985. "Discrimination in Recruitment, Admission, and Retention of Minority Graduate Students." *Journal of Negro Education* 54(4):526–536.

Richardson, Richard C., Jr., and Louis W. Bender. 1985. *Students in Urban Settings: Achieving the Baccalaureate Degree.* Washington, D.C.: American Association for Higher Education.

————. 1986. *Helping Minorities Achieve Degrees: The Urban Connection.* Tempe: Arizona State University.

Smith, Donald. 1980. *Admission and Retention Problems of Black Students at Seven Predominantly White Universities.* Washington, D.C.: National Advisory Committee on Black Higher Education and Black Colleges and Universities.

Thomas. Gail E. 1980. "Race and Sex Group Equity in Higher Education: Institutional and Major Field Enrollment Statuses." *American Educational Research Journal* 17(2):171–81.

————. 1985. "College Major and Career Inequality: Implications for Black Students." *Journal of Negro Education* 54(4):537–47.

Wilson, Kenneth M. 1981. "Analyzing the Long-Term Performance of Minority and Nonminority Students: Tale of Two Studies." *Research in Higher Education* 15(4):351–75.

ACHIEVEMENT/ASPIRATION/PREDICTION STUDIES

Alexander, Victoria D., and Peggy A. Thoits. 1985. "Token Achievement: An Examination of Proportional Representation and Performance Outcomes." *Social Forces 64(2):332–40.*

Allen, Walter R. 1980. "Preludes to Attainment: Race, Sex, and Student Achievement Orientations." *The Sociological Quarterly* 21:65–79.

Astin, Alexander W., and Lewis C. Solomon. 1979. "Measuring Academic Quality: An Interim Report." *Change* 11(6):48–51.

Braddock, Jomills H., and Marvin P. Dawkins. 1981. "Predicting Black Academic Achievement in Higher Education." *Journal of Negro Education* 50(3): 319–327.

Crain, Robert L., and Rita E. Mahard. 1978. *The Influence of High School Racial Composition on Black College Attendance and Test Performance.* National Longitudinal Study Sponsored Reports Series NCES 78–212. Santa Monica, Calif.: Rand Corp.; Washington, D.C.: National Center for Education Statistics.

Dawkins, Marvin P., and Jomills H. Braddock. 1982. "Explaining Outcomes for Black Students in Higher Education Using National Longitudinal Data." *Negro Educational Review* 33(3–4):146–160.

Epps, Edgar G., and Kenneth W. Jackson. 1985. *Educational and Occupational Aspirations and Early Attainment of Black Males and Females.* Atlanta: Southern Education Foundation.

Grevious, Carole. 1985. "A Comparison of Occupational Aspirations of Urban Black College Students." *Journal of Negro Education* 54(1):35–42.

Nettles, Michael T., A. R. Thoeny, and E. J. Gosman. 1986. "A Comparative and Predictive Analyses of Black and White Students' College Achievement and Experience." *Journal of Higher Education* 57(3):289–318.

ENVIRONMENT/SUPPORT PROGRAMS

Abbott, Kim, et al. 1982. "Counselor Race as a Factor in Counselor Preference." *Journal of College Student Personnel* 23(1):36–40.

Atwood, Nancy K., and William J. Doherty. 1984. "Toward Equity and Excellence in Math and Science Education." *Urban Review* 16(4):235–48.

Breland, Polly S., Michael Escott, Patricia H. Martin, and Phyllis Rubenfeld. 1987. "The Effective Counselor and the Disadvantaged Student: A View from Both Sides." *Journal of Negro Education* 56(2):212–220.

Fogelman, Billye S., and Wain Saeger. 1985. "Examining Sedlacek's Nontraditional Variables of Minority Student Success in a Summer Enrichment Program for Health Careers." *Journal of the National Medical Association* 77(7):545–49.

Follett, Charlene V., Wendy L. Andberg, and Darwin D. Hendel. 1982. "Perceptions of the College Environment by Women and Men Students." *Journal of College Student Personnel* 23(6):525–31.

Liao, Thomas T. 1983. "Using Computer Simulations to Integrate Learning." *Simulation and Games* 14(1):21–28.

Savitz, F. R., and A. Walls. 1986. "A Study of the Relationship between Utilization Patterns of Support Services and the Attrition and Retention Rates of Black College Students." *Psychology* 23(4):12–23.

Schmedinghoff, G. J. 1977. "Counseling Black Students in Higher Education—Is It a Racial, Socioeconomic, or Human Question." *Journal of College Student Personnel* 18(6):472–77.

RACIAL ATTITUDES PERCEPTIONS

Allen, Walter R. 1984. "Race Consciousness and Collective Commitment among Black Students on White Campuses." *Western Journal of Black Studies* 8(3):156–66.

Frisbie, Lynn H. 1980. "A Study of Racism and Sexism at Georgia Southwestern College." *Integrated Education* 18(5–6):61–64.

Morris, Lorenzo, et al. 1981. *Equal Educational Opportunity Scoreboard: The Status of Black Americans in Higher Education, 1970–1979.* Fourth ISEP Status Report, Part I. Washington, D.C.: Howard University, Institute for the Study of Educational Policy.

Pomales, Jay, et al. 1986. "Effects of Black Students' Racial Identity on Perceptions of White Counselors Varying in Cultural Sensitivity." *Journal of Counseling Psychology* 33(1):57–61.

Rosenthal, Steven J. 1980. "Symbolic Racism and Desegregation Divergent Attitudes and Perceptions of Black and White University Students." *Phylon* 41(3):257–66.

Rutledge, Essie Manuel. 1982. "Students' Perceptions of Racism in Higher Education." *Integrated Education* 20(3–5):106–11.

Sampson, William A. 1986. "Desegregation and Racial Tolerance in Academia." *Journal of Negro Education* 55(2):171–84.

Semmes, Clovis E. (Jabulani K. Makalani). 1985. "Minority Status and the Problem of Legitimacy." *Journal of Black Studies* 15(3):259–75.

Spaights, Ernest, Harold E. Dixon, and Susanne Nickolai. 1985. "Racism in Higher Education." *College Student Journal* 19(1):17–22.

CAMPUS ENVIORNMENTS/INSTITUTIONAL DIFFERENCES

Babbitt, Charles E., and Harold J. Burbach. 1979. "Perceptions of Social Control Among Black College Students." *Journal of Negro Education* 48(1):37–42.

Hemmons, Willa Mae. 1982. "From the Halls of Hough and Halstead: A Comparison of Black Students on Predominantly White and Predominantly Black Campuses." *Journal of Black Studies* 12(4):383–402.

Webster, D. S., R. L. Stockard, and J. W. Henson. 1981. "Black Student Elite: Enrollment Shifts of High-Achieving, High Socio-Economic Status Black Students from Black to White Colleges during the 1970s." *College and University* (Spring):283–91.

BLACK COLLEGES

Fleming, John E. 1976. *The Lengthening Shadow of Slavery.* Washington, D.C.: Howard University Press.

Hayes, John T. 1979. *Federal Agencies and the Black College and Universities.* Atlanta: Atlanta University, Resource Center for Science and Engineering.

Heintze, Michael R. 1985. *Private Black Colleges in Texas, 1865–1964.* College Station: Texas A&M University Press.

Hill, Susan T. 1985. *The Traditionally Black Institutions of Higher Education 1860 to 1982.* Washington, D.C.: Department of Education, National Center for Educational Statistics, U.S. Government Printing Office.

Moore, Dorothy G. 1981. "Student Perceptions of Traditional vs. Nontraditional Pursuit of Undergraduate Degrees." *Journal of Negro Education* 50(2):182–90.

Newby, James E. 1983. *Teaching Faculty in Black Colleges and Universities: A Survey of Selected Social Science Disciplines, 1977–1978.* Lanham, Md.: University Press of America.

Nichols, Otis C. 1981. "Inspiration, Aspiration, and Expectations of College Freshmen at Jackson State University." *College Student Journal* (Winter):384–86.

Powell, Christus N. 1981. "A Study to Determine the Influence of Certain Non-Cognitive Factors on Achievement of Freshmen Students Enrolled in a Predominantly Black State-Supported College." *Negro Educational Review* 32(2): 38–45.

Preer, Jean L. 1982. *Lawyers vs. Educators: Black Colleges and Desegregation in Public Higher Education*. Westport, Conn.: Greenwood Press.

Smith, Susan L., and Kaye W. Borgstedt. 1985. "Factors Influencing Adjustment of White Faculty in Predominantly Black Colleges." *Journal of Negro Education* 54(2):148–63.

Thompson, Daniel C. 1986. *A Black Elite: A Profile of Graduates of UNCF Colleges*. Westport, Conn.: Greenwood Press.

ENVIRONMENTAL/SOCIAL NETWORKS/INTERACTIONS

Asante, Molefi Kete, and Hana S. Noor Al-Deen. 1984. "Social Interaction of Black and White College Students: A Research Report." *Journal of Black Studies* 14(4):507–16.

Bennett, Christine. 1984. "Interracial Contact Experience and Attrition Among Black Undergraduates at Predominantly White Universities." *Theory and Research in Social Education* 12(2):19–47.

Feldman, Robert S., and Stanley Orchowsky. 1979. "Race and Performance of Students as Determinants of Teacher Nonverbal Behavior." *Contemporary Educational Psychology* 4(4):324–33.

Littig, Lawrence W., and Cardell E. Williams. 1978. "Need for Affiliation, Self-Esteem and Social Distance for Black Americans." *Motivation and Emotion* 2(4):369–74.

Patterson, Aldrich M., Jr., et al. 1984. "Perceptions of Blacks and Hispanics in Two Campus Environments." *Journal of College Student Personnel* 25(6):513–18.

Pittenger, Judith E., and Sharon L. Hunt. 1984. "Effects of Race Upon the Meaning of Leisure among University Students." *Journal of Negro Education* 53(1): 41–49.

Shingles, Richard D. 1979. "College as a Source of Black Alienation." *Journal of Black Studies* 9(3):267–89.

GRADUATE/PROFESSIONAL STUDENTS

Baratz, Joan C., and Myra Ficklen. 1983. *Participation of Recent Black College Graduates in the Labor Market and in Graduate Education*. Final Report.

Washington, D.C.: Educational Testing Service, Division of Education Policy Research and Services.

Blackwell, James E. 1975. *Access of Black Students to Graduate and Professional Schools.* Atlanta: Southern Education Foundation.

Braithwaite, Ronald L., and Lula Beatty. 1981. "Minority Male Participation in Educational Research and Development: A Recruitment Selection Dilemma." *Journal of Negro Education 50(4):389–400.*

Brazziel, Marian E., and William F. Brazziel. 1987. "Impact of Support for Graduate Study on Program Completion of Black Doctorate Recipients." *Journal of Negro Education* 56(2):145–151.

Frierson, Henry T. 1981. "Minority Participation in R&D: Developing an Undergraduate Feeder System." *Journal of Negro Education* 50(4):401–406.

Hall, Marcia L., and Walter R. Allen. 1982. "Race Consciousness and Achievement: Two Issues in the Study of Black Graduate/Professional Students." *Integrated Education* 20(1–2):56–61.

Hall, Marcia L., Arlene F. Mays, and Walter R. Allen. 1984. "Dreams Deferred: Black Student Career Goals and Fields of Study in Graduate/Professional Schools." *Phylon* 45(4):271–283.

Pruitt, Anne S. 1984. "G*POP and the Federal Role in the Graduate Education of Minorities." *Journal of Negro Education* 53(2):106–113.

WOMEN'S ISSUES

Houston, Lawrence N. 1980. "Predicting Academic Achievement among Specially Admitted Black Female College Students." *Educational and Psychological Measurement* 40(4):1189–1195.

Mednick, M. T., and G. R. Puryear. 1975. "Motivational and Personality Factors Related to Career Goals of Black College Women." *Journal of Social and Behavioral Sciences* 21:1–30.

TESTING BIASES

Green, Robert L., and Robert J. Griffore. 1980. "The Impact of Standardized Testing on Minority Students." *Journal of Negro Education* 49(3):238–52.

Rock, D. A., et al. 1982. *Construct Validity of the GRE Aptitude Test Across Populations—An Empirical Confirmatory Study.* Princeton, N.J.: Educational Testing Service, Graduate Record Examinations Board.

Scheuneman, Janice. 1985. *Exploration of Causes of Bias in Test Items.* Princeton, N.J.: Educational Testing Service, Graduate Record Examinations Board.

FACULTY ISSUES

Bagley, Ayers. 1984. *The Black Education Professoriate.* Portland, Ore.: Soc. Professional Educators.

Ciervo, A. V., and R. E. Janifer. 1984. "Present Dim, Future Bright: A Report on Minority Professionals at Majority Institutions." *Currents* 10:30–33.

Elmore, C. J., and Robert T. Blackburn. 1983. "Black and White Faculty in White Research Universities." *Journal of Higher Education* 54(1):1–15.

London, D. B. G., A. Palmer, and P. H. Lolotsi. 1984. "The Black Educator as a Participant in the University's Role as Moral Authority." *College Student Journal Monograph* 18.

McKay, N. 1983. "Black Woman Professor—White University." *Women's Studies International Forum* (2):143–47.

Newby, James E. 1982. "Goals in Teaching Undergraduates in Black Colleges and Universities: Professional-Centered or Client-Centered." *American Sociologist* 17(2):113–18.

Parker, Woodroe M. 1980. "Black Faculty Collaboration toward Black College Students' Improvement." *Journal of Non-White Concerns in Personnel and Guidance* 8:56–61.

Wharton, Clifton R., Jr. 1980. "Reflections on Black Intellectual Power." *Journal of Black Studies* 10(3):279–94.

Appendix B

Data Sources and Description

Quality of Data

Although the data collected in the National Study of Black College Students rank among the best currently available on African American college students, these data—like those from all studies—have some weaknesses. Most problematic in this respect is the relatively low response rates overall. Perusal of Tables B.1 through B.5 reveals, however, that for several institutions, data collection waves, or subpopulations, the response rates are comparable to the 50- 60-percent average rate characteristic of survey studies conducted on Black students during this decade (Allen 1986).

For example, in the 1982 white schools' first-year student sample, the graduate/professional student response rate was 47 percent, and the undergraduate response rate was 40 percent (Table B.2). Similarly, the 1985 black schools' follow-up student sample response rates for undergraduates was 45 percent and 54 percent for graduate/professional students (Table B.5).

The difficulty with these data arises from the fact that certain years and subpopulations were characterized by low response rates. Conventional social-science wisdom and approaches would argue for the exclusion of these problem groups from the analysis. If we took the easiest route, we would restrict this study to 1982 undergraduates (and the 1985 follow-up) or to graduate/professional students. Such a decision would pump up response rates and remove this serious point for criticism of the study. This is an option that we reject, however, preferring instead to argue our conviction that the subpopulation and study years with problematic response rates should not be peremptorily dismissed from the sample.

271

TABLE B.1
Return Rates
Spring 1981 Predominantly White Schools
Undergraduate and Graduate/Professional Respondents

School	Mailed Questionnaires	Returned Questionnaires	Response Percentage Rates
University of Michigan, Ann Arbor			
−Undergraduates	507	130	25.6
−Graduate/Professional	207	87	42.0
Total:	714	217	30.4
University of North Carolina, Chapel Hill			
−Undergraduates	513	183	35.7
−Graduate/Professional	219	94	42.9
Total:	732	277	37.8
University of California, Los Angeles			
−Undergraduates	522	143	27.4
−Graduate/Professional	253	85	33.6
Total:	775	228	29.4
State University of New York, Stony Brook			
−Undergraduates	256	58	21.7
−Graduate/Professional	100	41	41.0
Total:	367	99	27.0
Arizona State University			
−Undergraduate	363	67	18.5
−Graduate/Professional	84	22	26.2
Total:	447	89	19.9
Memphis State University			
−Undergraduates	388	114	29.4
−Graduate/Professional	100	24	24.0
Total:	488	138	28.3
Grand Totals:			
−Undergraduates	2,560	695	27.0
−Graduate/Professional	963	353	37.0
Total:	3,523	1,048	30.0
Adjusted Grand Totals (Minus SUNY and ASU)			
−Undergraduates	1,930	570	30.0
−Graduate/Professional	799	290	37.0
Total:	2,709	860	32.0

TABLE B.2
Return Rates
Spring 1982 Predominantly White Schools
Undergraduate and Graduate/Professional Respondents

School	Mailed Questionnaires	Returned Questionnaires	Response Percentage Rates
University of Michigan, Ann Arbor			
—Undergraduates	216	82	38
—Graduate/Professional	140	94	67
Total:	356	176	49
University of North Carolina, Chapel Hill			
—Undergraduates	362	188	52
—Graduate/Professional	123	67	54
Total:	485	255	53
University of California, Los Angeles			
—Undergraduates	264	119	45
—Graduate/Professional	118	56	47
Total:	382	175	46
State University of New York, Stony Brook			
—Undergraduates	149	46	30
—Graduate/Professional	64	16	25
Total:	213	62	29
Arizona State University			
—Undergraduate	146	64	30
—Graduate/Professional	36	18	50
Total:	182	82	45
Memphis State University			
—Undergraduates	487	163	33
—Graduate/Professional	210	80	38
Total:	697	243	35
University of Wisconsin, Madison			
—Undergraduates	327	160	49
—Graduate/Professional	95	55	58
Total:	422	215	107
Eastern Michigan University			
—Undergraduates	363	80	22
—Graduate/Professional	81	21	26
Total:	444	101	23
Grand Totals:			
—Undergraduates	2,314	902	39
—Graduate/Professional	867	407	47
Total:	3,181	1,309	41
Adjusted Grand Totals (Minus SUNY and EMU i.e., lowest response rates)			
—Undergraduates	1,802	776	43
—Graduate/Professional	722	370	51
Total:	2,524	1,146	45

Return Rates
Spring 1983 Historically Black Schools
Undergraduate and Graduate/Professional Respondents

School	Mailed Questionnaires	Returned Questionnaires	Adjusted Percentage Return
North Carolina Central University			
−Undergraduate	634	147	23
−Graduate/Professional	223	66	30
Total:	857	213	25
Southern University			
−Undergraduate	350	79	23
−Graduate/Professional	167	42	25
Total:	517	121	23
Texas Southern University			
−Undergraduate	528	99	19
−Graduate/Professional	123	25	20
Total:	651	124	19
Jackson State University			
−Undergraduates	370	92	25
−Graduate/Professional	180	38	21
Total:	550	130	24
North Carolina A & T University			
−Undergraduate	372	106	28
−Graduate/Professional	83	23	28
Total:	455	129	28
Central State University			
−Undergraduate	572	114	20
−Graduate/Professional	0	0	0
Total:	572	114	20
Morgan State University			
−Undergraduate	569	100	18
−Graduate/Professional	161	41	25
Total:	730	141	19
Florida A & M University			
−Undergraduate	535	96	18
−Graduate/Professional	43	12	28
Total:	578	108	19
Grand Totals:			
−Undergraduates	3,930	833	21
−Graduate/Professional	980	247	25
Total:	4,910	1,080	22
Adjusted Grand Totals (Minus TSU, MSU, and FAMU i.e., lowest response rates)			
−Undergraduates	2,298	538	23
−Graduate/Professional	653	169	26
Total:	2,951	707	24

TABLE B.4
Return Rates
Spring 1985 Predominantly White Schools
Undergraduate and Graduate/Professional Respondents

School	Mailed Questionnaires	Returned Questionnaires	Adjusted Percentage Return
University of Michigan			
−Undergraduate	82	32	40
−Graduate/Professional	95	39	46
Total:	177	71	43
University of South Carolina, Chapel Hill			
−Undergraduate	188	54	30
−Graduate/Professional	67	30	51
Total:	255	84	35
University of Los Angeles, California,			
−Undergraduate	121	44	38
−Graduate/Professional	56	23	51
Total:	177	67	42
Memphis State University			
−Undergraduate	164	45	28
−Graduate/Professional	81	39	51
Total:	245	84	36
Arizona State University			
−Undergraduate	64	15	24
−Graduate/Professional	18	11	69
Total:	82	26	33
State University of New York, Stony Brook			
−Undergraduate	46	16	44
−Graduate/Professional	16	5	36
Total:	62	21	42
University of Wisconsin, Madison			
−Undergraduate	161	51	36
−Graduate/Professional	55	23	51
Total:	216	74	40
Eastern Michigan University			
−Undergraduate	80	26	37
−Graduate/Professional	24	3	14
Total:	104	29	31
Grand Totals:			
−Undergraduate	906	283	31.2
−Graduate/Professional	412	173	42.0
Total:	1,318	456	34.6

TABLE B.5
Return Rates
Fall 1985 Historically Black Schools
Undergraduate and Graduate/Professional Respondents

School	Mailed Questionnaire	Returned Questionnaire	Adjusted Percentage Return
North Carolina Central University			
−Undergraduate	149	66	47
−Graduate/Professional	55	34	64
Total:	204	100	52
Southern University			
−Undergraduate	72	29	42
−Graduate/Professional	31	13	43
Total:	103	42	41
Texas Southern University			
−Undergraduate	97	30	38
−Graduate/Professional	0	0	0
Total:	97	30	38
Jackson State University			
−Undergraduate	93	35	39
−Graduate/Professional	30	16	59
Total:	123	51	44
North Carolina A & T University			
−Undergraduate	100	53	55
−Graduate/Professional	14	8	62
Total:	114	61	56
Central State University			
−Undergraduate	109	58	58
−Graduate/Professional	0	0	0
Total:	109	58	58
Morgan State University			
−Undergraduate	126	63	55
−Graduate/Professional	26	13	52
Total:	152	76	54
Florida A & M University			
−Undergraduate	114	50	48
−Graduate/Professional	5	3	60
Total:	119	53	49
Grand Totals:			
−Undergraduates	860	384	44.7
−Graduate/Professional	161	87	54
Total:	1,021	471	50

The argument for retaining low-response-rate subgroups in this analysis can be supported on both theoretical and empirical grounds. From the theoretical viewpoint, this study was originally conceptualized as an exercise in model specification rather than as an hypothesis testing effort. We did not accept the notion that consensus existed over what questions were important to ask about Black student college experiences or the accompanying assumption that what the field now requires was empirical evaluation of these accepted propositions. Instead, we approached the study of Black students' college experiences as essentially uncharted terrain. Thus, this study's focus was largely exploratory. The goal of this research was to identify variables of key importance in the determination of student outcomes and to suggest how these variables might be interrelated.

Traditionally, social science has applied different response-rate expectations to exploratory research or to research aimed at the specification of theoretical models. Such studies often use data sets which are nonrandom, regionally restricted, or that were originally collected for a different purpose to create the overarching conceptual outline for a model. Once a model of the complex processes underlying Black students' college experiences and outcomes has been specified, *then* the next logical step will be to empirically evaluate this model.

This step is beyond the scope of data and study presented here. The larger, confirmatory, *next* study will require data drawn from diverse subpopulations of Black college students, data about institutional characteristics, data from faculty, possibly matching data on other-race students, and, of course, it will require data which are representative of the Black college student *and* data which have high-reponse rates.

It is our conviction that, for the purposes emphasized in this study, the quality of data is more than sufficient. Even where certain waves of data collection or specific subpopulations are associated with low response rates, the problem is not of sufficient magnitude as to disqualify this research from serious consideration. So, on theoretical grounds, a very strong case can be made for retaining within the analysis data collection waves and subpopulations with low response rates. Interestingly enough, there are also strong empirical grounds for retaining these elements in the research.

EXTERNAL COMPARISON OF DATA: NATIONALLY REPRESENTATIVE DATA SETS

In the course of this research, we have compared our sample to larger, more representative samples of college students. The results from these comparisons leave us confident in the conclusion that our data do provide in sizeable degree an accurate picture of the model Black college student. We have also undertaken internal comparisons in our sample, comparing different data collection waves and different subgroups to establish whether differences in response rates internal to the study translate into statistical different student profiles.

Comparison of the National Study of Black College Students (NSBCS) 1982-sample of Black freshmen (on white campuses) to the 1982-sample of freshmen from the American Freshmen survey revealed interesting parallels. "Each fall since 1966, the Cooperative Institutional Research Program (CIRP) has collected survey data to profile the characteristics, attitudes, values, educational achievements, and future goals of the students who enter college in the United States" (Astin 1987: 7). The annual sample consists of about 200,000 entering freshmen at a nationally representative sample of over 500 two and four year institutions.

Table B.6 provides a comparison on key indicators of our sample from 1982 freshmen to the 1982 freshmen data for all race students from the CIRP. Predictably the educational backgrounds of NSBCS students' mothers and fathers were lower than for the national survey. Fewer parents of NSBCS freshmen students were college graduates, and more had not graduated from high school. As regards high-school academic performance, the freshmen in our sample reported comparable grades in high school to those of students in the national sample. Nearly equal proportions of both samples fell in the highest and lowest categories of grade-point average. However, 33 percent of the national sample had grade averages of 3.0 or better, versus 26 percent of our sample.

A more specific comparison of NSBCS 1982 freshmen to a national sample of freshmen adds perspective to questions about the representativeness of our data. The College Entrance Examination Board produces an annual summary of the characteristics of "college-bound" seniors or secondary-school seniors who are registered for the Admissions Testing Program (Ramist 1984). This summary is broken down by race/ethnicity, gender and other relevant student characteristics.

Table B.7 provides a comparison on common variables of the 1982 NSBCS freshmen sample with the 77,137 Black students who participated in the 1983 Academic Testing Program nationally. The 1982 NSBCS freshmen reported educational backgrounds for their mothers and fathers which were very much in line with the patterns in the national sample. However, the parents of the NSBCS sample freshmen were slightly better-educated than the parents of freshmen in the national sample. In the NSBCS sample, 12.6 percent of the students had mothers who were college graduates versus 10.2 percent for the national sample. About 13 percent of the students in NSBCS had fathers who had graduated from college as opposed to 12.3 percent in the national sample.

TABLE B.6
Comparison of NSBCS Freshmen Sample
and American Freshmen Data for 1982

Mother's Education	American Freshmen Data Percentages	NSBCS Freshmen Data Percentages
Less Than High School	11.0	20.7
High School Graduate	48.5	38.9
Some College	14.6	19.3
College Graduate	25.9	21.1
	100.0	100.0

Father's Education	American Freshmen Data percentages	NSBCS Freshmen Data Percentages
Less Than High School	14.5	26.1
High School Graduate	34.2	38.2
Some College	13.4	16.2
College Graduate	37.9	19.5
	100.0	100.0

High-School Grade-Point Average	American Freshmen Data Percentages	NSBCS Freshmen Data Percentages
Less Than 2.5	40.3	35.2
Less Than 3.0	26.5	38.9
Less Than 3.5	25.9	19.6
Greater Than 3.5	7.5	6.3
	100.0	100.0

Source: American Freshmen Data are from the "Cooperative Institutional Research Program" files. Alexander Astin, Kenneth C. Green, and William S. Korn. 1987. *The American Freshman Twenty-Year Trends, 1966–85.* Los Angeles: University of California, Graduate School of Education, The Higher Education Research Institute.

The family income of NSBCS freshmen was predictably higher than that of Black freshmen in the national sample. Almost 20 percent of NSBCS students reported family income greater than $40,000 compared to 9 percent of the national sample. We would expect the NSBCS Black freshmen to be more affluent compared to the national sample, since they attend larger, more expensive, flagship state universities, while the national group includes students who attend two-year, less-expensive, smaller, and less academically prestigious institutions.

Finally, it is instructive to compare the characteristics of NSBCS University of Michigan students to the entire universe of Black University of Michigan students matriculating from 1975 through 1981. From 1975 through 1981, the University of Michigan has maintained computerized academic records on all students matriculating (Allen et al. 1989). The academic records of the 30,806 students participating in this study of student

TABLE B.7
Comparison of NSBCS 1982 Freshmen Sample and CEEB
College-Bound Seniors 1983: Black Students**

Mother's Education	CEEB Seniors Percentages	NSBCS Freshmen Percentages
Less Than High School	26.1	27.4
High School Graduate	38.2	26.4
Some College	16.2	19.5
College Graduate	10.2	12.6
Graduate/Professional School	9.3	14.1
	100.0	100.0

Father's Education	CEEB Seniors Percentages	NSBCS Freshmen Percentages
Less Than High School	20.7	21.0
High School Graduate	38.9	28.0
Some College	19.3	27.9
College Graduate	12.3	13.3
Graduate/Professional School	8.8	9.8
	100.0	100.0

Family Income	CEEB Seniors Percentages	NSBCS Freshmen Percentages
Less Than $12,000	39.5	27.8
Less Than $18,000	19.4	15.0
Less Than $30,000	23.2	26.2
Less Than $40,000	8.9	11.1
Greater Than $40,000	9.0	19.9
	100.0	100.0

**Source: Data for CEEB college-bound high-school seniors are from Leonard Ramist and Solomon Arbeiter. 1984. *Profiles: College-Bound Seniors, 1983*. New York: College Entrance Examination Board.

attrition through 1981 were updated until the last term of enrollment. A total of 1,738 Black students were included in this retention data file in 1981. It is to this group that our University of Michigan 1981 NSBCS sample is compared (Table B.8).

The NSBCS Black students reported high-school grades that were significantly better than the grades of Black students in the overall university retention file. A bit more than 49 percent of NSBCS students had high school averages of 3.5 or better, as compared to 31 percent of the total population of UM Black students. Even allowing for the inflation factor associated with self-reporting, this is still quite a large difference.

The academic performance level in college is also skewed in the direction of the NSBCS sample, although less so. Among the total sample of UM Black students, almost 24 percent report college grade-point averages of less than 2.0 (or "C") as compared to a bit more than 6 percent of the

TABLE B.8
Comparison of NSBCS 1981 Sample and University of
Michigan Retention File Data for Black Students

High-School Grade-Point Average	University of Michigan Retention File Percentages	NSBCS Percentages
Less Than 2.5	9.0 (153)	4.1 (26)
Less Than 3.0	21.8 (367)	15.9 (182)
Less Than 3.5	38.2 (644)	31.5 (187)
Greater Than 3.5	31.0 (521)	49.4 (234)
	100.0 (1685)	100.0 (629)

University Grade-Point Average	University of Michigan Retention File Percentages	NSBCS Percentages
Less Than 2.0	23.8 (394)	6.4 (42)
Less Than 2.5	32.1 (532)	30.0 (196)
Less Than 3.0	31.4 (519)	39.2 (256)
Less Than 3.5	10.6 (175)	20.7 (135)
Greater Than 3.5	2.1 (35)	3.7 (24)
	100.0 (1655)	100.0 (653)

Source: Data for University of Michigan are from Walter R. Allen and Jonathan Stern. 1989. *Update on Student Retention and Academic Progress at the University of Michigan, Ann Arbor 1978–1982: An Analysis of the Freshman Retention File Data.* Ann Arbor, Michigan: Center for Afro-American and African Studies.

NSBCS sample. Of course, some exaggeration of this difference results from the retention files' inclusion of last-term-of-enrollment grade-averages for Black students who eventually dropped-out or were expelled for poor academic performance.

Taken together, these comparisons suggest that our sample of Black students in the NSBCS data files are characterized by slightly higher socio-economic status than the norm for African American college students nationally and at the University of Michigan in particular. Still, there is sufficient similarity to support the argument that NSBCS students do not represent a complete anomaly. The students in the NSBCS sample do seem to be representative of the broader profile of Black college students in many important respects.

INTERNAL COMPARISON OF DATA

Turning our attention to the examination and comparison of internal differences in the NSBCS data files, we again find reason to down play the ultimate effects of nonresponse on the quality of these data as regards representativeness. Below, we report results from a comparison of the 1981 and 1982 data collections of the NSBCS. Since the response rates in 1981 were much lower, we were interested in examining the hypothesis of "no real difference" between the two years. We began with the hypotheses that the low response rate in 1981 did not unduly bias this sample as compared to the 1982 sample which had higher response rates. Nine of the sixteen variables compared resulted in significant differences between the 1981 and 1982 samples. Only two of these differences remained significant when only freshmen from 1981 were compared to the group of freshmen who constitute the 1982 sample. The overall picture, then, is one of great similarity between the 1981 and 1982 surveys in terms of student background, experiences, group consciousness and achievement.

The internal comparison of schools with different response rates in the NSBCS dataset produced mixed findings. For the most part, revealed differences in the 1981 data set were more a matter of degree. Thus, although high-school grade-point average was significantly different for North Carolina and UCLA, the actual difference was between averages of 3.5 and 3.3. The significant difference between the University of Michigan and Memphis State University on college grade-point averages was the difference between 2.7 and 2.6.

The comparison of 1982 schools with response rates greater than 40 percent to those below 40 percent was undertaken next. Of eight comparisons, only three achieved statistical significance (percent freshman, students with children and students from large cities). For the most part, these differences were either not systematic or of little substantive importance. Schools with response rates that exceeded 40 percent had a much larger fraction of freshmen respondents, as well as fewer students who were parents and fewer students from large cities. While these are important differences, they do not represent findings which substantially compromise these data.

Several background, undergraduate experience, group consciousness, and undergraduate achievement variables from the 1981 and 1982 undergraduate surveys were compared. It is important to note that the 1982 survey is not only separated by a year from the 1981 study, but that it involved a difference within campus sample, and included two additional campuses. The 1982 sample involved only newly enrolled students—that is, entering freshman and new transfer students. Thus, the 1982 survey is disproportionately composed of freshmen.

Second, in addition to the six campuses involved in the 1981 survey (the University of Michigan at Ann Arbor, University of North Carolina in Chapel Hill, University of California at Los Angeles, Memphis State University, Arizona State University at Tempe, and the State University of New York at Stony Brook) two more universities were included in the 1982 survey (University of Wisconsin at Madison, and Eastern Michigan University at Ypsilanti). Any differences in response patterns may, therefore, be the result of time of survey, sample composition, or the addition of two more universities to the 1982 survey.

In order to make more accurate comparisons two analysis strategies were pursued. First, we report tests for two comparisons: a comparison of the 1981 responses to those from a reduced version of the 1982 survey (1982R) which includes only the six universities used in the 1981 survey, and a comparison to the full 1982 survey (1982F).

Second, where significant differences emerge the 1981 freshman are then compared to the 1982R freshman. If a difference remains at this point then a "true" or "real" difference between the two studies can be inferred. The exact cause of such differences, however, may remain a source of speculation.

The main hypothesis is that there are no real differences between the two studies. The background variables considered are: gender, size of high school, high-school class rank, high-school GPA, and family income. The current undergraduate experiences variables considered are: class level; overall evaluations of Black student relations with white students, faculty, and staff; and experiences of discrimination. Four group consciousness variables are also considered. Two achievement variables are considered: current occupational aspirations and university GPA. All tests involve maximum likelihood chi-squares.

Are there significant differences between the two surveys in the background characteristics of the students? Of the six background variables considered, four show significant differences: class level, high-school class rank, high-school GPA, and family income. The difference in class-level composition is due to sampling design. The differences in high-school class rank are not large and disappear when only the freshman for 1981 and 1982R are compared. Similarly, the differences in high-school GPA are not large. Indeed, the difference is significant only when 1981 and the 1982F samples are compared, and it disappears when 1981 and 1982R are compared. This difference does not appear when just freshman from the two latter samples are compared. There is a significant difference in reported family incomes that remains when the maximally similar 1981 and 1982 freshmen are compared. The 1981 sample apparently has more students with family incomes below $15,000. There were no differences between surveys by gender or size of high school.

Of the four undergraduate-experience variables considered, only one shows a significant difference. Both the 1982R and 1982F results show a tendency to rate overall Black students' relations with white faculty more positively than did students in the 1981 survey. This difference, however, vanishes when only freshman from the 1981 and 1982R samples are compared. Ratings of overall black students' relations with white university staff and students, as well as reports of experiences of discrimination, were similar for all comparisons.

All four group-consciousness variables examined reveal significant differences between the 1981 survey and 1982R and 1982F samples. The general pattern is for the 1982R and 1982F samples to appear more conservative and less group-conscious. None of these differences hold up, however, when just 1981 and 1982R freshman are compared.

Are there differences between the surveys in undergraduate achievements? Although there are no differences in occupational aspirations, the 1982R and 1982F samples have significantly more students with low GPAs. This difference holds up when just the 1981 and 1982R freshman are compared.

In sum, nine of the sixteen variables considered resulted in significant differences between the 1981 and 1982R samples (ten of sixteen if 1981 and 1982F are compared). Only two of these differences (aside from class-level composition) remain significant when comparing just the freshmen from 1981 and 1982R samples: family income and university GPA. Neither of these differences is very large. Both are under 10 percent. The overall picture, then, is one of great similarly between the surveys in terms of students' backgrounds, experiences, group consciousness, and achievement.

The empirical results from the external and internal comparisons of the NSBCS data essentially support our conclusions from the examination of theoretical rationales for including data from low-response groups in this analysis. What we lose by excluding these data would seem to far outweigh any resulting gains. Both theoretical and empirical considerations provide compelling arguments for retaining these data in the study. In conclusion, our position is that the extensive, comprehensive nature of the National Study of Black College Students data files makes them appropriate for use in the specification of a model of Black college students' experiences and outcomes—in spite of the low response rates of certain subgroups in the data files.

Notes and References

FOREWORD

References

Anderson, James D. 1988. *The Education of Blacks in the South, 1860–1935.* Chapel Hill: University of North Carolina Press.

Gurin, Patricia, and Edgar G. Epps. 1975. *Black Consciousness, Identity, and Achievement: A Study of Black Students in Historically Black Colleges.* New York: Wiley.

Hart, Philip S. 1984. *Institutional Effectiveness in the Production of Black Baccalaureates.* Atlanta: Southern Education Foundation.

Jencks, Christopher and David Riesman. 1968. *The Academic Revolution.* New York: Doubleday.

Patel, Narenda H. 1988. *Student Transfers from White and Black Colleges.* Lanham, Md.: University Press of America.

Shade, Barbara. 1982. "African American Cognitive Style: A Variable in School Success?" *Review of Educational Research.* 52(2):219–244.

Tinto, Vincent. 1975. "Dropout from Higher Education: A Theoretical Synthesis of Recent Research." *Review of Educational Research.* 45(1):89–125.

INTRODUCTION

References

Allen, Walter R. 1982. "Black and Blue: Black Students at the University of Michigan." *LS&A Magazine.* Ann Arbor: University of Michigan, Dean's Office, College of Literature, Science and the Arts. 6(1):13–17.

————. 1985. "Black Student, White Campus: Structural, Interpersonal and Psychological Correlates of Success." *Journal of Negro Education.* 54(2):134–147.

————. 1986. *Gender and Campus Race Differences In Black Student Academic Performance, Racial Attitudes and College Satisfaction.* Atlanta: Southern Education Foundation.

American Council on Education. 1988. *Minorities in Higher Education.* Washington, D.C.: Office of Minority Concerns, American Council on Education.

Anderson, James D. 1984. "The Schooling and Achievement of Black Children: Before and after *Brown* v. *Topeka,* 1900–1980." Advances in Motivation and Achievement JAI Press 1:103–122.

Astin, Alexander N. 1982. *Minorities in American Higher Education: Recent Trends, Current Prospectives and Recommendations.* San Francisco: Jossey-Bass.

Astin, Helen, and Patricia H. Cross. 1981. "Black Students in White Institutions." Gail E. Thomas, ed. *Black Students in Higher Education in the 1970's.* Westport, Connecticut: Greenwood Press. 30–45.

Blackwell, James E. 1982. "Demographics of Desegregation." Reginald Wilson, ed. *Race and Equity in Higher Education.* Washington, D.C.: American Council on Education. 28–70.

Braddock, Jomills and Marvin P. Dawkins. 1981. "Predicting Black Academic Achievement in Higher Education." *Journal of Negro Education* (Summer):319–325.

Deskins, Donald R. Jr. 1983. *Minority Recruitment Data: An Analysis of Baccalaureate Degree Production in the U.S.* Totawa, N.J.: Rowman and Allanheld.

Durkheim, Emile. 1925/1961. *Moral Education: A Study in the Theory and Application of the Sociology of Education.* New York: Free Press.

Fleming, Jacqueline. 1984. *Blacks in College: A Comparative Study of Students' Success in Black and in White Institutions.* San Francisco: Jossey-Bass.

Friere, Paulo. 1982. *Pedagogy of the Oppressed.* New York: Continuum.

Gurin, Patricia, and Edgar G. Epps. 1975. *Black Consciousness, Identity and Achievement: A Study of Students in Historically Black Colleges.* New York: Wiley Press.

Hall, Marcia, Arlene F. Mays, and Walter R. Allen. 1984. "Dreams Deferred: Black Student Career Goals and Fields of Study in Graduate/Professional Students." *Phylon* 45(4):271–283.

Morris, Lorenzo. 1979. *Elusive Equality: The Status of Black Americans in Higher Education.* Washington D.C.: Howard University Press, Institute for the Study of Education Policy.

National Advisory Committee on Black Higher Education and Black Colleges and Universities. 1980. *Still a Lifeline: The Status of Historically Black Colleges and Universities, 1975–1978.* Washington D.C.: U.S. Department of Education.

National Center for Education Statistics. 1982. *Fall Enrollment in Colleges and Universities, 1980.* Washington, D.C.: U.S. Department of Education.

Nettles, Michael, et al. 1985. *The Causes and Consequences of College Students' Attrition Rates, Progression Rates and Grade Point Averages.* Nashville, Tenn.: Higher Education Commission.

Pearson, Willie, and LaRue C. Pearson. 1985. "Baccalaureate Origins of Black American Scientists: A Cohort Analysis." *Journal of Negro Education.* 54(1):24–34.

Peterson, Marvin, et al. 1978. *Black Students on White Campuses: The Impacts of Increased Black Enrollments.* Ann Arbor: The University of Michigan, Institute for Social Research.

Smith, A. Wade and Walter R. Allen. 1984. "Modeling Black Student Academic Performance in Higher Education." *Research in Higher Education.* 21(2):210–225.

Thomas, Gail E. 1981. (Ed.) *Black College Students in Higher Education: Conditions and Experiences in the 1970s.* Westport, Conn.: Greenwood Press.

———. 1984. *Black College Students and Factors Influencing Their Major Field Choice.* Atlanta: Southern Education Foundation.

Thomas, Gail E., James M. McPartland, and Denise C. Gottfredson. 1980. *The Status of Desegregation and Black-White Participation in Higher Education.* Report No. 598. Baltimore, Md.: Johns Hopkins University, Center for Social Organization of Schools.

Woodson, Carter G. 1933 / 1969. *The Miseducation of the Negro.* Washington, D.C.: Associated Publishers.

CHAPTER 1

Note

*This project is supported by funds received from the Office of the Vice Provost for Minority Affairs at the University of Michigan in Ann Arbor.

References

Bloom, Allan. 1987. *Closing of the American Mind.* New York: Simon and Schuster.

Deskins, Donald R., Jr. 1984. "Achievement, Disappointments, and Prospects: Minority Graduate Students at Michigan." *Rackham Reports.* (Spring):1–2.

Gamson, William A., and Andre Modigliani. 1987. "The Changing Culture of Affirmative Action." *Research in Political Sociology.* 3:137–177.

Hirsch, Eric. D., Jr. 1987. *Cultural Literacy: What Every American Needs to Know.* Boston: Houghton Mifflin.

National Center for Educational Statistics. 1975–76, 1976–77, 1978–79, 1980–81, 1982–83, and 1984–85. *Data on Earned Degrees Conferred from Institutions of Higher Education by Race, Ethnicity, and Sex.* Washington, D.C.: Higher Education General Information Survey (HEGIS).

———. 1976, 1978, 1980, 1982, and 1984. *Racial, Ethnic, and Sex Enrollment Data from Institutions of Higher Learning.* Washington, D.C.: Higher Education General Information Survey (HEGIS).

U.S. Bureau of the Census. 1980. *Census of Population, 1980.* Washington, D.C.: U.S. Government Printing Office.

U.S. Department of Commerce. 1962, 1970, 1980, and 1986. *County Business Patterns for the United States.* Washington D.C.: U.S. Government Printing Office.

Wattenberg, Ben J. 1987. *The Birth Dearth: What Happens When People in Free Countries Don't Have Enough Babies?* New York: Pharos Books.

Western Interstate Commission for Higher Education. 1988. *High School Graduates: Projections by State, 1986 to 2004.* Boulder, Col.: WICHE.

Wilson, William J. 1987. *The Truly Disadvantaged: The Inner City, The Underclass and Public Policy.* Chicago: University of Chicago Press.

CHAPTER 2

Note

*A presentation to the Southern Sociological Society's annual meeting in Knoxville, Tenn., in April 1984.

References

Freeman, Richard G. 1976. *Black Elite: The New Labor Market for Highly Qualified Black Americans.* New York: McGraw Hill.

Higher Education General Information Survey (HEGIS). 1975, 1976, 1980, 1981. *Racial, Ethnic and Sex Enrollment Data from Institutions of Higher Learning.* Washington, D.C.: National Center for Education Statistics.

————. 1975, 1976, 1980, 1981. *Data on Earned Degrees Conferred from Institutions of Higher Education by Race, Ethnicity and Sex.* Washington, D.C.: National Center for Educational Statistics.

Hodgkinson, Harold. 1983. "Guess Who's Coming to College: Your Students in 1990." (Report). Washington, D.C.: National Institute for Independent Colleges and Universities.

Institute for the Study of Educational Policy. 1981. "Equal Educational Opportunity Scoreboard: The Status of Black Americans in Higher Education 1970–79."

U.S. Bureau of the Census. 1973A. "Educational Attainment: March, 1972" *Current Population Reports,* ser. P–20, no. 243. Washington, D.C.

————. 1973B. "Persons of Spanish Origin in the United States." *Current Population Reports,* ser. P–20, no. 250. Washington, D.C.

————. 1981. "School Enrollment—Social and Economic Characteristics of Students: October, 1974." *Current Population Reports,* ser. P–20, no. 286. Washington, D.C.

CHAPTER 3

Notes

1. In some cases, dichotomous dummy variables in simple linear regression equations may create estimation problems. This is especially true when the distribution on a dichotomous dependent variable is highly skewed. However, this was not the case for the present dependent measure where 51 percent of the total sample indicated a major in the natural and technical sciences. Thus, ordinary least-squares regression was viewed as appropriate for this analysis.

2. The number of Blacks in the sample who were enrolled in predominantly white institutions was too small to construct separate regression equations for Blacks in public versus private white institutions.

References

Allen, Walter R. 1981. "Correlates of Black Student Adjustment, and Aspirations at a Predominantly White Southern University." Gail E. Thomas, ed. *Black Students in Higher Education: Conditions and Experiences in the 1970s.* Westport, Conn.: Greenwood Press.

————. 1986. *Gender and Campus Race Differences in Black Student Academic Performance, Racial Attitudes and College Satisfaction.* Atlanta: Southern Education Foundation.

Angle, J., and D. A. Wissman. 1981. "Greater College Major and Earnings." *Sociology of Education* 54:25–33.

Berryman, Sue E. 1983. *Who Will Do Science?* New York: The Rockefeller Foundation.

Blackwell, James E. 1981. *Mainstreaming Outsiders: The Production of Black Professionals.* Bayside, N.Y.: General Hall, Inc.

Braddock, Jomills H. 1981. "Desegregation and Black Student Attrition." *Urban Education* 15:403–418.

Cebula, Richard J., and Jerry Lopes. 1981. "Determinants of Student Choice of Undergraduate Major Field." *American Educational Research Journal* 19: 303–312.

Davis, James. 1966. *Undergraduate Career Decisions.* Chicago: Aldine Publishing Company.

Fox, Lynn. 1976. "Women and the Career Relevance of Mathematics and Science." *School Science and Mathematics* 26:347–353.

Gottfredson, L. S. 1978. *Race and Sex Differences in Occupational Aspirations: Their Development and Consequences for Occupational Segregation,* Report No. 254. Baltimore, Md.: Johns Hopkins University, Center for Social Organization of Schools.

Gurin, Patricia and Edgar G. Epps. 1975. *Black Consciousness, Identity, and Achievement: A Study of Students in Historically Black Colleges.* New York: Wiley.

Herzog, Regula A. 1982. "High School Seniors' Occupational Plans and Values: Trends in Sex Differences 1976 through 1980." *Sociology of Education* 55:1–13.

Holland, J. L. 1966. *The Psychology of Vocational Choice: A Theory of Personality Types and Model Environments.* Waltham, Mass.: Blaisdell.

Kerchoff, Alan C., and Richard T. Campbell. 1977. "Social Status Differences In the Explanation of Educational Ambition." *Social Forces* 53(3):701–714.

Kerlinger, E. N., and E. J. Pedhazur. 1974. *Multiple Regression in Behavior Research.* New York: Holt, Rinehart, and Winston.

Koch, James V. 1972. "Student Choice of Undergraduate Major Field of Study and Private Internal Rates of Return." *Industrial and Labor Relations Review* 26:680–685.

Maccoby, B. E., and C. N. Jacklin. 1974. *The Psychology of Sex Differences.* Stanford, California: The Stanford University Press.

Olivas, Michael A. 1979. *The Dilemma of Access: Minorities in Two-Year Colleges.* Washington, D.C.: Howard University Press.

Portes, A., and K. L. Wilson. 1976. "Black-White Differences in Educational Attainment." *American Sociology Review* 41:414–431.

Rosenfeld, Rachel A. 1980. "Race and Sex Differences in Career Dynamics." *American Sociological Review* 45:583–609.

Sells, L. W. 1976. "The Mathematics Filter and the Education of Women and Minorities." Paper presented at the annual meeting of the American Association for the Advancement of Science. Boston, Mass.

Thomas, Gail E. 1980. "Race and Sex Differences and Similarities in the Process of College Entry." *Higher Education* 9:1979–2202.

————. 1981. "Student and Institutional Characteristics as Determinants of Prompt College Graduation for Race and Sex Groups." *The Sociological Quarterly* 22:327–345.

————. 1983. *The Access and Success of Blacks and Hispanics in U.S. Graduate and Profession Education.* Washington, D.C.: National Academy Press.

————. 1984. *Black College Students and Factors Influencing Their Major Field Choice.* Atlanta: Southern Education Foundation.

Thomas, Gail E., K. L. Alexander, and B. K. Ekland. 1979. "Access to Higher Education: The Importance of Race, Sex, Social Class and Academic Credentials." *School Review* 87:133–156.

Trent, William T. 1983. *Race and Sex Differences in Degree Attainment and Major Field Distributions from 1975–76 to 1980–81.* Baltimore, Md.: The Johns Hopkins University, Center for Social Organization of Schools.

Turner, Ralph H. 1960. "Sponsored and Contest Mobility and the School System. *American Sociology Review* 25:855–867.

Vetter, Betty E., and Eleanor L. Babco. 1986. *Professional Women and Minorities.* Washington, D.C.: Scientific Manpower Commission, Manpower Data Resource Service.

Werts, C. E. 1966. *Career Changes in College.* Evanston, Ill.: National Scholarship Corporation.

Willingham, Warren W. 1970. *Free-Access to Higher Education.* New York: College Entrance Examination Board.

CHAPTER 4

References

Aiken, L. R. 1964. "The Prediction of Academic Success and Early Attrition by Means of a Multiple Choice Biographical Inventor." *American Educational Research Journal* 1:127–35.

Anastasi, A., J. J. Meade, and A. A. Schneiders. 1960. *The Validation of a Biographical Inventory as a Predictor of College Success.* Princeton, N.J.: College of Entrance Examination Board.

Astin, Alexander W. 1964. "Personal and Environmental Factors Associated with College Dropouts among High Aptitude Students." *Journal of Education Psychology* 55:219–227.

Ayers, I., and R. W. Bennett. 1964. "University Characteristics and Student Achievement." *The Journal of Higher Education* 54:517–531.

Beasley, S. R., and W. A. Sease. 1974. "Using Biographical Data as a Predictor of Academic Success for Black University Students." *Journal of College Student Personnel* 15:201–6.

Clark, K. B., and L. Plotkin. 1964. *The Negro Student at Integrated Colleges.* New York: National Scholarship Service and Fund for Negro Students.

Pascarella, E., and P. Terenzini. 1980. "Student-Faculty Informal Contact and College Outcomes." *Review of Educational Research* 50:545–595.

Scott, C. M. 1933. "Background and Personal Data as Factors in the Prediction of Scholastic Success in College." *Journal of Applied Psychology* 22:42–49.

Sedlacek, W. E., G. C. Brooks, and L. A. Mindus. 1968. "Black and Other Minority Admissions to Large Universities: Three-Year National Trends." *Journal of College Student Personnel* 9:177–179.

Stanley, J. C., and A. C. Porter. 1967. "Correlation of SAT Scores with College Grades for Negroes Versus Whites." *Journal of Educational Measurements* 4:199–218.

White, A. J., and D. E. Suddick. 1981. "Five Years after Matriculation: A Comparison of Grades and Attrition of Black and White College Students." *Journal of College Students Personnel* 22:177.

CHAPTER 5

Note

*This chapter is a synopsis of a longer report by Walter Allen, *Gender and Campus Race Differences in Black Student Academic Performance, Racial Attitudes and College Satisfaction,* published in 1986 by the Southern Education Foundation in Atlanta, Ga.

References

Abramowitz, Elizabeth A. 1976. *Equal Educational Opportunity for Blacks in U.S. Higher Education: An Assessment.* Washington, D.C.: Howard University Press.

Blackwell, James E. 1982. "Demographics of Desegregation." Reginald Wilson, ed. *Race and Equity in Higher Education.* Washington, D.C.: American Council on Education. 28–70.

Fleming, Jacqueline. 1984. *Blacks in College: A Comparative Study of Students' Success in Black and White Institutions.* San Francisco: Jossey-Bass.

Gurin, Patricia, and Edgar G. Epps. 1975. *Black Consciousness, Identity, and Achievement: A Study of Students in Historically Black Colleges.* New York: Wiley.

Rehberg, Richard, and David Westby. 1967. "Parental Encouragement, Occupation, Education and Family Size: Artifactual or Independent Determinants of Adolescent Educational Expectations." *Social Forces.* 45:362–373.

Thomas, Gail E. 1984. *Black College Students and Factors Influencing Their Major Field Choice.* Atlanta: Southern Education Foundation.

CHAPTER 6

Notes

1. Census definitions were used to categorize schools: Among predominantly white schools, 1 = South (East and West South Central, and South Atlantic), or 2 = West (Pacific and Mountain), with all others regarded as 3 = North. For the historically Black schools, 1 = Mississippi and North Carolina (southern states without large cities), 2 = Florida and Louisiana (southern states with large cities), and 3 = Texas and Maryland (Border states with large cities). This formulation of region is necessary because of the preponderance of Blacks in southern, four-year, public institutions (Mingle 1981).

Among white schools, the size of the student body which distinguishes small and large schools is a twenty-five thousand total student population. Among Black schools, this division is accomplished at seven thousand students. For white schools, a graduate, research-oriented, *and* flagship institution in a state's university system was designated to be of the higher caliber. A research- and graduate-oriented, but *not* a flagship school, was considered of higher quality than a state university without a research tradition (that is, one whose historical mission was training undergraduates or "teacher training"). Black schools are rated for prestige according to their effectiveness in producing baccalaureates. See Hart (1984) for details.

2. To make this question consistent with the others, the numerical value of the response scale was reversed.

3. Purists may question whether the NSBCS data, as construed here, violate the assumption of multivariate normal distributions and/or equal group covariances. Klecka (1980) and others advise that these conditions are of greatest importance when dealing with a small sample (Bibb and Roncek 1976; and Huberty 1975). The

695 cases from the white schools and 888 cases from the Black institutions in the NSBCS data set offer greater latitude in the rigors with which these assumptions are held. Moreover, the percentage of correct classifications here among the white schools is 50.9 percent (or 34.6 percent better than chance, given the unequal sizes of the groups); and among the Black schools, 45.6 percent (a 27.5 percent improvement). This indicates that any violation of assumptions is not very harmful—although, as always, caution should be used in interpreting the results—and that efforts to use alternative formulations or otherwise improve on the data will have only marginal effects on the quality of results (Klecka 1980:62).

4. The original Wisconsin model found a nonrecursive relationship between aspirations and attainment. Rather than risking error by the arbitrary declaration of a causal order for the sake of replicating previous methodologies, the choice here is to allow for the joint dimensionality of the educational outcomes, and to use the analytical technique most appropriate for this dependent variable arrangement. Given the other advantages, the loss of direct comparisons with previous statistical outcomes is a small price to pay for the capture of aspirations and attainment in a form more like the one implied by Sewell et al. (1970) and Sewell and Shah (1968).

5. In the path analysis, Wisconsin-type model tradition, the heuristic model posits that the relationships between independent and dependent variables exist in a definite temporal order, indicative of causality. The discussion to follow focuses on the correlational connections between independent and dependent variables because that is all that the statistical operations will allow. However, readers are reminded that, in the cases of the sociodemographic, ability, and institutional variables, the temporal relationships between these independent variables and the dependent variables are definitive.

6. As expected, these results are similar to earlier findings using these data (Smith and Allen 1984; and Smith and Moore 1983).

References

Allen, Walter R. 1985. "Black Students, White Campus: Structural, Interpersonal, and Psychological Correlates of Success." *Journal of Negro Education* 54(2):134–147.

Bibb, R., and D. W. Roneck. 1976. "Investigating Group Differences: An Explication of the Sociological Potential of Discriminant Analysis." *Sociological Methods and Research* 4:349–379.

Epps, Edgar G., ed. 1981. *Black Students in White Schools.* Worthington, Ohio: C. A. Jones

Frazier, Edward F. 1957. *Black Bourgeoisie.* Glencoe, Ill.: Free Press.

Gottfredson, Denise C. 1981. "Black-White Differences in the Educational Attainment Process: What Have We Learned?" *American Sociological Review* 46:558–572.

Gurin, Patricia, and Edgar G. Epps. 1975. *Black Consciousness, Identity, and Achievement: A Study of Students in Historically Black Colleges.* New York: Wiley.

Hart, Philip S. 1984. *Institutional Effectiveness in the Production of Black Baccalaureates.* Atlanta: Southern Education Foundation.

Huberty, C. J. 1975. "Discriminant Analysis." *Review of Educational Research* 45:543–598.

Klecka, W. R. 1980. *Discriminant Analysis.* Beverly Hills, Calif.: Sage.

Mingle, J. R. 1981. "The Opening of White Colleges and Universities to Black Students." Gail C. Thomas, ed, *Black Students in Higher Education.* Westport, Conn.: Greenwood Press.

Porter, J. N. 1974. "Race, Socialization, and Mobility in Educational and Early Occupational Attainment." *American Sociological Review* 39:303–316.

Sewell, W. H., et al. 1970. "The Early Occupational Status Attainment Process: Replication and Revision." *American Sociological Review* 35:1014–1027.

Sewell, W., and V. P. Shah. 1968. "Education and Childrens' Educational Aspirations and Achievements." *American Sociological Review* 33:191–209.

Smith, A. Wade, and Walter R. Allen. 1984. "Modeling Black Student Academic Performance in Higher Education." *Research in Higher Education* 21(2):210–225.

Smith, A. Wade, and E. G. J. Moore. 1983. "Racial Identification and Attainment among Black Collegians." Paper presented at the meeting of the American Sociological Association, Detroit, Mich.

Tinto, Vincent. 1975. "Dropout From Higher Education: A Theoretical Synthesis of Recent Research." *Review of Educational Research* 45(1):89–125.

Treiman, D. J., and K. Terrell. 1975. "Sex and the Process of Status Attainment: A Comparison of Working Men and Women." *American Sociological Review* 40:174–200.

Turner, Ralph H. 1960. "Sponsored and Contest Mobility and the School System." *American Sociological Review* 25:855–867.

CHAPTER 7

References

Allen, Walter R. 1982. *Winter 1981 Study of Black Undergraduate Students Attending Predominately White, State-Supported Universities.* Ann Arbor: University of Michigan, Center for Afro-American and African Studies.

Allen, Walter R., and Winifred Nweke. 1985. *1983 Survey of Black Undergraduate Students Attending Predominantly Black, State-Supported Universities.* Ann Arbor: University of Michigan, Center for Afro-American and African Studies.

Astin, Alexander W. 1982. *Minorities in American Higher Education: Recent Trends, Current Prospectives and Recommendations.* San Francisco: Jossey-Bass.

Fleming, Jacqueline. 1984. *Blacks in College: A Comparative Study of Students' Success in Black and White Institutions.* San Francisco: Jossey-Bass.

Gurin, Patricia and Edgar G. Epps. 1975. *Black Consciousness, Identity and Achievement: A Study of Students in Historically Black Colleges.* New York: Wiley.

Hedegard, J. M. and B. R. Brown. 1969. "Encounters of Some Negro and White Freshman with Public Multiversity." *Journal of Social Issues* 25(3):131–144.

Thomas, Gail E., ed. 1981. *Black Students in Higher Education: Conditions and Experiences in the 1970s.* Westport, Conn.: Greenwood Press.

CHAPTER 8

References

Andrews, G., C. Tennant, D. M. Henson, and G. E. Vaillant. 1978. Life-Event Stress, Social Support, Coping Style, and Risk of Psychological Impairment. *Journal of Nervous and Mental Disease* 166(5):307–316.

Cobb, S. 1976. "Social Support As a Moderator of Life Stress." *Psychosomatic Medicine* 38:300–314.

Dean, S., and N. Lin. 1977. "The Stress-Buffering Role of Social Support: Problems and Prospects For Systematic Investigation." *Journal of Nervous and Mental Disease* 165(6):403–417.

Fleming, Jacqueline. 1984. *Blacks in College: A Comparative Study of Student Success in Black and White Institutions.* San Francisco: Jossey-Bass.

Hammer, M., S. Makiesky-Barrow, and L. Gutwirth. 1978. "Social Networks and Schizophrenia." *Schizophrenia Bulletin* 4(4):522–545.

Henderson, S., P. Duncan-Jones, M. McAuley, and K. Ritchie. 1978. "Social Bonds in the Epidemiology of Neurosis: A Preliminary Communication." *British Journal of Psychiatry* 137:463–466.

Kaplan, B. H., J. C. Cassel, and S. Gore. 1977. "Social Support and Health." *Medical Care* 15(5):47–58.

Miller, P., and J. Ingham. 1976. "Friends, Confidants, and Symptoms." *Social Psychiatry* 11:51–58.

Thoits, P. A. 1982. "Conceptual, Methodological, and Theoretical Problems in Studying Social Support as a Buffer Against Life Stress." *Journal of Health and Social Behavior* 23(6):145–159.

CHAPTER 9

Note

*An earlier version of this paper was presented at the American Educational Research Association, San Francisco, Calif., April, 1986. The authors are grateful to Walter Allen and several anonymous reviewers for their helpful comments on earlier drafts of this manuscript.

References

Anderson, E., and F. Hrabowski. 1977. "Graduate School Success of Black Students From White Colleges and Black Colleges." *Journal of Higher Education* 68:294–303.

Berryman, Sue E. 1983. *Who Will Do Science?* New York: The Rockefeller Foundation.

Blackwell, James E. 1981. *Mainstreaming Outsiders: The Production of Black Professionals.* Bayside, N.Y.: General Hall, Inc.

Braddock, Jomillis, and Marvin P. Dawkins. 1981. "Predicting Black Academic Achievement in Higher Education." *Journal of Negro Education* 50(3):319–327.

Hall, Marcia, and Walter R. Allen. 1982. "Race Consciousness and Achievement: Two Issues in the Study of Black Graduate/Professional Students." *Integrated Education* 20(1–2):56–61.

National Center for Educational Statistics. 1983. *Participation of Black Students in Higher Education: A Statistical Profile from 1970–71 to 1980–81.* Washington, D.C.: U.S. Department of Education.

Nettles, Michael T. 1987. "Black and White College Student Performance in Majority White and Majority Black Academic Settings." J. Williams, ed. *Title VI Regulation of Higher Education: Problems and Progress.* New York: Teachers College Press.

Nettles, Michael T., A. Thoeny, E. Gosman and B. Dandridge. 1985. *Causes and Consequences of College Student Performance: A Focus on Black and White*

Students' Attrition Rates, Progression Rates and Grade Point Averages. Nashville, Tenn.: Tennessee Higher Education Commission.

Scott, R., and M. Shaw. 1985. "Black and White Performance in Graduate School and Policy Implications of the Use of Graduate Record Examination Scores in Admissions." *Journal of Negro Education* 54(1):14–23.

Thomas, Gail. 1985. *Access and Success Status of Blacks and Hispanics in U.S. Graduate and Professional Education.* New York: Ford Foundation Report.

Trent, William, and Jomills Braddock. 1987. "Trends in Black Enrollment and Degree Attainment." J. Williams, ed. *Title VI Regulation of Higher Education: Problems and Progress.* New York: Teachers College Press.

CHAPTER 10

Notes

*Much of the work for this chapter was done while the first author was a postdoctoral fellow in the Bush Program in Child Development and Social Policy, University of Michigan at Ann Arbor from 1984–1985, and the second author was a Rockfeller Foundation Postdoctoral Fellow. We would like to thank Timothy Wilkens and Roland McKoy for research assistance and Mary Kirkland for her help in the preparation of the data set.

1. We should make clear from the outset that we are not suggesting that there is a sufficiently large pool of Black Ph.D.s from among which schools can easily choose. The lack of representation of Blacks on the faculties of the nation's major colleges and universities is, first and foremost, a function of American higher education's failure to produce an adequate supply of Black Ph.D.s. But, even though the pool is too small to achieve any real parity (however that may be defined), the argument we make is that the search and hiring procedures now in effect serve to exacerbate the problem.

2. The following discussion draws heavily on the masterful biography of Just by Kenneth R. Manning (1983). A general account of the exclusion of early Black scholars is found in Winston (1971).

3. Parallel analyses were conducted with the graduate, professional, and combined (graduate and professional) students with virtually identical results. We report the findings from the analyses which use the combined data set because of the greater statistical power which the larger sample provides.

References

Alvarez, Rodolpho. 1973. "Comment (on Jose Hernandez, Jay Strauss, and Edwin Driver. The Misplaced Emphasis on Opportunity For Minorities And Women In Sociology)". *The American Sociologist* 8:124–126.

Blackwell, James E. 1981. *Mainstreaming Outsiders: The Production of Black Professionals.* Bayside, New York: General Hall, Inc.

Caplow, Theodore, and Reece McGee. 1958. *The Academic Marketplace.* New York: Basic Books.

DuBois, W. E. B. 1940/1968. *Dusk of Dawn.* New York: Schocken.

Duster, Troy. 1976. "The Structure of Privilege and Its Universe of Discourse." *The American Sociologist* 11:73–78.

Edwards, Harry. 1970. *Black Students.* New York: Free Press.

Exum, William H. 1983. "Climbing the Crystal Stair: Values, Affirmative Action, and Minority Faculty." *Social Problems* 30(4):383–399.

Fleming, John E., et al. 1978. *The Case for Affirmative Action for Blacks in Higher Education.* Washington D.C.: Howard University.

Gilford, Dorothy M., and Joan Snyder. 1977. *Women and Minority Ph.D.s in the 1970s: A Data Book.* Washington D.C.: Commission on Human Resources, National Research Council, National Academy of Sciences.

Glazer, Nathan. 1975. *Affirmative Discrimination.* New York: Basic Books.

Gottfredson, Denise C. 1981. "Black and White Differences in the Educational Attainment Process." *American Sociological Review* 46:558–572.

Hirschorn, Michael W. 1989. "Doctorates Earned by Blacks Decline 26.5 Per Cent in Decade." *Chronicle of Higher Education* 34(21):A1–A32.

Lewis, Lionel S. 1975. *Scaling the Ivory Tower.* Baltimore: Johns Hopkins University Press.

Manning, Kenneth R. 1983. *Black Apollo of Science: The Life of Ernest Everett Just.* New York: Oxford University Press.

National Center for Educational Statistics. 1988. *Digest of Educational Statistics.* Washington D.C.: U.S. Government Printing Office.

Prager, Jeffrey. 1982. "Equal Opportunity and Affirmative Action: The Rise of New Social Understandings." *Research in Law, Deviance and Social Control* 4:191–218.

Rafkey, David. 1971. "The Black Academic in the Marketplace." *Change* 6(10):65–66.

Smelser, Neil, and Robin Content. 1980. *The Changing Academic Marketplace.* Berkeley: University of California Press.

Sowell, Thomas. 1975. *Affirmative Action Reconsidered: Was it Necessary in Academia?* Washington, D.C.: American Enterprise Institute for Public Policy Research.

Turner, Ralph H. 1960. "Sponsored and Contest Mobility and the School System." *American Sociological Review* 25:855–867.

Winston, Michael R. 1971. "Through the Back Door: Academic Racism and the Negro Scholar in Historical Perspective." *Daedalus* 100:678–719.

CHAPTER 11

References

American Association of State Colleges and Universities. 1985. *Student Aid and Minority Enrollment in Higher Education.* Washington, D.C.: American Association of State Colleges and Universities.

American Council on Education. 1984. *Third Annual Status Report on Minorities in Education.* Washington, D.C.: American Council on Education.

Anderson, James D. 1984. "The Schooling and Achievement of Black Children: Before and after *Brown* v. *Topeka,* 1900–1980." *Advances in Motivation and Achievement* (JAI Press) 1:103–122.

Blackwell, James E. 1981. *Mainstreaming Outsiders: The Production of Black Professionals.* Bay Side, N.Y.: General Hall, Inc.

Fleming, Jacqueline. 1984. *Blacks in College: A Comparative Study of Students' Success in Black and White Institutions.* San Francisco: Jossey-Bass.

Hedegard, James, and Donald Brown. 1969. "Encounters of Some Negro and White Freshmen with a Public Multiversity." *Journal of Social Issues* 25(3): 131–144.

Miller, Doris, and Patricia O'Connor. 1969. "Achiever Personality and Academic Success among Disadvantaged College Students." *Journal of Social Issues* 25(3):103–116.

National Research Council. 1984. *Survey of Earned Doctorates.* Washington, D.C.: National Research Council.

CHAPTER 12

References

Bell, Derrick. 1983. "Learning from Our Losses: Is School Desegregation Still Feasible in the 1980s?" *Phi Delta Kappa* (April): 572–575.

Chesler, Mark, Bunyan I. Bryant, and James E. Crowfoot. 1981. *Making Desegregation Work.* Beverly Hills, Calif.: Sage Publications.

Cohen, Elizabeth. 1980. "Design and Redesign of the Desegregated School." Walter Stephan and Joe Feagin, eds. *School Desegregation*. New York: Plenum. 251–280.

Cohen, Michael. "Instructional, Management and Social Conditions in Effective Schools." Allen Odden and L. Dean Webb, eds. *School Finance and School Improvement Linkages in the 1980s*. Washington, D.C.: American Educational Finance Associates. Forthcoming.

DuBois, W. E. B. 1935. "Does the Negro Need Separate Schools?" *Journal of Negro Education* 4:328–335.

Edmonds, Ronald. 1979. "Effective Schools, for the Urban Poor." *Educational Leadership* 37:15–24.

Epps, Edgar G. 1974. *Cultural Pluralism*. Berkeley, Calif.: McCutchan Publishing Corp.

Glazer, Nathan, and Daniel Patrick Moynihan. 1963. *Beyond the Melting Pot*. Cambridge, Mass.: MIT Press.

Hare, Bruce R. 1982. "Development and Change Among Desegregated Adolescents: A Longitudinal Study of Self-Perception and Achievement." Department of Sociology, State University of New York at Stony Brook. Working Paper No. 820504.

Hare, Bruce R., et. al. 1983. "Crossing the Brook: Desegregated Education at the State University of New York at Stony Brook." Paper presented at the American Educational Research Association Meetings, Montreal, Canada.

Hawley, Willis, D., ed. 1982. *Effective School Desegregation*, Beverly Hills, Calif.: Sage Publications.

Hawley, Willis, D. 1983. "Effective Educational Strategies for Desegregated Schools." *Peabody Journal of Education* 59(4):207–322.

Kopan, Andrew. 1974. "Melting Pot: Myth or Reality?" Edgar G. Epps, ed. *Cultural Pluralism*. Berkeley, Calif.: McCutchan Publishing Corp.

Levine, Daniel U., and Eugene Eubanks. 1983. "Instructional and Organizational Arrangements at an Unusually Effective Inner-City Elementary School in Chicago." Paper presented at the annual meeting of the American Educational Research Association, Montreal, Canada.

Orfield, Gary. 1975. "How to Make Desegregation Work: The Adaptation of Schools to their Newly Integrated Student Bodies." *Law and Contemporary Problems* 39:314–340.

Pearce, Diana M. 1980. *Breaking Down the Barriers: New Evidence on the Impact of Metropolitan School Desegregation on Housing Patterns*. Washington, D.C.: National Institute of Education.

————. 1983. "Beyond Busing: New Evidence on the Impact of Metropolitan School Desegregation on Housing Segregation." Paper presented at the annual meeting of the American Sociological Association, Detroit, Mich.

Purkey, Stewart, and Marshall Smith. "Effective Schools—A Review." *Elementary School Journal.* Forthcoming.

Sizemore, Barbara, Carlos Brossard, and Birney Harrigan. 1983. *An Abashing Anomaly: The High Achieving Predominantly Black Elementary School.* Pittsburgh: University of Pittsburgh.

Slavin, Robert. 1983. "Team Assisted Individualization: A Cooperative Learning Solution for Adaptive Instruction in Mathematics." Paper presented at University of Pittsburgh Leaning Research and Development Center.

Washington, Booker T. 1970. *Up From Slavery.* 22nd ed. New York: Bantam.

CHAPTER 13

References

Association of American Medical Colleges. 1982. *AAMC Curriculum Directory.* Washington, D.C.: Association of American Medical Colleges.

————. 1987. *Minority Students in Medical Education: Facts and Figures III.* Washington, D.C.: Association of American Medical Colleges.

Frierson, Henry T. 1984. "Impact of an Intervention Program on Minority Medical Students' National Board Part I Performance." *Journal of the National Medical Association* 76:1185–1190.

————. 1986. "Two Intervention Methods: Effects on Groups of Predominantly Black Nursing Students' Board Scores." *Journal of Research and Development in Education* 19(3):18–23.

————. 1987. "Combining Test-taking Intervention with Course Remediation: Effects on National Board Subtest Performance." *Journal of the National Medical Association* 79:161–165.

Hubbard, John P. 1978. *Measuring Medical Education.* Philadelphia: Lea and Febiger.

McQuaid, E., and M. Kane. 1981. *The State Board Test Pool Examination for Registered Nurse Licensure.* Chicago: Chicago Review Press.

Overstreet, L. P. 1983. "A Study of the Efficacy of Reinforcement Courses for Graduate Nurses on Success in Passing the State Board Test Pool Examination in Georgia." *Journal of Nursing Education* 22:28–31.

Ramist, L., and S. Arbeiter. 1985. *Profiles, College-Bound Seniors.* New York: The College Board.

Rolph, J. E., A. P. Williams, and A. L. Lanier. 1978. *Predicting Minority and Majority Medical Student Performance on the National Board Exam (R–2029–HEW).* Santa Monica, Calif.: The Rand Corporation.

Vetter, Betty E., and Eleanor L. Babco. 1986. *Professional Women and Minorities.* Washington, D.C.: Scientific Manpower Commission, Manpower Data Resource Service.

CHAPTER 14

Notes

*Funding for the Biology Student Center project was provided by the following administrative units of The University of Michigan:

1. The office of the Vice-President for Academic Affairs,
2. The College of Literature, Science, and the Arts,
3. The Department of Biology,
4. The Center for Research on Learning and Teaching, and
5. The office of the Vice-Provost for Information Technology.

Three animated tutorials on the subjects of protein synthesis, meiosis, and the lac operon have been licensed for commercial distribution in Apple II and IBM PC compatible versions.

Reference

Kleinsmith, Lewis J. (1987). "A Computer-Based Biology Study Center: Preliminary Assessment of Impact." *Academic Computing.* 2(3):49–50, 67.

CHAPTER 15

Note

I am grateful to Walter Allen, Thomas Holt and Rudy Lombard for their valuable suggestions in improving the section "Color, Difference and Culture."

References

Carnoy, Martin. 1974. *Education as Cultural Imperialism.* New York: D. McKay Company.

Farley, Reynolds, and Walter R. Allen. 1987. *The Color Line And The Quality of Life In America*. Oxford: Oxford University Press.

Freire, Paolo. 1970. *Pedagogy of the Oppressed*. New York: Seabury Press.

Gleick, James. 1988. *Chaos, Making a New Science*. New York: Penguin Books.

Illich, Ivan D. 1971. *Deschooling Society*. New York: Harper and Row.

Kunjufu, Jawanza. 1985. *Countering the Conspiracy To Destroy Black Boys*, vols. I and II. Chicago: African American Images.

Madhubuti, Haki R. 1990. *Black Men Obsolete, Single Dangerous? The African American Family in Transition: Essays in Discovery, Solution and Hope*. Chicago: Third World Press.

Ogbu, John. 1978. *Minority Education and Caste: The American System in Cross-Cultural Perspective*. New York: Academic Press.

Ong, Walter. 1982. *Orality and Literacy*. New York: Methune Press.

Takaki, Ronald, ed. 1987. *From Different Shores: Perspectives in Race and Ethnicity in America*. New York: Oxford University Press.

Woodson, Carter. 1933/1969. *The Miseducation of the Negro*. Washington, D.C.: Associated Publishers.

Contributors

Walter R. Allen is Professor of Sociology at the University of California, Los Angeles. Dr. Allen's degrees in the field of sociology are from Beloit College, (B.A., 1971) and the University of Chicago (M.A., 1973; Ph.D., 1975). In 1978–79 he completed postdoctoral study in Epidemiology at the School of Public Health, University of North Carolina-Chapel Hill. His honors include the Rockefeller Foundation Postdoctoral Fellowship (1982–83), Senior Fulbright Lecturer-University of Zimbabwe (1984, 86), United Negro College Fund Distinguished Leadership Award (1985), American Educational Research Association Distinguished Scholar Award (1987), and the University of Michigan Faculty Recognition Award (1988). Dr. Allen is cited for distinguished achievement in *Who's Who in the Midwest* (1988, 89); *Who's Who in America* (1988, 89); *Men of Achievement* (1987); *Outstanding Young Men of America* (1982) and *Who's Who Among Young Americans* (1976). He has held teaching appointments at the University of Michigan (1979–1989), the University of North Carolina, Chapel Hill (1974–79), Howard University (1975), Duke University (1976), the University of Zimbabwe (1984–86) and Wayne State University (1988). His research and teaching focus on family patterns, socialization and personality development, race and ethnic relations in higher education. Among his more than fifty publications are *The Colorline and the Quality of Life in America* (co-authored with R. Reynolds Farley), and *Beginnings: The Social and Affective Development of Black Children* (coedited with Geraldine Brookins and Margaret Spencer).

Jomills Henry Braddock II is a Director of the Center for Research on Effective Schooling for Disadvantaged Students, a Principal Research Scientist at the Center for Social Organization of Schools/Center for Research on Elementary and Middle Schools, and a Professor of Sociology, at Johns Hopkins University. His broad research interests encompass issues of ine-

305

quality and social justice including extensive examination of the long-term effects of school desegregation on Black young adults. He has written numerous articles, book chapters, and research monographs on these topics. Dr. Braddock's work has been published in the *Harvard Educational Review, Journal of Social Issues, Journal of Negro Education, Sociology of Education, Phi Delta Kappa, International Journal of Sociology and Social Policy, Youth and Society,* and *Review of Research in Education.*

Robert Bob Davis is a professor of sociology at North Carolina A&T State University. With a Ph.D. from Washington State he did postdoctoral work at the University of Wisconsin-Madison in the Institute for Research on Poverty and the Center for Demography and Ecology. His areas of specialty include suicide, homicide, poverty and education-related issues. A New Orleans native, Davis has lived in Greensboro, North Carolina since 1970. He is currently the Director of A&T's Institutional Self-Study and is finishing a term as president of the North Carolina Sociological Association. Davis is on the board of the North Carolina Poverty Project and is a member of the North Carolina Youth Suicide Study Commission. Davis is also actively involved in the American Sociological Association (ASA), the Association of Black Sociologists (ABS) and the Southern Sociological Society (SSS). He describes himself as an avid runner and jazz fan.

Donald R. Deskins, Jr. is Professor of Urban Geography and Sociology at The University of Michigan where he received a B.A. with distinction in 1960, an M.A. in 1963, and a Ph.D. in 1971. He has held several administrative posts at the University and served on numerous committees, receiving the University's Faculty Recognition Award, the Leonard F. Sain Esteemed Alumni Award and the Distinguished Faculty Governance Award. He is a member of numerous professional societies and his most recent service on national committees is as a member of the National Research Council's Panel on the Decennial Census Methodology. His publications are numerous and his most recent research is focused on the analysis of the restructuring of American industry and its impact on society. Dr. Deskins is also interested in the public policy implication of changing academic enrollment and trends in degree production in the United States.

Edgar G. Epps is the Marshall Field IV Professor of Urban Education at The University of Chicago (since 1970). He has previously held faculty positions at Tuskegee Institute (1967–70); The University of Michigan (1964–67); Florida A & M University (1961–64), and Tennessee State University (1958–61). He was educated at Talladega College, Atlanta University, and Washington State University where he earned the Ph.D. degree in sociology. His books include *Black Students in White Schools; Race Relations:*

New Perspectives; Cultural Pluralism; and *Black Consciousness, Identity and Achievement.* He has authored or co-authored many articles on sociological and psychological factors that influence achievement and motivation.

Henry T. Frierson is a professor at the University of North Carolina. He was based in the Office of Educational Development and the director of Learning Assessment Laboratory. He is now Dean in the Graduate School and he is also a clinical professor of educational psychology in the School of Education. He received his bachelor's and master's degrees from Wayne State University and a Ph.D. in educational psychology from Michigan State University.

Ruby Gooley is Assistant Professor of Sociology and Coordinator of Applied Sociology Program at Georgia State University. She is currently pursuing research on the status of Blacks in American society, gender and racial identity in Black women, the family life of older Blacks and the effects of counseling on children of imprisoned mothers. Dr. Gooley received her degree from the University of Michigan at Ann Arbor.

Jo Anne Hall is Assistant Librarian at the University of Michigan and the Librarian at the Center for Afro-American and African Studies. She is a co-editor of *Black American Families, 1965–1984: A Classified, Selectively Annotated Bibliography.* She has research interests in bibliographic and computer-assisted instruction and its applications to Afro-American and African studies. She has initiated and participated in cooperative research/ bibliographic projects with teaching faculty. Dr. Hall received her B.A. degree from University of Dubuque, Dubuque, Iowa, her M.L.S. degree from State University of New York at Albany, and Ph.D. degree from the University of Michigan. She has worked as a librarian at University of Vermont at Burlington and as an institute librarian at Jackson State University, Jackson, Mississippi.

Nesha Z. Haniff was born in Guyana. She is the author of *Blaze A Fire: The Significance Contributions of Caribbean Women.* Her scholarly interest is the history of ideas as they affect the study of women and people of color. She shares her time between projects in the Caribbean and her position as Adjunct Assistant Professor at the Center for Afro-American and African Studies and the University of Michigan.

Bruce R. Hare is Professor of Sociology and Afro-American Studies and Chair of the Department of Afro-American Studies, Syracuse University. He earned the B.A. from the City College of New York and the M.A., Ph.D. degrees from the University of Chicago. His research focuses on adolescent self-esteem, racial identity and the sociology of education. His publications appear in the *American Journal of Psychiatry,* the *Journal of Negro Education* and the *Journal of Intercultural Relations.*

Kenneth W. Jackson is Associate Professor and chair of the Department of Sociology and Social Work at Texas Southern University. He received his undergraduate degree from Texas Southern and earned his Ph.D. from the University of Chicago. His primary areas of interest are race and ethnic relations and research methodology.

Jerome Johnston is Associate Research scientist at the Institute for Social Research and Senior Researcher at the National Center for Research to Improve Postsecondary Teaching and Learning (NCRIPTAL). His research over the past 18 years has focused on child and adolescent development, and how it is shaped by the family, the school, and television. In recent years his work has focused on computers and learning. His books on this topic include a guide to research methods (*Evaluating the New Information Technologies*) and a summary of several decades of research on the impact of radio, television, and computers on student learning (*Electronic Learning: From Audiotape to Videodisc*). His central interest today is describing the contextual features associated with effective use of computers in the classroom.

Lewis J. Kleinsmith is currently an Arthur F. Thurnau Professor of Biology at The University of Michigan, where he has served on the faculty since receiving his Ph.D. from Rockefeller University in 1968. His research interests have included studies of differentiation and growth control in cancer cells, the role of chromosomal proteins in gene eukaryotic gene regulation, and control of gene expression during development. He is the author of over 130 publications, including the textbook *Principles of Cell Biology* and several educational software programs. Among the honors he has received are a Guggenheim Fellowship, the Henry Russel Award, a Michigan Distinguished Service Award, several citations for outstanding teaching from the Michigan Students Association, a Thurnau Professorship, and a Best Curriculum Innovation Award from the EDUCOM Higher Education Software Awards Competition.

Westina Matthews is Vice President of Corporate Staff and Manager of Corporate Contributions and Community Affairs at Merrill Lynch & Co., Inc. She also serves as Secretary of the Merrill Lynch & Co. Foundation, Inc. Ms. Matthews came to the worldwide financial services firm in 1985 to head the corporate contribution program after extensive experience in education and foundation work. Born in Chillicothe, Ohio, she graduated with a B.S. in education from the University of Dayton in 1970. While teaching elementary school for six years in Yellow Springs, Ohio, she earned a master's degree in education from Dayton in 1974. Ms. Matthews proceeded to earn a Ph.D. from the University of Chicago in 1980 and then served as a post-doctoral fellow at both Northwestern and Wisconsin. In 1982 she joined the Chicago Community Trust where she became senior program officer. Ms. Matthews is the newly elected chair of the Contribution Advisory Group, the membership organization for corporate contributions managers based in the greater New York City area. She recently became a Board Member of the Ms. Foundation. She also served as Secretary for the New York Regional Association of Grubstakers and is a member of the Governor's Advisory Committee on Black Affairs. In 1989, Ms. Matthews was selected as a Harlem YMCA Black Achiever in Industry and was one of the 1989 Salute to Women In Industry honorees from the National Council of Negro Women.

Roslyn Arlin Mickelson received her Ph.D. in the sociology of education from the University of California, Los Angeles in 1984. Presently she is Assistant Professor of Sociology and Adjunct Assistant Professor of Women's Studies at the University of North Carolina at Charlotte. Her research interests include race, gender, and class equity in educational processes and outcomes. She is the author of *Why Does Jane Read and Write So Well?: The Anomaly of Female Achievement* and *The Attitude-Achievement Paradox Among Black Adolescents*, both of which recently appeared in *Sociology of Education*. Her current project is a National Science Foundation funded examination of corporate-sponsored school reform and its implications for educational equity.

Michael T. Nettles became Vice President for Assessment for The University of Tennessee System in 1989. Dr. Nettles has recently conducted a three-year study, supported by the Ford Foundation and the Southern Education Foundation, on the factors related to students' college performance. This study included colleges and universities in ten states. The findings from the research are presented in the final report: *The Causes and Consequences of College Students' Performance: A Focus on Black and White Students' Attrition Rates, Progression Rates and Grade Point Averages*, which was published by The Tennessee Higher Education Commission, Nashville, Tennessee, and his book, *Toward Black Undergraduate Student Equality in American Higher Education*, which was published in 1988 by Greenwood Press. Currently Dr. Nettles is directing two research projects in the area of graduate education. One is supported by the Office of Educational Research and Improvement (OERI) and is concerned with comparing the experiences and performance of minority doctoral students with those of majority doctoral students. The second project, supported by the Graduate

Record Examination Board (GRE), is concerned with assessing the impact of financial assistance, financial indebtedness and other factors upon the decisions of GRE examinees to attend graduate school, professional school, or to seek employment.

Melvin L. Oliver is an Associate Professor of Sociology and Associate Director, Center for the Study of Urban Poverty at UCLA. Professor Oliver earned his B.A. in 1972 at William Penn College in Iowa and his M.A. and Ph.D. in 1974 and 1977 in sociology at Washington University in St. Louis, Missouri. His areas of research interest include interethnic race relations, urban social networks, the urban underclass, and poverty and wealth. His work has appeared in such journals as *Social Problems, Sociological Quarterly, Review of Black Political Economy, Urban Geography* and *Urban Review.*

Cheryl Presley is a research assistant with the Center for Afro-American and African Studies and a Ph.D. candidate in the Higher and Adult Continuing Education Program at the University of Michigan. She received her B.A. and M.Ed. from Colorado State University in Social Work and Adult Education. Her research interests include the impact of organizational structures on student achievement and issues related to African American students at predominantly white universities. Presley is an active member in the Association for the Study of Higher Education (ASHE), American Association for Higher Education (AAHE), the American Association of University Women (AAUW) and Delta Sigma Theta Sorority. She describes herself as one who enjoys the arts and sports.

A. Wade Smith is Associate Professor of Sociology at Arizona State University. In addition to work on educational attainment among Blacks, he is investigating the potential effects of class cleavages on the overall fabric of public opinion and especially on the attitudes and values of Blacks. He is participating in the development of new racial attitude measures for the 1990 General Social Survey. Dr. Smith serves on the editorial boards of the *American Sociological Review* and the *Journal of Marriage and the Family.* His article "Education as a Determinant of Social Class Among Black Americans" appeared in the *Journal of National Education.*

L. Alex Swan is Professor of Clinical Sociology and Dean of the College of Arts and Sciences at Texas Southern University in Houston, Texas. He is the author and editor of six books including *The Practice of Clinical Sociology and Sociotherapy, The Politics of Riot Behavior, Families of Black Prisoners,* and *Survival and Progress: The Afro-American Experience.*

Gail E. Thomas, who received her Ph.D. from the University of North Carolina at Chapel Hill, is professor of sociology at Texas A&M University.

Her main fields of interest are gender and racial differences in educational access and attainment as well as the stratification and institutional processes which impact minorities. Dr. Thomas is currently engaged in research on how race and gender affect the choice of college majors and career orientations. Dr. Thomas is also interested in the institutional practices of recruiting and retaining minorities in various educational programs. She serves on a variety of national committees and task forces designed to address the problems and monitor the progress of minorities in higher education. She has published extensively in a variety of journals including *Sociological Quarterly, Sociological Spectrum, Harvard Educational Review, Science Education Journal of Negro Education* and *International Journal of Higher Education.* She is also editor of two books: *Black Students in Higher Education* (1981: Greenwood Press) and *American Race Relations in the 1980s and 1990s: Current Status and Future Projections* (1990: Hemisphere-Taylor-Francis).

William T. Trent is associate professor of educational policy studies and sociology at the University of Illinois at Urbana-Champaign. His current research interests include equity issues in higher education, the desegregated schooling experience, race, class and cultural implications for educational attainment, as well as core problems in teaching.

Index

313